TRANS-SIBERIA

INSIDE THE GREY AREA

PADDY LINEHAN

SUMMERSDALE

Summersdale Publishers Ltd
46 West Street
Chichester
West Sussex
PO19 1RP
UK

www.summersdale.com

Printed and bound in Great Britain.

ISBN 1 84024 114 4

To Anne Healy for reading what I wrote and
to Irene Yates for helping me to write it better.

N
ARCTIC OCEAN
MOSCOW
KIROV
PERM
EKATERINGBURG
URAL
MOUNTAINS
OMSK
NOVOSIBIRSK
KRASNOVARSK
IRKUTSK
BAIKAL
ULAN
UDE
SAKHALIN
ISLAND
JAPAN
BLACK SEA
TURKEY
CASPIAN
KAZAKHSTAN
MONGOLIA
CHINA
IRAN
AFGHANISTAN
PAKISTAN
TIBET
INDIA
BURMA
PACIFIC
OCEAN
500
0
MILES
1000

Chapter One

The bee dropped out of the wildflowers, heavy and malicious, swinging around my head in a deep, droning rage. I took flight. The fear was so overpowering that no sound came though my brain was giving orders to scream. I was hopelessly outclassed. Even at my top speed he overtook with ease. He'd swing out past me, hang there for a moment, double back, wwwhuuu-ooooomm past my ear and fall behind to pick up momentum for a fresh attack. The Russian killer bee!

In the distance I had seen a family working. Sheer panic propelled me at them. Saliva was strangling my breath and I didn't think I would make it. My hands were flailing the air and I only touched the ground every third or fourth step. Yards short, I dived and came to a skidding halt in their midst. Hands, now still and wrapped around my head, dulled my cries of HELP! HELP! HELP!

Nothing. Then the Russian words I'd rehearsed for robberies . . . *pomogite menya*! *pomogite menya* . . . *pomo-gi-t-e m-e-n-y-a*!

Silence.

I cautiously periscoped out, scanning the air. No bee, just five frightened Slav children in careless summer rags crowding their father's legs for protection from the madman. The fearless mother stood apart, stout arms resting on wooden rake.

I rose slowly.

The children huddled closer to their father. Drained, I tried to say that a HUGE swarm of killer bees had chased me and I was very lucky to be alive. Only their eyes moved in darts. I couldn't translate so I spread my arms and buzzed and droned menacingly. The children loosened out and one said, 'BBZZ . . . zzz . . . zzz'; another giggled. Mother understood. She said something, buzzed and slapped her stout arm with a resounding clatter. The BBZZ . . . zzz . . . zzz girl did the same, then the Giggler and then all the others laughed and slapped their sunburnt arms too. The crescendo of slapping and laughing told me I had been pursued by something harmless that even a small child wouldn't fear. For a moment I contemplated sticking to my story of a near death experience. I counted possible support; the odds were impossible so I slapped my arm, echoed what I heard mother say and, with relief, joined in the glee.

It was almost the end of day anyway but the invasion by a man from outer space brought their labour to an irreversible halt. As we walked together towards the village, which was home to the workers of the collective land around, the children boldened. Long before we arrived the younger ones had all touched me and the competition was on for 'first to risk holding his hand'. The Queen, she was no more than five, won. Though her eye was no higher than my waist, she tried to match my step. Ambition made her tumble and she erupted in mirth.

Mama and Papa sat me on a long wooden stool with their blond, burnt brood and fed me steaming *borsch*: soup. They asked me a hundred questions. I didn't understand a single one. They put me to sleep in a comfortable crevice near the open fireplace. There was no fire because it was warm summer in the Pushkin Hills. The tired family soon purred in slumber. The wooden house was small and the tune took hold . . . they slept in key.

Lying awake, I pondered my limitations. Was it all a crazy idea? My knowledge of the language was almost nil. This place was only barely Russia, just a few miles from the Estonian border. Real, distant, far-off Russia, the Russia I wanted to see, stretched seven thousand miles east. This was the shallow end of the pool where amateurs paddled. A simple, pastoral place for writing poetry, cutting hay and picking flowers. I wanted to go into the deep water of far-off Siberia; I had pioneering ambitions, yet here, in the gentle, rolling Pushkin Hills, I had been frightened near to death by a bee.

Sharply, four blasts of a train's whistle pierced the dark and sleeping symphony. I didn't know that there was track or station anywhere near this humble village. 'It must be an omen,' I thought.

It had all begun, so many years before, when I had just finished secondary school. I was holidaying with a friend in the west of Ireland; it rained for days. We were eighteen and unused to idleness. With nothing to do but peer at the wetness, I bought a second-hand book in the local Post Office. I wasn't too selective; there were only four to choose from. One was a book about an escape from a gulag in a place called Siberia. Those two words: 'gulag' and 'Siberia' made my mind up for me. I wasn't familiar with either word but I liked them both.

Both sinister.

I wasn't far into the book when my fascination increased. A gulag was a place where prisoners were kept. But they weren't bad people. The prisoners were the goodies; it was the wardens who were bad. It seemed the only bad thing that the prisoners did was to disagree with powerful men in high places. These powerful men, it seemed, were all corrupt and were very far from cold Siberia.

It seemed that these poor innocent prisoners had spent weeks and weeks in dire conditions on trains, cattle-boxes, being transported to this very far-off Siberia. The book suggested that Siberia was created for punishment. It was incredibly cold and dark most of the time. Even then I was confused as to whether it was a real place, or one created by the evil people to punish the courageous and outspoken.

The story intrigued me. The escapee had a job working in the house of one of the cruel wardens. He told the warden's wife of his plans of escape and she was in a terrible dilemma. She was pulled and dragged between duty to her husband, who was about the best of the wardens, and the dictates of her conscience that told her that the prospective escapee had committed no crime and deserved a break. In fact, the book told you that even though the wardens were by and large a bad lot, many of them were themselves there for punishment for not totally conforming with the corrupt regime in far-off Moscow. After much agonising, this warden's wife made up her mind: she'd help him. She provided him with an axe-head. She said: 'It is the only thing I have ever stolen and I know I will regret it for the rest of my life.' He walked for four months and eventually ended up in India. I was fascinated. From Siberia to India. I couldn't wait to get home to search the atlas for this Siberia place.

I didn't find it. I found Russia and I found India and I joined them with finger-drawn lines, but the possibilities were limitless. Russia is huge. In the old atlas I counted eleven little clocks, all indicating different times. I discovered that when it was one o'clock in the afternoon in Moscow it was already tomorrow at the other end of the vast expanse called Russia. Siberia didn't feature; it could be anywhere. These eleven hours measured the great distance left to right; up and down it was also huge. I concentrated on the upper fringes of unfamiliar coastline. Or was it real coast? Could there be water away up there or was it always ice? Big blocks of the stuff like the thing that had sunk the Titanic.

I couldn't really disentangle this Russia place at all. It was spread all over the pages. There was Russia and the Union of Soviet Socialist Republics and there were a whole lot of countries down towards India with indistinct boundaries and names ending in 'stan'. I didn't know if they belonged to the USSR or if they were real countries. I got the feeling that the map-maker was probably not sure either. The borders were vague and the shapes doubtful. The colours were hardly colours at all. Map-makers, in general, display a distinct prejudice. England, Australia and North America are plonked right in the middle of pages and coloured vibrantly: pinks, blues and duck-egg greens. But when you venture east of Europe things turn spooky. Colours become muddy, borders doubtful and names rare. Large tracts are coloured light brown, dark brown and darker brown. Pages meet with scant respect for the lands they portray. The few place-names that exist are speared with staples or stitched. And the shapes are a disgrace. Nothing like Europe.

Europe looks so pretty. It's full of interest and humour. Italy's long leg is action-frozen, just about to kick Sicily into the Mediterranean sea. Norway and Sweden reach down, a cartoon serpent, mouth open, ready to gobble up the hand-puppet, Denmark. The British Isles are a pair of doggies sitting on their hind-legs, looking out in anticipation across the broad Atlantic to promising lands, and Greece dips south in islanded luxury to bask in the exotic, warm waters of the Aegean. But, to the right of Europe, map-makers look as if they've run out of colour and imagination. The rest of the land mass, to the east, drifts into a brown, boggy wedge. I pored over this boggy wedge for a long time. Failing to find Siberia, I put it on hold.

Over the years I covered all the nicely coloured bits. I dabbled in the Pacific and ducked in the Atlantic and even paddled in the South China Sea, but at the back of my head always there was this Siberian place that I had to find out about. It was not easy. I asked people, 'Do you know where Siberia is?' and the answer was always the same: 'Oh, Siberia is very cold . . . frost and snow all the time.'

When in 1992 the Berlin wall fell, I saw an opening. The world peered through the wreckage at the forbidden land, the 'evil empire'. Barriers conceive curiosity about what is beyond. Churchill's christening of the barrier that lay between the area of Soviet influence and the Western world as 'the iron curtain' fortified this curiosity. The curtain now had a hole in it through which one could just spy what might be beyond. What we had in our sights was not Siberia, it wasn't even Russia, yet the door was open a slit. If they allowed this to happen maybe they would allow people to go there and find out where Siberia was. I thought I'd head in that direction and get some information there.

I made preparations. These took a while. I learnt how to read the Cyrillic alphabet and I got someone to invite me to visit Russia. This is necessary in order to get a visa, so it was 1995 before I actually got to Russia. From there I thought it would be no trouble. Ho, ho!

The man who invited me was a professor at the University of St Petersburg and even he didn't know where Siberia was. University professors aren't paid very well in Russia. In 1995 they got twenty-five dollars a week. Salaries are always quoted in dollars because the rate of inflation is such that in roubles it is meaningless. In 1995 there were 4,500 roubles in a dollar. So the professor was not a well-off man, though he had business instinct. He advertised his services over the Internet. Russians took easily to this new mode of communication. Though the telephone network was lame, it was extensive. Russians are given to long conversations over great distances so the Internet is an extension of an existing custom. The professor's invitation, in duplicate, arrived simultaneously at my home and at the Russian Embassy in Dublin. There, on production of my copy, a visa was issued. It doesn't go into one's passport like most visas; it is a separate little booklet like a driver's license that gives one permission to go to St Petersburg. Whether it entitles one to travel farther afield is a question I was never clear on and did not push for clarification. Using it and Aeroflot I presented myself to the professor, Alexei, and his wife, Tamara.

Their apartment, though obviously a mere section of a former extensive warren, was still grand. I was amazed that such an opulent place had such a dilapidated entrance. It was an unlit burrow reeking of pee and excrement. Inside the apartment was interesting; old, two-bathroomed and though on the ground floor, full of steps: from my inner room there were two steps up to one of the bathrooms, two more steps down and two up again to Alexei's office, where he moodily watched a green-flickering screen for other visa-seekers, and three more stone ones up to Tamara's kitchen. She hummed tunefully over brewing pots and broke into a handsome and toothy smile and a 'Hi! How are you?' that sounded like she really wanted to know. She looked naturally glamorous even without make-up and in the kitchen she had natural class. Her father was a surgeon and had been sent to Uzbekistan in the fifties when Tamara was a young girl. She shook her head when I asked for more information on what sounded like exile and said dinner would be ready in just a few minutes.

Her dinners were magnificent. Issuing invitations was obviously a lucrative business. I was unusual in that I stayed in their home; most invitees were farmed out to host families who got six of the twenty-five dollars that Alexei charged for each night. He was a rather hard man, his wife a charming lady. I stayed with them for a couple of weeks and always brought the conversation around to Siberia. Alexei got angrier and angrier. 'Go to the Hermitage, go to Peterhof, walk along the Fontanka, what is it about this Siberia – it is very cold there. Frost and snow all the time.'

I did go to the Hermitage and Peterhof and I walked the Fontanka and then I got restless again and started to ask for some more distractions. He took me to the *banya*. I didn't want to go. There were two showers in the apartment. *Banya* sounded like a stony public bathhouse and I said I'd rather wash at home. 'Wash! It is not only for washing, you'll see,' Alexei responded with a relaxed smile untypical of the man.

Women stood in the street outside selling feniks. These are bundles of birch twigs and my uncertainty grew. I had visions of lardy-white men beating and bettering each other to see who was most macho. Inside, my fears dissipated in the luxuriant, indolent atmosphere of indulgence. They plodded around in easy nakedness, relaxed, earthy and altogether at home. The locker-room was more like a club. There were marble slabs and marble stools and some men played chess while others ate and drank. They talked easily, like cats purring. I asked Alexei what they talked about and he said: 'Politics and sport but the ballet too and music.' The range of Russian conversation is wider than in the West. 'The Arts', is not the domain only of the rich and educated, a *pas de deux* is as likely a topic of conversation for men as a good soccer pass. In a wooden room of heat we used the feniks. The ambient atmosphere surprised me but I fell in with it and felt oh-so-good. Lashing oneself with feniks was not the masochistic act I had envisaged. It made me tingle and feel I was looking after myself. Then Alexei and I together, in a companionable mode we could not muster at home, dived into a boxy, green-tiled, icy pool.

The *banya* brings out the best in Russian people. There are between twenty and thirty in St Petersburg and two or three in almost every town across Russia. Strangely,

Moscow has only one and it has the reputation of being Mafia territory. The *banya* is a kind of institution and impossible to describe objectively. Public bathhouse, sauna or steam room carries seedy connotations that insinuate themselves into any description of *banya*, but there is no seediness. Most have separate floors for men and women and separate family rooms. There are attendants who clean and bring coffee or tea. In some areas there are women attendants in the men's section and they don't flinch at prolonged conversations with naked men. These conversations were so natural and uninhibited it took me a while to pinpoint that it was a tad unusual.

Alexei was pleased at my pleasure in the *banya*, he thought I had settled in. On different days he took me to four different ones in different areas each with its individual atmosphere. It was like going to the pub.

I said nothing about you-know-where for a long time but then I couldn't resist any longer so I said, 'Not saying that I am going, but if one wanted to go to Siberia how would one go? Just for curiosity.'

He just left the kitchen.

Tamara, his wife, was more tolerant. She was also a romantic and understood when I told her about the book I had read years ago, but no, she would not advise it. Russia was a dangerous place now, especially for foreigners. Siberia was out of the question, I should stay in big centres like St Petersburg and maybe Moscow, but even that was dangerous. 'Stay in St Petersburg.' I had two months.

In the beautiful city of St Petersburg, the period from late May until late July is called *Belly Nochi*: White Nights. It hardly gets dark at all. The street lights don't come on for two months. It is completely bright at midnight. At two a.m. it becomes dusk and stays like that until three when it begins to get brighter again. People walk Nevskiy Prospekt, the main street, all night. There are unsmiling men with mobile phones who drive Land Rovers and seem constantly to be being stopped by police. I'm told they are Mafia. They hang around doorways of hotels and expensive shops.

There are prostitutes.

They are very beautiful and their profession is less obvious than in European or American cities. Their conversation with prospective clients is friendlier than that of their European sisters. This is doubly surprising because Russians, in general, are distant. They reserve friendly greetings for well-established friends.

There are women who sell things: *babushkas*. Like the *banya* they are a Russian institution that more or less defies description. Literally, the word means grandmother but its use is far more extensive than that. *Dadushka* is grandfather but the word does not have parallel implications. *Babushka* is definitely feminine but beyond that it is hard to be specific. Usually old but not necessarily: a woman of forty might qualify if she were fat, experienced and wise, while one of seventy might not if she were pinched and cranky. A *babushka* is warm, kind, loving and caring but not soft and not demonstrative of her affection. She is almost omniscient. You could never 'put one over' on a *babushka*. Heavens! Who'd try? They're stolid and Russians use the word with a stolid, respectful reverence. *Babushka*, as well as being a beautiful word, is a Russian phenomenon. They are entrepreneurs, seers, weather forecasters, medics and psychologists all in one. Wise beyond belief; I would trust every one of them with my life. One Russian friend, finding me in a quandary about something, shrugged his shoulders and said, 'Ask a *babushka*, they know everything.' It was one of those chance remarks that cleared up for me exactly what a *babushka* is: a woman who has seen everything and has all the answers. Most of the selling women are *babushkas*.

They take up their positions in the late evening. They congregate in one spot, forming something like a queue, and they sell everything: bottles of beer, packets of cigarettes, holy pictures and every imaginable item of used clothing. Shoes, second-hand ones especially. Shoes are a very personal item of dress. Their sale seems to be a personal intrusion. I looked at the shoes and tried to guess their history from the shape etched there. Then I learned that the Russian word for shoes is *botinki*. It sounded appropriate . . . little booties. The word has an affectionate and diminutive ring to it. I liked these Russian words. I set myself the goal of learning ten new ones every day.

When I had three hundred I decided to venture further. My host and hostess tried to stop me. They said I would be robbed. They said no one would sell me a train ticket because foreigners weren't supposed to go outside St Petersburg. The professor said his invitation only covered me for St Petersburg. I insisted I had to go.

At the railway station, people made it sound difficult too. I didn't know what they were saying but there was a lot of *nyet*, a word I was to become very used to. Eventually one large lady (not a *babushka*) gave up, just to get rid of me. She sold me a ticket to Pskov. I liked the name and it was the right distance away, about four hours. It is a small city near the border with Estonia. I walked its streets until I found the place where the selling women congregated. And there I met Ida.

She was sixty, which she called *starry*: old. Her hair was carefully dyed nut-brown. She had an unusually slim figure for a woman of her years. Despite food shortages, Russian women tend to be large. Ida wasn't, though in every other respect she was *babushkic*. I picked her for her figure and dress as they indicated she had been somewhere other than Pskov. I said, '*Ya chotu komnata spat*,' and waited for what seemed like a few hours. It was my first attempt at a sentence in Russian: 'I want a bedroom.' My heart thumped and I was perspiring under the arms, then in slow motion she said something starting with *da*.

I could have kissed her for joy.

I didn't understand the rest of what she said but I had a yes. Later, I discovered I was even luckier than I realised at the time. Had I known the scarcity of spare beds, even spaces in beds, not to mind rooms, I would have been more apprehensive. I'm sure Ida was the only woman in that large gathering of sellers who could have accommodated me. Seconds later, her friend Rima arrived. Rima spoke fluent English. In the old system these two friends had been couriers, guiding tourists around nearby Estonia. Ida spoke German and Rima, English. The English-speaker was decades younger, blonde, deserted of husband and with one son.

Ida had an apartment on the fourth floor of a typically grim block on Luxembourg Ulitsa. It was, like herself, neat, tasty and a little different from the average. The hall was small and tidy. There was a line of slippers and two hooks for coats. To the left was a wardrobe-sized bathroom and further inside, a blue kitchen. Many Russian kitchens are oil-painted shiny blue. This room was crowded with gurgling, whooshing pipes. There were large ones and small ones, all painted blue and all showing rust through the paint.

The living-room was large and had a tiny balcony that was full of Ida's washed clothing, patched and neatly sewn. There were two glass cabinets of books and a menagerie of ornaments. Lots of little glass animals and vases that looked Venetian.

One of the vases was blue. It was very attractive; its blueness made it a focal point and it seemed to indicate better times.

On the wall there was a wooden cuckoo clock with chains. Then there was the bedroom, very small with a two-foot wide bed. Here was another cabinet of books and more ornaments. There was a door between the living-room and bedroom, ajar. The opening was decked with hanging strips made from cut-up cigarette boxes woven into an unending 'W'. Ida drew them aside as if she were saying, 'Welcome to the casbah.' It was obviously her own bedroom but she and Rima laughed and tut-tutted: 'Of course not . . . Ida never sleeps here . . . she sleeps at her son's place to help with the baby-sitting . . . ha, ha!' Their prods and nods told me the story. Rima would find a space for her friend Ida while the foreigner took the bed. They would share the spoils.

Ida was a dear and sensitive lady who could make a meal out of nothing. It hurt her to have to take money. In the *starry system* it was different, people didn't think of money, no one would dream of expecting money for a bed or food.

The *starry system*, the old system, of course means Communism.

It is still at the core of every conversation in Russia. Under Communism everyone had a job. There was no unemployment. Wages were low, choices were few, but everyone had food. Ida preferred the old system. They hadn't much but what people had they shared. Now!

'Pshaw – everything is money.' Rima translated Ida's words, but she couldn't convey the thoughts and sentiment because she was mercenary. She tried to induce me into hiring a friend who had a car to show me around. In the English learnt to tell foreigners how good things were she told me of monasteries, monks and bells, the chimes and the wild flowers; of the good and *safe* times we'd have in her friend's small, but comfortable, car cruising the countryside and the Pushkin Hills. We'd visit the poet's house and without any of the threats of robbery faced by other less lucky tourists we'd linger in the woods with picnics packed by Ida. To my 'How much?' she answered twenty-five dollars a day plus petrol and raced on with exaggerated blonde courier smile to say 'how wonderful' it would be, 'how memorable' and 'how lucky I was to be in safe hands and among friends.' She quoted me an exorbitant price (two months' salary for a teacher in one day to her friend). I hadn't wanted to go by car anyway but I would have found it difficult to reject her offer had it been reasonable. As it was it gave me the excuse to huff indignantly about how capable I was of looking after myself and of my great affection for walking hills and fields alone. Her latent nastiness surfaced (if she lived to be a hundred Rima would never be a *babushka*). 'It is not safe for foreigners . . . you will be robbed . . . we will not be responsible, will we Ida?' The older lady pretended business, stirred pots and opened the window even further, saying it was *ochean topley*. I asked Rima what that was and she spat back: 'Very hot.'

They left me for the night and I browsed through the books. I knew a word here and there. I could change the authors' names into English letters. I saw something impossible and slowly transliterated P-U-S-H-K-I-N. I yelped with joy. Then D-O-S-T-O-Y-E-V-S-K-Y, then G-O-G-O-L and when it got easier I had Turgenev, Trifinov and Chekhov.

I was to learn that most Russians had an appreciation of literature akin to Ida's. I asked her to teach me Russian. She said Rima would because she knew English. I said I wanted her, Ida, to teach me. She shrugged reluctantly, feeling bad about taking what she wanted her friend to have.

We swapped phrases. She'd say: '*Idyom v magazini*,' and I'd say: 'We go to the shops.' Then we'd head off together each one mouthing the other's language. She pronounced shops, cheops. 'Vee ghow tsu tse cheops.'

We wound our way through overgrown lots and between apartment buildings; we zig-zagged among broken-down cars and skips and ducked through arched passageways to the places where *moloko* (milk) was *dyeshyovii* (cheaper) and *yaits* (eggs) were *svezhii* (fresh). It was a day's work to collect *chleb* (bread), *kartofel* (potatoes), *moloko* and *yaits*. Ida bargained and harangued and tried not to let me see her counting what was left after each purchase. On the way home in the evening we visited her son's *kvartera* (apartment) and, with a nonchalant shrug, unloaded half of what was bought. Her daughter-in-law would say, '*Spasiba spasiba spasiba*,' thank you, thank you, thank you, and Ida would convincingly shrug that it was nothing. '*Na zdrovye*,' to health, she'd say. Then back at our *kvartera* she'd wave a wand over our gathering and put me to eat in the main room where I could look out over the balcony. Rima always turned up for the food.

One evening I was working on a child's book as I ate and I became impatient with a word. I went to the kitchen for help. The friends were eating, with their fingers, from the same plate. Ida was embarrassed.

Washing was a problem. Ida's bathroom was scrubbed clean. The tub was full of plastic containers, which were full of clothing separated according to colour. These had to be removed. There were also plastic buckets of water in readiness for water cut-offs. We put these in the living-room and it was then the real challenge began. The turned-on tap released the gas that, ignited, heated the water. Trouble was that the tap was in the bathroom while the heater was in the kitchen. There was no jet so when the tap was turned on Ida had to stand by with a match to light the released gas. The builders of these apartments took no risks with people's health. Getting hot water called for a well-orchestrated duet. Ida and I had difficulty synchronising. I told her the words 'off' and 'on'. She told me '*otkluchyon*' and '*vkluchyon*'. But neither of us was sure which were the corresponding pairs: on was *otkluchyon* and off was *vkluchyon* or was it off for *otkluchyon* and on for *vkluchyon*?

In practice it was a disaster. I stood ready to dart into the spray and shouted, '*vkluchyon*'. From the kitchen, at the ready, Ida answered with an 'off', I ducked in, froze, ducked out, shouted '*otkluchyon*', she answered, 'off – *nyet* – on', it whooshed to life, I darted in, burnt, shouted '*vkluchyon*' she switched off . . .

Ablution was hazardous but my vocabulary grew and I boldened. I thought I'd put my new words to the test in the real country.

Giving up on deterring, Ida loaded me down with vitals and, from her little balcony, pointed out the hills to the east. She was a sensitive lady and I read uncertainty, or an undercurrent of guilt in the pointing. Though she preferred the *starry system* and was still a Communist party member (she attended meetings many days and marched with the red flag), she had reservations and some guilt about the expansionist policy of the old Soviet Empire.

Russians still harbour mixed feelings about the lost Baltic States of Estonia, Latvia and Lithuania. These were annexed in the period of Communist expansionism. These nationalistic states quickly and proudly reverted to their independence when Communism fell in 1992. Though she wasn't pointing to these republics, but to the closer Pushkin Hills, the guilt of an occupation she did not agree with showed. She covered it up with excessive superlative gestures about the closer Hills called after the famous poet who lived and wrote there.

I set out to walk for some days in the Pushkin Hills. They form the area between Pskov and the Estonian border. It is a dreamy countryside of wild flowers and monasteries. These flowers are among Russia's greatest treasures. They are yellow, pink and mauve and impossible blues. Blue flowers like velvet that can provide busy bees with rich reward and a curious foreigner with much embarrassment.

It was these beautiful flowers that had led me to be in this simple house among this simple family who had saved my life. And now a ghost train was sending out a signal in four blasts. I knew almost no Russian and I had been scared near to death by a bee but I believed in miracles and omens so I drifted off to sleep and dreamed of Siberia. I was lost in blizzards. I strangled bears with my bare hands. I heard the hollering of pursuing dogs and I used the axe-head the warden's wife had given me to inscribe my name on a tree so that if I died while I slept the world would know I'd died in the cause of freedom and justice. Triumph was mine and I was just making the final breakthrough to the warm land of India when they wakened me.

Mama replenished my food stocks. Children danced as sober Papa carefully indicated a safe direction for another day of walking. The little ones laughed and shouted advice I didn't understand until the Queen spread her arms and buzzed around me with mock menace. The others took it up and they bzzzz . . . ee . . . ddd and wove off to the fields for their chores as I headed for the opposite horizon.

I stayed in a village near an army barracks and sat in the square on Sunday when the soldiers' parents and girlfriends visited with parcels. In the evenings I watched the partings. One soldier chewed gum right through the goodbye kisses. His lips smiled but a tear overflowed and coursed down. Two years later I thought of him when a young girl told me the awful things that had happened to her boyfriend soldier.

Russian youth, boys and girls, wear clothes well. These valiant soldiers wore their uniforms with style. Even though the material is poor they can manage to appear dashing. Some can be rough too, but most are not. Like soldiers everywhere their *raison d'être* is war so they must look tough; custodians of boundaries must be ever-vigilant for lurking enemies. These soldiers ranked higher than most of the species. Their too-large tunics were tucked and gathered at the back and tied with wide, sash-like belts. They pushed out their chests and strutted. They smoked, chewed and punctuated their words with derisory spurts of laughter: 'Fwha.' They threw their legs out from them in strides and you'd think, 'Maybe they'll click their heels.' They didn't and it might be because the boots are made of cardboard. Like the men themselves they look tough but close up they're made of soft material.

I stayed in a monastery where they treated me like a beggar and for a night with a teacher, who treated me like a prince. He pretended to the villagers that he spoke

English. I didn't understand his words but his deeds were the best of Russian hospitality, rarely experienced by a stranger who stays in the main cities. Then I walked back over the Pushkin Hills to Ida's. Despite the years of Communism, when religious practice was forbidden, I was never out of sight of the familiar onion domes of an Orthodox Church. And, as I was to experience in another form later in Siberia, they always occupy the horizon and are as magnetic, if not so elusive, as the pot of gold at the end of the rainbow. When you get to one an even more promising one appears on the next horizon. It always has something more to offer: stars on its dome, or one made like a decorative blob of icing on a cake, or one with a double glittering cross and bells. *Kolokolniy zvon* (the sound of bells) never fails to draw.

The monks are dark, bearded and mostly grim. They look like they know for sure that it was only by the skin of their teeth that they were saved from eternal damnation under an atheistic state. My smiling approaches were nearly always rejected. The older men with grey spade-beards just turned and shuffled off to the dappled shade of a tree to offer counsel to an acquiescent *babushka*. Younger men were slightly more responsive but never warm or sure of themselves. Giving time to a free foreigner with little purpose other than small chat was at some kind of odds with the gravity of monkhood. And these monks are always going, never still. Striding solemnly here and there and back again, passing each other but too deep in inner thought to see each other at all. There are stalls selling things: tinny icons, strings with knots, scapulars, medals and beads on strings for praying. The stalls are manned by the younger monks but these also are too distracted with the seriousness of life to talk. It is now fashionable for students to become monks. As young as nineteen they grow beards, wear greenish-black robes and severe black hats and shed the joy of youth. Soldiers of Christ are less attractive than the ones with cardboard boots.

When I returned Ida had collected some new children's books. My favourite was *Uncle Fyodor, Dog and Cat*.

Uncle Fyodor is a small boy, they call him Uncle Fyodor because of his wisdom. The three eponymous characters set out *peshkom*: on foot. They take their belongings in spotted rag bundles hooked to sticks over their shoulders. They march off in protest against dictatorial parents to find freedom. And just like the man in the Siberian book, they succeed.

It strengthened my resolve.

Ida counselled me against my resolution. She said Siberia was *ochen kolodnay, e ochen daleko*: very cold and very far. She said I should go to Suzdal, the centre of the area near Moscow famous for its monasteries and cathedrals. Rima said I should stay in a hotel there. She would if she had plenty of money like me. All foreigners had plenty of money. Ida said no, I should stay with her friend, she would phone her. And she did, straight away. Despite poverty, Russians have no inhibitions about using the phone. In the old system every apartment had a phone. All local calls were free and even long-distance ones were ridiculously inexpensive. Ida phoned her friend and I was to go the next day.

Lighting is seldom good in Russian apartments. Bulbs are of clear glass and the flimsy filament can be seen glowing dimly. It is seldom too bright to stare at. Ida's was reasonable but not very good. I studied *Uncle Fyodor, Dog and Cat* late. I sought to improve the light by transferring to the area under the clear glass bulb. Dragging the table across, I toppled the blue glass 'Venetian' vase. It crashed to smithereens on the painted concrete floor.

It was probably very valuable. It could have been an heirloom.

This lovely woman who had little would be broken-hearted. I gathered the pieces in a pile and debated how to break the news.

An announcement? No. I'd leave the evidence for a discovery. I changed my mind and the exhibit for my prosecution many times. I'd lie down, close my eyes, jump up, change things around and lie down again. It couldn't be worse. The nicest thing in the whole apartment in a million mocking, shining pieces. There was a silence such as I had not noticed any other night. All the neighbours must have heard and they were all waiting, breath held, for Ida to walk in and shoot the foreigner. I drifted into a nightmared half-sleep. I saw her tear-stained face cracked with grief and, in the background, Rima leering: 'Sue him . . . sue him . . . sue him . . . foreigners have plenty of money!'

I awakened in anguish and paced. A shard lodged in my bare foot and I bled. Like a plunderer of tombs I was hoist by my own petard.

At eight a.m. the cuckoo poked out its head. Instead of eight separate calls he stuck in a strangled, continuous, derisory croak.

When Ida arrived I croaked too. Words failing, I presented the fragmented pile. For a moment she was silent. When she saw my anguish she threw her head back in laughter. It was a convincing performance and then this beautiful woman turned and spat over her left shoulder. She must have spoken in Russian but it is in English I remember the dismissal of such things as glass vases: 'That is what I think of glass vases, Paddy.' And in case I still had any doubt, which I had, she spat venomously once again. To Ida, of a few prized possessions, nothing mattered as much as people.

She and Rima walked me to the railway station and took no notice of what I said about Siberia. They weren't even dismissive any more; the idea was ridiculous beyond rational argument.

To get to where I was going I had to go back to St Petersburg. I spent one night there and then took another train to Vladimir. No trouble this time, I had learnt my lines and I didn't even look at the seller as I asked for a single to Vladimir. I arrived in rain so heavy that I could not get to the bus station by walking. I did not know the time of buses to Suzdal anyway, so I reluctantly put myself into a room like a corridor, on the fourth floor of an awful hotel at twenty dollars a night. The whole place was terrible; thin and tall and standing alone but looking like it could do with adjacent buildings for support. The woman at the desk suited the establishment, a barking, bony woman of many *nyets*. The foyer was gloomy and tall too. Its only illumination came from fluorescent tubes so high up their light was almost lost altogether. The floor was a sticky, steamrolled, synthetic marble. A much-stained red carpet runner ran its length dankly to the diamond-mesh lift door. It didn't work. I spent what was left of the day watching black and white TV lying on an iron bed wrapped in a grey blanket.

Next day was sunny. The local bus to Suzdal was really local. Everyone knew each other. They didn't talk much but when they complained it was obvious that they had shared much hardship – yesterday wasn't *their* only bad day. The bus was full so I stood all the way which made me an even more obvious stranger, yet I never got a glance. And I was the only one with a bare head although it was a lovely day. The women all had headscarves and the men a variety of dark soft caps and beanies which they shuffled about their heads occasionally with bark-like, gnarled hands.

My hosts lived walking distance from the town and they must have waited for me at every bus for two days. Their children, initially shy, romped and yelped by the time we reached the wooden house with the blue shutters and potted plants. Anna and Mikhail now owned the land they farmed and though Anna spoke good English I could not understand the process by which once collective land was now becoming private property. What they had now was a plot that her parents had had in the old system, but much had been annexed to it. In the old system people were allowed a small piece of private land much like the *dacha* or allotment plot rights of city dwellers.

At first by day I did my walking. The area is more widely known in the West than that around Pskov. It is the centre of what is known as the Golden Circle and is famous for its monasteries. I'd lost interest in monasteries in close up, monks depressed me; I preferred viewing them as things on the horizon. The summer was getting late and people sold mushrooms all around the streets of Suzdal. They looked strange and inedible, like sponge or pumice stone. I avoided them. Sated with monasteries and the sight of mushrooms I stayed at home and helped Anna and Mikhail. They appreciated it. Their land was home to two cows, three pigs and a brown harem of laying hens ruled over by a strutting cock. His comb was scarlet and he, it appeared, forgot his species because he goose-stepped.

Anna made butter and cheese and did a hundred things with eggs. One of last year's pigs hung in smoked strips from the kitchen ceiling. The walls were lined with jars of radishes and gherkins and unrecognisable things.

I liked their town and its surrounds and they were very pleased with that. I liked all of Russia and they were pleased with that. They had two beautiful children whom I adored and they were also pleased with that. It wasn't until I told them that I wanted to go to Siberia that, protectively, they drew in their stock and children.

I told Anna in English and she told Mikhail. He changed. He turned white and he shivered.

'*Seber ochen kolodnay ochen delako*.'

He drew young Mikhail closer. '*Ochen delako*,' he repeated, reaching out for young Anna. Around the yard he seemed to be telling the hens about my mad ideas and after he had a few words with the rooster it crowed wildly though it was past noon.

The situation was grave. They went to bed early and left me with *Uncle Fyodor, Dog and Cat*.

People didn't understand him either. He wanted to go live in the woods with his dog and cat, but Mama and Papa laughed it off as a crazy dream. So he put his few possessions in a spotted bit of cloth, hooked it to a stick, put it over his shoulder and, with his dog and cat, set off to live in the woods. They found an abandoned cottage, cleaned it up and lived happily, if not forever after, at least for a considerable time. I told Uncle Fyodor I admired his resolve and that, some day, I would follow his example.

I repeated my plans to Anna and Mikhail. They were silent. They took me to the bus and only when I was safely aboard, safely out of influence, did they allow their lovely children to wave with abandon at the weird stranger.

I had been warned against Moscow: dangerous, expensive . . . 'You'll get lost.' It is big and difficult to get around initially. I found the Intourist Office. It is a survivor of the Soviet system when its main function was to keep the foreign tourist a good distance from his Russian comrades. In those times there was no choice; if you wanted to go to Russia, the only option was to be forced to stay in tourist hotels where you were secluded from locals. They have extended only slightly what they offer. Now they have posters, advertising, but their mind is still set on packages in awful hotels with standard tours. The lady there did know Siberia. She said I could fly to Krasnoyarsk or Novosibirisk and there I could have coach tours and stay in a high-rise hotel. She said it would have a games room and a cleaning service and that there was a hairdresser in the basement. One could have a sandwich in the middle of the night and watch TV in bed. I was afraid she was going to say that I could get CNN news of what was happening in the White House. She didn't, but she was surprised that I wasn't interested in what she had to offer. I said I wanted to go there alone by bus or train. She went into a paroxysm and called her colleagues to circle around. 'No bus . . . buses only for short trips in Russia . . . train, yes, but only for Russian people . . . not even for ordinary Russian people but for rough Russian people who aren't afraid of wild savages.' She got worse when she heard me try to say a few Russian words.

So I went back on the street and I nearly gave up, thought maybe I would go to Torremolinos in the South of Spain and have sandwiches and room service there.

But then I met Sasha.

Sasha is short for Alexander in Russian. He had but one arm and a chest full of medals: testimony to service to his country. He was standing under a statue of a man on horseback on Treverskaya Street. The statue leans forward, pointing with outstretched hand at a building which is now the city hall. This man's name is Prince Yuri Dolgoruki. Yuri of the long arm. He is supposed to have founded Moscow.

Sasha was selling maps. He had no English so he halted a passing student and co-opted him, in good old Soviet fashion, to do the translation. I asked him if he knew where Siberia was; I told him I wanted to go there. It had been over thirty years since I'd read the book about Siberia and from Sasha came my first positive response.

His eyes lit up. He opened a map and spread it on the pavement. He ordered the student to stand on one corner of it, the way old Russian men order young people, and he put a bundle of his merchandise on another corner. Then the two of us got down on hands and knees and pored over it, like two children playing with toy soldiers.

He uttered a series of names that, for me, turned fiction into fact. Ekateringburg, Omsk, Krasnoyarsk and Irkutsk.

His bony index finger traced a path across the mighty land mass ending in that other winning post of addicted travellers, Vladivostock. The impossible was made easy by his familiarity with the place. It wasn't uncertain pointing in directions he didn't know in practice. He had been there. He was born there, in Komsomolskay-na-Amur.

Boldened with the enlightenment, I slid a finger up north where the dots, indicating towns, thinned out and the lines of road and rail became dimmer and dotted. I thought this might be where my man had escaped from. I was keeping an eye down to the Himalayas and figuring out how far he would have gone in four months. Sasha shook his head, slowly at first. Then when I got impossibly far north he said a sharp '*Nyet, nyet*' and, placing the shaking claw of his single hand over my lost finger, he dragged it back to reality on the shores of Lake Baikal. This was the possible Siberia, the beautiful Siberia. '*Krasevee* Baikal.' Beautiful Baikal, he uttered reverently.

It was to be a while yet before I knew exactly what he meant. First he said I must learn real Russian. He didn't understand my few words. He traced his finger along the line of the Urals and, with an inclusive sweep over the ten time zones beyond, he said, '*Ezdecs loody goveryat tolka po Rooskey*.'

Here people speak only Russian.

Then, before I bought the map from him he did a lovely thing. He directed me to put my foot on the map. With his one hand he manipulated it around until my heel was just beyond the Urals. In this position my toe was pointing at Irkutsk on Lake Baikal and he said something which I thought was, 'See! You are fated to go here, your foot indicates it.'

Or maybe he said something else, because our translator had lost patience and left. The corner that he had anchored now flapped in the wind under the statue of the man with the long arms who founded Moscow.

Chapter Two

But it wasn't until two years later that I finally got going to Siberia. In the interim it was very difficult to ascertain what exactly was happening in Russia. Some were declaring it to be the great new market. Others opined that its natural resources were so vast it would flood the Western world with cheap minerals and oil. Speculators were poised – anxious to make a killing. I was still worried about its geography.

The atlas I had used before was old, I thought I'd try a different angle so I bought a globe. I played with this new round world. I spun it and twirled it and examined all its lines and curves. At night I shone a torch on it to simulate its day and night and season cycles. Next day I turned it upside down and rid myself of one more prejudice: there is no top or bottom to our planet; it is an illusion we create. We call the northern hemisphere 'top' because that is where we are from; it is where all the discoverers originated so it becomes 'top'. But the other half is just as top. Consider the sky. It is up. Even Australia's sky is up. But if we apply the conventional top/bottom terminology then from our half Australia's sky is down. So even the globe prioritises. And my new world also had the old colour prejudice I had found in the atlas. From the Arctic Ocean to Iran and Afghanistan, from Poland to the Pacific: all brown. Fifteen countries all brown. In the early nineties a mathematical proof was discovered to support the existent theory that any map, no matter how complicated, may be filled in using only five colours so that no two adjoining countries will be the same. Then it is visually easy to differentiate. The people who made my globe and all the maps I have ever seen decided there was no necessity to differentiate the countries of the former Soviet Union, no one wanted to distinguish them, it seemed. They didn't matter so they were left the same colour. All the nice paint had been used up on the rest of the world and Russia and its fourteen neighbours were left in muddy mourning, a kind of punishment for the sin of Communism. In an effort to counter this imbalance I released the earth from the crescent spine that held it.

My world fell apart; burst open in the middle, erupted along its equator and fell in two halves on the floor. I found myself staring down on it from above: a world of two tops. I could see it all at once.

Eureka! Russia and Siberia became less remote from the rest of the world. I saw Canada just a hop across the North Pole and Alaska only a step away from Siberia. Russia and the US are close neighbours . . . only fourteen miles apart at the closest point. Japan is even closer, seven miles from Russia's Sakhalin Island to Hokkaido in Japan. Norway shares a thirty-mile border with Russia. All this jumped up at me from the floor. Flat maps can give very false pictures. Even globes, if you inspect them pivoted and head-on. When you spin a globe while it is still one piece the place you are looking at runs away from you, goes around the bend and you see no more of it until it comes out the other side. With my two hemispheres on the floor I couldn't spin the world at all but I could simulate its movement by walking around it. Nothing ever went out of view. I sauntered around the equator without ever losing sight of any country. I kept my eye on Russia. I'd leave it via Europe and cross the Atlantic, wander stateside all the way to sunny California and sneak up on the Old Bear unexpectedly from its rear-end eastern shore and all the time no part of it would have left my sight at all.

For years I had tried vainly to track the twinkling stars but they kept shooting away from me. Every night they were in different spots. The sky was moving around. It wasn't until I found out that the Northern Star was like a drawing pin that held the sky up and that the heavens rotated around this pin that I succeeded in locating what I wanted. The Northern Star was the stationary point. Poles are the only stationary point on planet Earth. They are the drawing pins that we spin on, the fixed points of reference. Now the North Pole focus gave me a better bearing on the northern half of Earth. I didn't have to let one country out of my sight while looking at another. I was able to look at all the brown bits and at the same time away down as far as India on one side and Mexico on the other. All of Europe, Arab Africa, Japan, China and even Singapore were in a single view. The brown blob had taken her place among the nations of the world.

I mentally shaded in all the countries that end in 'stan'. To compensate for years of obscurity I had Kazakhstan fluorescent pink, Uzbekistan emerald green, Tajikistan orange and the others equally festive. Even the Arctic Ocean had been neglected. It wasn't bright and blue like the Pacific or Atlantic, it was a whitish grey and lumpy so I wished it turquoise and standing over it beheld from above my new Russian world, adjusted for colour, contrast and without any roll.

I had a better perspective on Russia's geography but still knew little of its people and the ebb and flow of its affairs. I didn't want to delve into serious, heavy tomes. What books I had seen on its history were forbidding. They either had boring titles with dates or were bound in shades of brown that matched the old maps. Then, as serendipitously as my erupting globe, I came upon a school project. A teenage group had written just what I wanted. It was in simple language and illustrated in lively colour. They even named it well: *The Last Shortest Remake of Russian History Ever Written*. It was in instalments and posted around their classroom wall. It was helpful.

The first instalment was devoted to Genghis Khan, his plunder mania and his conquest of almost all that is now Siberia: all the 'stans' and everything right up to the Urals. He was quoted in giant, multicoloured font: 'THE GREATEST PLEASURE IS TO VANQUISH YOUR ENEMIES AND CHASE THEM BEFORE YOU (cerise), TO ROB THEM OF THEIR WEALTH (green) AND SEE THOSE DEAR TO THEM BATHED IN TEARS (plain black mourning), TO RIDE THEIR HORSES AND CLASP TO THE BOSOM THEIR WIVES AND DAUGHTERS (red for sin).'

There was a chasm of five centuries between the first and the second instalment, which was devoted to Napoleon's defeat at the battle of Leningrad. Next was Nicholas I (1825 – 55) whose reign was here dedicated to the Decembrists who the authors obviously identified with: 'This group of intellectuals tried their damnedest to create a constitutional monarchy and reform civil society and wrench from the czars their abusive power. They were BANISHED (violet) to Siberia, many to a town called Irkutsk where their influence is still experienced in the form of schools of languages and institutes of higher learning.'

I had already come across the Decembrists. It seems the Decembrists didn't share the map-seller Sasha's rosy image of Irkutsk. One, Piotr Mukhanov, who was exiled to a village near Irkutsk said in a letter to his mother: 'This place has depressed me much more than prison has ever done. All nine prisons I was at (*sic*) were better than this settlement.' And later from another town even closer to Irkutsk he wrote again: 'It is a small town on the banks of the Angara, surrounded by impenetrable forests and devoid of plough lands and meadow, a wild, unpopulated desert, a most abominable place. And when the Governor General told me I would be sent to the worst place, he was speaking the complete truth for I have never seen a place worse than the Bratsk settlement, despite the fact that I have travelled all over Russia.'

There was a page on Marx, Engels and the Communist Manifesto and I noted with amusement that Russia had sold Alaska to the United States, depicted in a picture of a Cossack handing over Alaska to a top-hatted Uncle Sam who was handing over a bag of dollars and winking out at us.

Then we were straight into the First World War and out of it almost as quickly because of the Bolshevik's successful defeat of Czar Nicholas II and his family's BANISHMENT TO SIBERIA AND EXECUTION there in Ekateringburg. The untoward incident was gorily depicted with explicit graffiti of what Rasputin did to the Czarina. The artist was clearly concerned with historical accuracy, as this type of uncompromising representation is exactly what supporters of the Czar found written on the walls when they arrived at the scene two days after the assassination of the Romanovs. Someone had speculatively added that the history of the world would be different if they had not been 'tardy'. Then the founding of the Soviet Republic, which a short time later became the USSR.

Joseph Stalin got two pages, well, one and a half really because Trotsky with an ice pick sticking out of his back occupied the second half of the second page. There was a crowd of onlookers with sombreros all shouting '*Viva Mexico*', all in the interests of accuracy of location of course, and a smilingly complicit Stalin was like a stamp in the corner. The other half of this page consisted of a picture of Stalin herding hordes of bedraggled peasants over the Urals. The figure 30,000,000 had been scratched out and replaced with 47,000,000 in reference to the recent revision upwards, and in another half page he was shown stitching Lithuania, Latvia and Estonia on to the map of the USSR. And then an explosion and then Stalin lying dead. It perhaps needed to be pointed out that the matters were not related – the explosion was the first Soviet atom bomb in 1949 and the second was Stalin's unrelated death in 1953.

Nikita Khrushchev followed Stalin and was shown banging his shoe off a desk in the United Nations in 1960, after an American spy plane had been shot down over Russia and then he was depicted handing out apartments and telephones and boxy Lada cars to lines of people. It said that when the first lady in space told him she didn't really want to go because she was afraid of heights he assured her with a pat on the head that 'everything would be all right'. He was shown invading Hungary while Sputnik circled overhead with a hammer and sickle on it. The first satellite launched from Earth was Russian. And then a portrait of Yuri Gagarin: September 12th, 1961: First Man in Space.

From Khrushchev until Gorbachev Russia was ruled over by a succession of aged and ailing old men. There was a picture of a doddery Brezhnev on a state occasion in Red Square. Brezhnev's staff had a great fear that he would drop dead in public during one of those parades in Red Square. He had to be seen there so that people would know that he was alive. They wrapped him in fur hats and heavy coats and propped him up on the balcony and prayed that he wouldn't keel over.

Then there was Gorbachev and his wife Raisa, both loved by the West but detested by Russians. *GLASNOST* and *PERESTROIKA* flew in banners over Gorbachev's head, leading his people to freedom, and became the two best-known Russian words in the world. The Iron Curtain came down or, in theatrical terms, went up. Then the last picture painted an ironic similarity to the hordes that Stalin was driving over the Urals – the 'free' people of Russia with their hands out and bubbles over their head asking for *chleb*: bread.

Soviet scientists were well represented in *The Remake*. They were ahead in many technologies – but now are unemployed. The 1918 Revolution, in theory at least, saw the rise of the proletariat through the suppression of unearned title, power and privilege. But were there any winners in this new *glasnost* – openness – revolution? We in the West thought Gorbachev was the great director of the new show. Russians do not agree. People had become free to say what they thought; a doubtful wage for the complete disruption of a way of life that was at least certain. Then as now about half of Russian people think the *starry system* that Ida had so much time for, was better. They think Gorbachev got it wrong. That he made a mistake.

I was impressed. Like a good cartoon *The Remake* carried quite a punch. Something of the mystery and vagueness surrounding Russia was dissipated in what amounted to thirteen colourful instalments of eleven historical bits and two maps. It also confronted me with

Russia's enormity. The Russia depicted was a mere half of the Soviet Union. The European Russia that we are familiar with is a short fifth of this half. Siberia makes up most of Russia and, on this map, it was exposed in full frontal.

Two years later I arrived again, topped up with Linguaphone Russian and full of new hope. I confined myself to one small flight bag. I replaced my spare pair of trousers with a laptop computer. My Russian was good enough to be understood and I don't really know why I bothered to make prior arrangements about a place to stay in Moscow before setting out for Siberia. I read Igor's ad in a magazine of puzzles and curiosities that I subscribed to. It said: *Russian engineer, 30, with large comfortable apartment in Moscow will arrange visa and accommodation. Speaks fluent French and English.* It was like the professor in St Petersburg again and I should have avoided it but I wanted to be doing something.

Long before he started wagging his finger at me I knew I had made a mistake. He was waiting at Sheremetievo Airport. He stood there, in front of all the other waiting people, rigid and erect. He was handsome but glum and there wasn't a hint of a smile on his perfectly oval, symmetrical face. Every shiny black hair was slicked back and his shoes were black and shiny too. His hand rose in a stern greeting and it was marble in perfection. His wet, brown, piercing eyes picked me out straight away and he came to me and shook hands. His hand felt as it looked, fish cold and without blemish. There was no hint of work in it. Neither callous nor bump. Then he held up a perfectly manicured forefinger and wagged it. His head inclined with severity and he said, 'We waste no time but get bus; where your luggage?'

'This is all I have.' The incredulous eyes ran slowly over the small flight bag and came to rest in reprimand on my forehead. I felt I had to apologise: 'I'm sorry, but I never carry any luggage.' His disappointment pleased me because it was an emotion. It was the deepest emotion he displayed in the few days I was to share his apartment.

He pivoted on his leather soles and marched to the bus stop in a manner that demanded brisk pursuit. There was an interesting queue. Lots of baggage and bundles and bags and cases and people. It took some time to load the shaky machine because only half of the door opened. A dark-looking man with a moustache and a lot of bundles put a little pressure on the unyielding half, but he was firmly reprimanded by the large lady driver who roared restraint. She didn't leave her driving cubicle. The wheezing sound of the engine indicated that she had her foot on the accelerator and dared not take it off. I didn't know exactly what she said but it sounded like an expletive. Its effect on the dark man was so profound I thought it was worth knowing. I also thought I might thaw out Igor by asking him a question and showing how serious I was about perfecting the language. For two years I had been working with tapes – I wanted to hear real people speak this difficult and beautiful language.

'Igor, what did she say to that man?'

'Shhhhhhhhhhh . . .'

Everyone was silent and glum and looking nowhere. The ragged machine jerked away uncertainly and trundled down a wide highway. There were no lane markings, despite four lines of traffic moving in both directions. Our valiant blonde navigator stuck to the inside and allowed a continuous line of biscuit tin Ladas to overtake in a constant crackling whirr.

The metro was a lot better for progress, but no better for conversation.

'Igor, where's the name of the station written?'

'Not so loud!'

Much of modern Russian retail trade is conducted from kiosks in the vicinity of the metro stations. In Moscow everyone travels by metro, it is cheap, fast, extensive and amazingly efficient. One of the very few things that Russians are sure of is that the train will come. A digital clock on every platform tells how long it has been since the last train. Waits of more than two minutes are rare. Some stations are like art galleries; others like sculpture museums, all are constantly being cleared by diligent and uniformed sweepers. So metro station exits are good for business.

The kiosks vary. Many sell genuine designer clothes and jewellery. It is hard to believe at first. There are fine stores all over Moscow and St Petersburg where trendy assistants sell designer clothes at designer prices but these same items are available from small kiosks in the vicinity of stations or almost anywhere there are shoppers. Kiosks can vary from upturned boxes to clapboard cupboards to modern architect designed chrome-and-glaze gazebo-like constructions. There could be a line of plywood stalls selling Coca-Cola, hotdogs, flowers, vodka, bras, shoes, shampoo and Nike runners, followed by a honeycomb section of modern, ritzy, hexagonal kiosks selling Levi jeans where beautiful girls pout and inspect their manicure while quoting prices that sound like they have at least one zero too many. The older kiosks will have an amazing range: washing-up liquid, videos and TVs, holy pictures, toilet paper, turnips and always vodka.

Outside this metro station there were lines and lines of kiosks selling CDs and coats and high boots and Adidas trainers for a hundred dollars. There were stalls selling tomatoes and cucumbers and a few with Walkmans and some with labelled Italian leather coats. And then some old Russian *babushkas* sitting on makeshift stools surrounded by a wide selection of vegetables and old plates and the inevitable used shoes, the *botinki*.

I stopped and showed interest in their produce and these *babushkas* smiled and joked. I nearly cried with relief. I enthusiastically gushed out a few malformed sentences. Igor came to a full stop. His jaw dropped and I thought he was in awe of my language. Then he gripped my shoulder and almost lifted me like a crane. His manicured hands had surprising strength. He hushed me in front of him, away from the lovely ladies. He was beside himself with outrage that I spoke to them.

'You must not talk to strangers! They know you are foreign. They are thieves, all thieves. They want to rob you. Quick. We must get trolley bus.' So Igor and I jumped across a wide brown puddle to get on to another bus driven by a clone of the valiant blonde. Almost all Moscow bus drivers are female, fat, blonde, red-nailed and glum. My romantic reminiscences of wild flowers and bees, of Ida Pskov and hill-walking were wilting in this reality.

The suburbs of all Russian cities are grim. Even the centres can be grey but the suburbs are awful. Thousands of people are crammed into badly constructed high-rise apartments. In the fifties it was Khrushchev's Soviet dream that every Russian family would have an apartment and a car. All the same. It would be an empire greater than any other in the history of mankind. An empire of the people where everyone had equal rights, equal opportunity and got equal reward for their labour. Everyone was to own a flat. There was to be no class distinction. Flats were to vary in size only depending on family size and needs. They were the same as Ida's in the Pushkin Hills and, though I never saw them, they would be the same in Vladivostok and in Kamchatka that poked down to Japan. Like a mould that cuts out cookies over and over again, the same blocks of flats had replicated themselves all over the Soviet Union. With little respect to tradition, location or environment they rose up out of the steppes; a monument to a lost dream of a flat for every family irrespective of race, colour, creed or location. Kazaks,

Tatars, Chechnyans or Buryats were to be boxed equally in locations as varied as they were distant. Here in suburban Moscow their awfulness is exaggerated by their sheer number. They go on forever like a repeat pattern in bad wallpaper. Miles upon miles of the same grey blocks. It is hard to know how people can pick any mark that distinguishes their block from the others. I often wondered how people knew where to get off the bus. At first I counted stops, perhaps they did too, but later I didn't have to. Igor's block was more stark, more rigid, more ominous, but most of all, more lonesome than the rest. Strangely, Ida's block in Pskov was architecturally similar but, in reality, another world. Her aura gave it a glow.

Igor led me to the passageway of his apartment block. It was probably no worse than others I had seen but I had forgotten how terrifying they are. It was dreadfully dank and fetid. The light that reluctantly shone on the opening was not enough to show in much detail the caked dirt on the wall but it was hard to believe that what was visible could have been accumulated in the thirty or forty years this block had stood here. There was graffiti, cans, bottles, discarded clothing and the remains of a shopping trolley. I had to paw around for the railing that Igor told me existed. It was a cold, damp, metal affair that came a little bit with me, no longer solidly anchored in whatever concrete thing once held it. My foot encountered steps . . . one . . . two . . . and then no more banister. It was a dank cave. My outstretched hands touched a living thing coming the other way and I screamed just as the metal cage that called itself a lift opened its door and cast out a dim glow. Igor tugged me into it and pushed a shaky button. The lift doors slammed shut and we were dragged up to the fourth floor by twanging, stretching cable. He kept his eyes unswervingly on the floor numbers displayed above the buckled door, though they revealed nothing except a raw wire protruding through the loop of the number six. He used two keys to open a blue metal door to a corridor that led to four apartments. A cat sat staring at us from the top of an abandoned metal-grey cupboard. As Igor produced his ring of keys like a warden, looking all around for spies, the cat spat and bolted. I wondered if I was entering Dracula's den. I knew nothing of this strange man. No one knew where I was. I wouldn't be missed for months.

As in all Russian apartments there were two doors, one right up against the other. The outer is like the armour plating of a security van full of bolts and rivets and the inner, in complete contrast, is often padded, plush and sometimes even deep-buttoned like a chesterfield couch. When the outer one is opened you think you are entering a bordello. Privacy starts here – or rather when one is safely inside, chained, locked and bolted shut. Igor's outer door had two locks and the inner, three. He was not really excessive in this; all inner doors have at least two locks that need keys as well as bolts on the inside. Indoors he took off his shiny shoes and stepped into slippers. Russians never wear street shoes inside. His glare indicated that I should do likewise. I had no slippers. He nearly said tut, tut. I could see it on his lips but he bit it back. He brought me a large pair, like snowshoes, and I thought maybe he did it on purpose; if I had to make a run for it they would slow me down. There wasn't any place to run to, we were on the fourth floor and the double door was bolted, double-locked and bolted again. The outer door always has a peep-hole.

These doors and locks are something of a metaphor for the Russian personality. Though they constantly complain of the necessity for such security, I feel it is more a physical manifestation of a psychological barrier that they like to maintain. They're all private. Igor was sinister.

Then he took me into the living-room and sat me on the couch that was to be my bed. Above it was a carpet covering the whole wall. The opposite wall was covered with bookshelves, built-in cupboards and wardrobes. One stood ajar. It had long, slinky, shimmering costume items and he quickly shut it and stood with his back to it. I had only caught a glimpse but it was enough to make out the heavy drapes of a black cape.

'I will take your money because it is not safe for you to have it.' My mind raced. Most of it, I said, was in travellers' cheques and plastic. I was thinking to myself what a ridiculous line to try, if he couldn't see into my mind by day, definitely when night fell he'd know all. The corners of Igor's mouth slipped down a centimetre and I saw with great relief that the teeth were still human. Then he went on so much about the money and how to get it out of me I relaxed, because Dracula would not have such an interest in mundane things.

I had a money belt around my middle, rigid with crisp new dollar bills. Russians won't take dollars unless they are new. Probably because they are in such great need they can't take a chance. But I didn't tell Igor this. I said most of my money was in travellers' cheques. I had some cheques but very few. They are little used in Russia. It is very much a cash society. I carried a small amount because it is a good idea to have a variety of money travelling anywhere but the bulk of what would take me to Siberia and back was swaddled around my middle like the explosive of some self-destructing fanatic. If they went, I went with them. It is a sad irony that what was so long resisted, the US and its trappings, had now its ultimate symbol, the greenback, as the only reliable means of exchange.

The word rouble has such a nice earthy resonance. It sounds like real money that is earned honestly by the sweat of one's brow compared to the fast-buck wages of the shady deal. But it was the bucks that Igor was interested in.

I survived the night with just a few nightmares. Before I could sleep I had to check out the wardrobe. The 'cape' was a large lady's evening dress and stole. Obviously it belonged to someone who loved pretty things.

The next day Igor marched me off to a bank of his choice to turn these clinical travellers' cheques into real bread. I hedged and insisted on changing only a couple of hundred. I licked up to him saying that I was taking his warning seriously and that I wouldn't want to be walking around with all that cash on me. 'Especially,' I said, 'with all those black people around.' It killed me to say it but I knew it would sound genuine to him.

Racism is a very serious problem in all of Russia. People from the Caucasian countries: Azerbaijan, Armenia, Georgia and Chechnya are called 'black people', altogether inappropriately since they are yellow-brown or Arab-looking. What is most disturbing is that black automatically means inferior. Even lovely Ida in Pskov called them the 'black people'. It was the only phrase she used with anything other than great kindness. *Loody cheornay*.

Every Russian person I met thinks this way. They never conceive it possible that some white people may not share their view. As far as they are concerned, anyone who is not white-skinned is inferior and has no rights. In a Moscow hostel I met a black American student of music. He was studying the piano. I spoke to him about racism. He said: 'It's worse in Russia than it is Europe, it's worse in Europe than it is in America, and it's very bad in America.' I could see he had been hassled so much that he had stopped believing that any white man was truly egalitarian. I felt cheapened by the inclusiveness, but I understood.

At the moment Chechnyans fall in for the most contempt. Azerbeijanis (mostly known as Azeriis) and Armenians have independent homelands now but not the Chechnyans. Their land is on an important oil-line route. It is commercially important for Russia to keep Chechnya – she has lost thousands of reluctant soldiers in the cause. Those in power and those without, to a man and woman, hate Chechnyans. Even Ida. Yet the Chechnyans are prevented from establishing their independence. Trouble is, Russia loves black oil but hates 'black' Chechnyans.

Later I befriended a Chechen street artist and we walked together around the city. On every block we were stopped by police. His papers were requested and closely inspected, I wasn't asked for anything. The sad irony being that he is a Russian citizen while I am a foreigner. When I told this to Russian people the only thing that amazed them was that I was talking to a 'black man'.

So I took advantage of this sad situation to explain to Igor why I wasn't changing much money. In reality, I had a couple of reasons. I didn't want to stay with him because he was humourless and his world was full of danger and demons. Also I wanted to keep some travellers' cheques. I paid him for a few days' lodging and knew I'd invent an excuse to pull out.

As soon as I met his mother, Nina, I knew who owned the costume in the wardrobe. She was a delight, but she only came in the evenings to prepare food for the next day before going to her own place. This had been her home, Igor had been married and she had moved out. He was now divorced. She was very round and bouncy and carried many colourful bags. She'd drop them down while she grappled with the double door and her large bundle of keys.

It was a very warm June in Moscow. By the time Nina conquered the lift and the double door, perspiration was beaded on her lip. She had no English but sometimes surprised with the odd word. 'H-o-a-t,' she'd say as she kicked off her shoes and slipped her chubby toes into shocking pink furry slippers with shiny buckles. She was an eye surgeon by profession, a cook by nature. In the Western world it is fairly easy to match someone with their profession. Not so in Russia, especially with older people. You'll meet a stout-block woman, almost a *babushka*, whom you'll expect to be a homemaker, stitcher, cook, a gatherer of food, and she'll turn out to be a marine biologist or perhaps an architect. It may be that career counselling didn't feature big in Soviet education or it may be that in the West career category is largely determined by your lineage. In the Soviet Union the needs of the state determined one's trade. Nina was a most unlikely eye surgeon. It would be easier to imagine her kissing the 'bold eye better' than wielding a scalpel. She performed eight operations a day and received thirty dollars a month. She made it sound like a fortune.

She was a welcome relief from finger-wagging. In no time the place was full of warmth and aroma. She'd overload the small kitchen table with strawberries, mushrooms, carrots, mint, cucumber and juicy berries in a hundred hues. She'd glide into the sitting-room, laden down with bowls of cherries sunk in cool water and plonk them on my desk with a playful little-girl curtsy and the fake admonition: 'All eat!' Then she'd waltz back to her cubicle kitchen and her little black and white TV where she'd watch ancient Mexican gypsy movies. The Russian soundtrack is dubbed in, the Spanish or English audible in the background. She'd draw in her breath with outrage at the carry-on of the baddies, her chores would come to a halt with indignation, then she'd release it in a gush as good inevitably triumphed. She'd skate around the little floor space in tight circles like a sugar plum fairy. She'd conjure up succulent dishes and land them on the table with a trill as she sang along with the heroine. Then, holding her round and dimpled hand mid-air, she'd turn her head to one side in admiration and anticipation.

Then she'd eat; and how she'd eat!

She'd slurp up all the juices and roll her eyes in ecstasy. She'd noisily suck her fingers one after the other. Then she'd summon Igor and me to partake and I'd wonder anew about inheritance. He'd poke things about the plate with a fork, a metallic extension of his long, manicured finger, placing lots of bits and pieces to one side as unfit for human consumption. She must have seen it a million times and yet I'd see her react as if it was his first rejection. It's in Russian but her face and dimples tell as much as the words: 'Awh Igor . . . such a piece of bacon you put aside . . . tut, tut, tut.'

Her *dacha*, a sort of country garden, was the source of her culinary ingredients. I thought *dachas* were places where czars and presidents rested or waited for coups.

Not so. A *dacha* is really a garden, a country place. In Soviet times every citizen had a right to a plot of land in the country to grow their own fruit and vegetables. Even through the ideals were egalitarian, in practice party officials got convenient places with nice residences. Ordinary mortals got a patch of earth to do with what they could. Nina, I gathered, was no party favourite; her *dacha* was modest. I begged her to take me there to help her. It took time. She didn't believe I'd like it, it was hard work, we could only go at the weekend.

Nina called for me very early. She had lots of bags folded up inside a strong hessian one. Her soft, fleshy, powdered face twitched in little eddies. I was strange company for her; I could see she was afraid I was going to be disappointed with the day. We walked along earthy paths, through little copses to a lonesome, seldom-used bus stop. Moscow has this curiosity of escaped countryside close to its centre. You'll find large patches of rough and weedy land and you'll find it hard to believe you're not somewhere else altogether, miles and miles from any town. You'll hear no city noises and you might come to a broken concrete road you'll think hasn't been used for generations. Nina and I traversed such a tract. She talked of the hard life, *gizn trudney*, which is *de rigueur* conversation for anyone on the way to work in Russia. It's like a mantra, which they mumble over and over again. Nina said it in many different ways but without self-pity. She thought life was wonderful. And then we came to that broken concrete road and a broken bus picked us up at a broken stop sign.

It took almost two hours to arrive at a destination. The other passengers were all going to *dachas* too – I could see by the empty bags and glean from the conversation. Nina didn't share her son's distrust of people, she talked to everyone. She varied her tone to suit the disposition they displayed. She shook her head in sorrow with bent *babushkas*; she threw her head back in laughter with teenage girls and tut-tutted seriously with the blonde driver in admonition of bad-mannered youths pushing an exit. Every now and then she glanced sideways at me, a little unsure, and then patted my knee playfully saying something like: 'It won't be long now.' And then we were in real countryside.

Alighting at the terminus she sailed like a dhow down a pathway skirting a stream. Then, listing playfully to starboard, arms spread out like wings and making childish engine sounds, she sailed through an unseen opening into Her *Dacha*.

When I caught up with her she was standing in the middle of it, facing me proudly, arms still spread out, but now in a curtsy pose that said: 'Allow me to present My *Dacha*.'

There were drills of potatoes and patches of cabbage and beetroot. There were marrows and cucumbers and bright red tomatoes. There were clustered bushes of berries and plums and blossoms and up left My Little House. Humble yet imposing it watched over things when she was away. Its wooden bits had aged to a sage grey and, raised off the ground on solid stones, it both owned and belonged to where it stood. She had customised it on location from bits and pieces drawn from building sites and dumps. It had outgrown its low caste origins and, costumed in hessian and with an aged chintz door flap, nicely underplayed a central role. For years I had thought a *dacha* was a mansion in the country belonging to a rich person. Like *banya* and *babushka* the real thing has to be experienced to be known. This was real *dacha* – not just the building but the berries the fruits and vegetables the earth the stream the clear air and Nina with her bags and baskets.

My Little House harboured crude implements and provided repose. Inside there was a garden fork with a missing prong, a spade and shovel and a triangular weeding thing with a branch handle, still barked in spots and hand-polished with labour. There was a bucket, once enamelled, and two other galvanised ones with circular metal bits screwed in to stop leaks. We started with these and watered. I fancied I could hear the sigh of relief as the vegetables soaked it up. Then I painfully translated my idea of piping the water from the stream to a tank on top of the shed and letting gravity do the work of watering. She chirped in support of my wisdom and only reluctantly mentioned the lack of electricity. We weeded and hoed and picked and plucked and repaired to the Little House for rest. She offered me the table but I insisted: 'No! You table, me floor.' When I awakened she already had our buckets, baskets and bags all lined up, full of glistening fruit and veg. And an extravagant bunch of flowers mixed with reeds, weeds and tall grass.

Nina was a real *babushka* but her son was her total opposite. I couldn't take the restrictions. Keys were a problem. He waited up at night rather than give me keys. His whole demeanour was a problem. At some stage in his engineering (he was now unemployed) he had to work in Siberia but he refused to talk about it. He silenced my questioning with a raised hand, palm out: Stop! I was bursting to know but all I got was: 'Awful . . . mosquitoes, had to wear a scarf over my mouth.' Further pleading got a double-handed STOP.

I had to find another place to stay.

In Ireland, while learning Russia's language and reading her history, I had met a young man called Maxim. He was studying at the department of Celtic studies at Trinity College. In one of Dublin's main libraries every Saturday a room is set aside for those interested in speaking Russian. No one is in charge, people just turn up and talk. The assemblage was interesting. There was an Iraqi researching Irish folk medicine, a beautiful, sophisticated medical doctor who sidetracked any queries about her origin, a Tatar who claimed to be from Tajikistan, and a Tajiki who claimed the Tatar couldn't be from Tajikistan because he didn't know the language, and then there was Maxim. He stood head and shoulders above the rest of us in stature, confidence and esoterica. I invited him to my home, promising to show him parts of my country I thought beautiful. In return I expected practice in speaking Russian.

He came. He spoke English, Gaelic and Sanskrit and strongly advised me to abandon Russian. I wasn't doing it justice. It hurt him to have to listen to me. Even Russians, he said, unless well-educated and from the right background did terrible things to the language. He said my Gaelic wasn't bad and my English passable.

Our lakes, rivers and mountains made him chuckle; they were as nothing compared to what I'd find in Russia if I returned. I asked him if I might stay with him if I did. 'In summer?' Anybody who knew anything about the finer things in life wouldn't be found dead in Moscow during the summer. But he had an aunt he said, 'not real aunt but kind of aunt' whom I might call on if I was really, really stuck for somewhere to stay. She was 'odd' he said . . . kind of odd.

She turned out to be nicely odd and snobby as anything. Her apartment was on the ground floor, half an hour from Red Square. Perfect! No lift, no hallway, her front door was single with one lock and one key which she handed over without hesitation. Odd indeed!

She was disdainful of everything. Quietly and sighingly disdainful of the Communist past, which had reduced all to the ranks and mode of the workers, and the present chaos that had reduced the unfortunate workers to paupery. She worked in some office dealing in financial products, which I didn't understand. She did it for her sanity and 'to help people' she told me, touching her forehead lightly with the back of her hand. She aspired to grandeur. She whispered her noble past and raised her brow in quest of condolence for what had happened to Her People. I didn't quite understand this either and suspected she was dreaming much of it. Her claim of noble lineage ran right up to the czars. I was a little afraid to ask for clarification of what I did not understand, because she had the power to relegate me to the rank of imbecile with the silent lift of a single eyebrow.

She had a black poodle with a protruding lower jaw and fleas. He scratched with vigour and dedication until the place vibrated. And he did it on my bed, which, as in Igor's, was a converted couch in the living-room. All Russian apartments have such couches.

Like Igor's also there were books. Larissa's living-room was completely lined with enclosed bookshelves. She had an impressive collection on ballet and music and poetry by Pushkin. Like Ida, she also had Dostoyevsky and Chekhov, but her most impressive tomes were connected with theatre.

She took down one on period costume and held it open and out from her, like a director. She mentally donned each costume and performed. She posed her free hand variously to suit the creation. With a limp wrist and tilting jaw she became a ballerina. She turned the page and made an 'O' of her mouth and inflated her chest to become an opera star. Then she was the sad and fading Czarina, tiredly waving to her subjects. The next page showed a peasant costume so she slammed the tome shut . . . performance concluded.

She rested a lot in her darkened room, door ajar. This room was to the right, off the tiny hall and impossible not to pass. She lay in a swoon on a large, fluffed-up, high bed dimly lit by a lamp made from a crinolined doll, the poodle on his back, naked, belly up, beside her. But when he got the urge to scratch he left his mistress' bed in a dash to mine and shook the flat from there. Her hair was dyed dark and cut straight with a fringe and a centre parting. It was too young for her wrinkled, heavily made-up face. She talked a lot on the phone in hushed, secretive importance. By phone she summoned her nephew Maxim ('Poor Maxim will be delighted . . . no blood relation . . . oh! No! Poor Maxim . . .') to show me Moscow and dissuade me from going to Siberia: 'Awful people, criminals, rough too.' I was a little embarrassed at the prospect of meeting him and trying to explain or lie about the reason I had taken up his offer of staying at his 'aunt's' house, but I needn't have worried. It didn't even occur to him to enquire. And he mustn't have remembered that he told me he would be in his 'country residence' for the summer. I'm sure he had none and I suspect Larissa was all he had for family. It appeared to me in this case and many like it in Russia that often people are unsure exactly how related they are to the cast that surround their lives. Men leave their wives frequently. Marriage is entered into and departed from with alacrity. It isn't taken seriously. I have spoken to a few young men who 'think' they will marry on Friday but they're not sure, *mozhet bit*: perhaps. Offspring of broken unions are often raised by 'aunts' who may be blood relations or sympathetic friends of abandoned wives. But if Maxim was no blood relation of Larissa then snobbery and disdain are clearly environmental.

He never mentioned Siberia but promoted Moscow. He promoted it as he went on to say that his visit to Dublin had been very useful indeed because it gave him an appreciation of what he had in Moscow. But he was embarrassed by his people and their great ability to say *nyet*. Everywhere in Moscow it is the favourite word.

'Can you change 100,000 roubles?'

'*Nyet*.'

'Can you tell me the way to . . .'

'*Nyet*.'

'Nice day isn't it?'

'*Nyet*.'

Nyet. It is the word that is most important to them. They will often say it and then go ahead and supply the information or service requested.

Red Square is the heart of Moscow and it is vast, about 400 metres long and 300 metres wide. At one end is St Basil's Cathedral. It's the famous one with eight colourful onion domes and one steeple which features in most guides to Moscow. Ivan the Terrible was so impressed with it he had the architects who designed it blinded to prevent their producing anything to equal it elsewhere. We entered the square from the far end under the golden eagles of Iverskaya Church. The famous Gum Store forms almost all the left side of the square. Centre right is Lenin's tomb and behind it a wall. Though it is long, high and sturdy it understates the splendour of what lies behind: the Kremlin. I used to think Red Square and the Kremlin were one. Later I thought the Kremlin was in the square. Fortunately I hadn't said any of this to Maxim. Though I knew he thought my going to Siberia was insanity, he would have dispatched me there with haste had he been aware of my ignorance. Moscow's Kremlin is ninety walled acres of churches, vaults, palaces, museums and a plethora of other architectural gems. Government buildings are here too. The castellated walls curl around to form palaces where czars dwelled, and look-out boxes for those who protected them. The whole place glistens with gilded domes and echoes with gongs and chimes. And yet there are lovely, little, quiet places where you can get lost in; small cobble-stoned alcoves with maybe a tiny, whitewashed church that looks like it escaped from some humble village.

Russians are justly proud of all of this. They know there is nowhere else on Earth like it: nowhere as splendid, nowhere as beautiful and nowhere that God has such a personal interest in. He performed many miracles to design and construct it and as many again to protect its treasures from the elements and marauding enemies. Were it not for His personal intervention, they tell you, there would be no Kremlin, no Red Square and no Moscow.

Maxim showed me his miraculous city. Almost everything of any interest or importance in Moscow has a miracle to go with it. Their miraculous stories are a little vague. Sometimes it is difficult to see the significance of the miracle or its connection to what is being illustrated by it. Much of Russian heritage is centred on religion. Though suppressed under the Communist system, most of its monuments have survived and there is a resurgent interest in things religious and in young men joining monasteries. Maxim said he was thinking of being baptised *mozhit bit*: maybe.

The main gateway to the Kremlin is called the Saviour Tower. Its miracle: A blind nun had a dream in which she saw dead patron saints rise up from their graves inside the Kremlin and leave through this gate. They were abandoning the city, which was under siege by the Crimean, Khan Mengli-Girei. They were carrying a statue of the Saviour. At the gate they were met by other dead saints on their way in who persuaded the ones on the way out not to leave but to stay and pray for the sinners of Moscow and its salvation. They did, and that day the Mongols were defeated. Now the statue is over this gate and people passing take off their hats and bless themselves.

These miracles sounded like the ones of my own Irish youth. I had been brought up in rural, pre-TV Ireland where entertainment consisted of listening to storytellers. They came rambling across the damp fields and sat around open fires telling and retelling stories of saints and demons and devils appearing unbidden. They frightened and thrilled me. I sat in the hob fascinated, and when finally taken by the heat and sleep and transferred to my feather bed my dreams filled in the endings. These Russian stories had different kinds of endings and there were bits of sequence missing. Other ingredients were added just for visual effect. Their stories are better staged than the Irish ones. Ours were for the spoken word, theirs are for theatre. All the positions must be filled in, even if they are superfluous to the story. The stage must be dressed. The stories are cryptic and often contain an obscured message. I couldn't figure out the significance of the nun, or her blindness, and where the miracle was if it was all only a dream. Maxim was appalled at my questioning. 'It's a miracle,' was all he'd concede to my request for clarification. In my school days priests chastised me for my questioning. They worried about my lack of real faith. I was known to search, unreasonably, for logic.

Maxim strongly suggested that my Celtic heritage left me a little deficient and I could hardly be expected to understand. But he continued to show me the sights and told me the miracles and added little magical, inexplicable snippets: Ivan the Terrible was married four times and in 1584 saw a cross-shaped comet and died a few days later. Peter the Great died on the eve of his wedding. The bell, as a summons to prayer, was used first in Moscow. Properly translated from the Russian, Peter the Great would be Bellicose Peter; Red Square properly translated is Beautiful Square. Lenin's mausoleum was first made of wood because they didn't know if the embalming process they used on the body would preserve it for long. Only when it did was it changed to stone.

Then he waxed serious to tell me the miracle of the Iverskaya Icon. In the fifteenth century its woman owner was visited by henchmen of the Emperor of Byzantium who said they were going to destroy the icon. Maxim didn't give a reason how they knew she had it – it was a miracle! 'She asked them to give her until morning. She took the statue to throw it into the sea but it didn't sink. It turned on its side and sailed away.'

The turning on its side was stressed but not explained. Her son went off and joined a monastery and told the monks about what had happened. They prayed and 200 years later one of them saw a pillar of fire in the water and sure enough it was the statue. They pulled it in and put it in the church but in the morning it was above the gate. They replaced it in the church many times but as soon as they shut their eyes off it went again, above the gate. I would have thought this was a fair indication that the icon didn't want to be in the church, that it wanted to be above the gate. But Maxim continued to tell me how one of the priests had a dream where someone appeared to him and said the statue didn't want to be in the church but above the gate.

I was impressed with the floating statue but Maxim told me that wasn't the real miracle, but rather it was the dream. Then there was a wooden church, which Napoleon tried to burn down, but rain put the fire out.

A miracle. The final miracle was how the Beautiful Square itself survived Stalin's intention to double its size by demolishing the Gum Store and the Cathedral of the Intercession of the Mother of God of the Moat. But Gum Stores survive. Most of the big designers from the West retail from within, selling their labelled goods at exorbitant prices. Strangely they are busy, but I don't know who's buying. My questions bring the answer: 'Shhhhhh . . . Mafia.'

It was my second time in Moscow. My second arrival seemed stranger than the first because this time I had come straight from Dublin instead of from Pskov and Suzdal. But now the buzz was back. I was beginning to burn away the strangeness. Memories of the first visit became a foundation and I was breaking through and communicating with the aura. Moscow as a whole is a dark and distant challenge, but divided into its constituent parts, it is easier to make contact. Even St Basil's strange circus onion domes are easy to separate. The confusion cleared and I began to see things in bits. I mentally disassembled it like a child's Lego architecture. Maxim and I developed a tenuous accord and I lowered my resistance to his sophist enunciation of Russian grandeur and greatness. I smiled and conceded and nodded and smiled. It is easier to be happy with what you have than get what you want.

Maxim believed cupolas are more personal and homely than spires. He said Orthodox churches are more like houses, especially when they are whitewashed. The

Russian word for cathedral, *khram*, comes from the Slavonic word *khoromy*, meaning house. Inside they have things fussy and gold for the gods and angels, but on the outside they are houses.

And I learned why Russian people don't smile a lot. It's not because they are humourless or sad, it is just their way. Smiles come later when you know them. The opposite to our way in the West where we smile a lot until we get to know people when contempt often takes over. Of course there are some like Igor who don't smile at all, but they are rare.

I wanted to go back to Treverskaya Street to the statue of Prince Yuri Dolgoruku to meet the one-armed man who had sold me the map that was going to lead me to Siberia. I wanted to go alone but Maxim was solicitous and, like most Russians, underestimated my ability to find my way.

It had been two years and I wondered if he would remember me. He didn't get the chance. In his place was a woman with a white scarf selling holy pictures and icons from an improvised table. Yes! she had know my friend Sasha but he hadn't looked after himself – '*ne beryeok sebya*' – and the hard winter had taken him. She made the sign of the cross and reverted her attention to the sale of her trinkets that would guide others to look after themselves or, failing to do so, would steer them to a better place, and if not that, then would at least provide her with the wherewithal to look after herself.

I had been dawdling. I hadn't much time on my hands and was anxious to test my Russian on a population that could put me right when I faltered, before exposing it to the other side of the Urals. But the discovery of the death of my director who, two years ago, had sold me the map, gave me the impetus to move. I felt unreasonably guilty for having lingered luxuriantly unaware of his departure to the ultimate destination. I only had to cross the Urals on a train; he had forded the Styx.

Maxim made no reference to my Siberian destination, such a gross, mundane goal didn't deserve the dignity of comment, but he was pleased with my mental progress after 'only two weeks in Moscow'. I was finally beginning to understand miracles.

Larissa talked a lot to the poodle about how stubborn and stupid I was for persisting with this crazy idea of going to Siberia while every civilised person, even criminals, was trying to get out of it. She kissed his damp protruding jaw and tut-tutted. 'My beautiful little dog wouldn't do a silly thing like that . . . no he wouldn't, he'd stay safe and comfortable with his mumsy in civilised Moscow. Big, rough, hungry Siberian dogs that eat people up . . . not like my little baby . . .'

It was mid-June and Larissa told me the season was well over. 'Winter is the time for the arts in Moscow.' But she said there was one final display of the best from all the dancing schools and she would try for tickets. She got them and declared that if I were to die in this crazy venture at least I would do it with a little culture.

She was very much at home in the theatre. Almost everyone was, despite its grandeur. The curtain went up and the billowy backdrop seemed as distant as a horizon. The first entrance was from up left to centre stage and the small, strong, dark male took three full marathon leaps to cover the distance. The orchestra sounded like it was overhead in the chandeliers. We sat not on tip-up seats, but on drawing-room chairs. First impression was of a great hall of Versailles. The chairs were in rows and numbered – but this was not immediately apparent. All the smiling and talking is saved for this place. In the interval, strangers talked to Larissa and she smiled down at them and whispered appreciation. She had borrowed a jacket for me from Maxim but she was still uncertain of what her friends would think. So she introduced me as her 'eccentric Irish friend – a scholar'. Then, if they were still doubtful, she'd add 'foreign'.

It was still bright when the performance ended and we strolled by the river before she deigned to enter 'the awful metro' to go home.

Maxim came part of the way with me in the morning. He was on his way to a library to look at some Sanskrit text. In the metro we talked about East and West. Muscovites don't consider themselves European. Officially the divide is marked by the Ural Mountains far to the east of Moscow but they ignore this technicality. They talk of Europe and America as 'the West'. Our relationship, Maxim's and mine, had traversed a fairly tight rope in the area of life comparison between Russia and the West. Because of my imminent departure I was disposed to a little patronage. 'I must admit the metro is excellent,' I said, to his obvious delight. We discussed the relative merits of other subway systems and I happily agreed that Moscow came out ahead in every respect except one. I was being very careful.

'And what is that?' he asked defensively.

'It is very easy to miss your station because the name appears in writing only once and if you don't catch the name over the public address you can easily pass it.'

'Ah yes,' he said. 'But in Russia you must be thinking all the time.' Then he added wickedly: 'In the West you don't have to think.'

It was cruel and unnecessary. Not think, indeed. I wanted to say: 'If Russians are such great thinkers how come the place is in such a mess?' But I didn't, I brooded.

Of course I'll never tell him, but gradually I came round. I started to admit to myself that maybe one had to be a little more circumspect to survive in Russia.

Chapter Three

It is hard for Europeans and Americans to appreciate the importance of the railway in Russian life. It is hardly an exaggeration to say that all long distance travel is done by train. Though Aeroflot is the largest airline in the world and Russia has an extensive domestic network, it only makes tiny inroads into rail travel. Airfares are modest for natives but still a lot more than they can afford. The people are afraid of accident on domestic routes. The record is appalling. The statistics of their disasters are lost in a haze born of hazardous life, but even Russians who admit to few fears avoid air travel if they can. They love to travel by train. They make vast preparations: cooking, packing and congregating for the send-off. In Soviet times rail fares were dirt-cheap. They now complain and say they can't travel any more – they say it's too expensive. Their fares seem cheap to me – mine does not.

Russians make no secret of their discrimination. They think black people are not the same as white people. They are inferior. They don't voice it, not because it is not nice but because they take it as universally understood. Even white people from what were once other Soviet countries are not to be trusted. They may be all right, but who knows? It's safer not to trust them. And Europeans and Americans? 'Well, they are not Russians.'

Foreigners pay more for their train tickets, so they buy them from different windows. The foreign queue is not the expected cluster of student back-packers, but an unfamiliar category of dark-skinned, weathered academics and people who look as though they have survived discrimination. The same window deals with people bound for all four corners of the former Soviet Union. They speak a mixture of unfamiliar tongues. Though Russian is understood throughout the former Soviet Union, all of the republics that comprised it had their own language. As well as Ukrainian, Latvian, Kazak, there were an estimated 150 other minor languages of little known ethnic origin. Most of the now independent republics have reverted to their individual language, sometimes with a patriotic zeal that nearly amounts to fanaticism. These former comrades – Uzbeks, Tajikis, Turkmen, Georgians – are now foreign and must pay the price of alienation at the same window as me. They stare with mistrust at the ticket-seller and she avoids their eye. She keeps her attention on a computer screen that almost mystically keeps track of seating. Prospective travellers, miles, even days down the line are accounted for and no duplication occurs. The seller doesn't talk to the ticket purchasers; she talks at a small mike, which transfers her words in cold, metallic, clipped phrases. Sitting in profile behind thick glass she is on a slightly elevated platform, which adds to the disdain of her office. When communication falters, she pivots the screen of information at the separating glass and taps it with a pencil.

There is no personal interest, advice or greeting. Ticketing is efficient, computerised and non-transferable.

Russian trains are numbered and the numbers go in pairs. For example, the 3 and 4 are one, both are the Moscow–Irkutsk train, but the 3 is eastbound from Moscow to Irkutsk while the 4 is the same train on its return journey from Irkutsk to Moscow. Odd numbers are eastbound. They are talked about with familiarity, like horses:

'The number 3 is very good; better than the 5 – my friend lost his wallet on the 5.'

'The 1 is quick, but full of Mongolians; they make everything greasy with their butter.'

'Don't take the 45, it's unlucky. So unlucky they changed its number; it's now the 44A but everyone knows it's the 45.'

'My uncle was going to take the 45 to visit his uncle in Komsomolskay-na-Amur and the night before his mother had a dream and she saw it diving over a bridge so she wouldn't let him take it and there was a fire under the seat he would have sat on.'

Railway stations are busy but orderly. People know their way around. Arrivals and departures are announced. Punctuality is amazing. Stations have individuality. Even if one isn't travelling oneself, it is worth visiting stations. Prospective passengers of each railway station give a good indication of the regions of this vast country. The one from which the Trans-Siberian trains begin also serves the detested southern, now independent, republics. The station policemen are busy with these black passengers; Armenians, Azeriis and a straggly bunch, looking like European gypsies. They are hauled into corners and crowded and scuffled until they reluctantly draw out their papers. Then they glare with haunted eyes, as the thumbing, uniformed officers pass the identities amongst themselves, searching for problems.

The policemen try to outdo each other in severity. One will scrutinise the document and throw a look of hatred over its owner as if to say, 'How could anyone as low as you exist?' He will then pass it to a colleague with a sidelong glance of suspicion. He'll rub his fingers together to rid them of any contamination contracted in the handling of their papers. The tension is such that at first I hold my breath for the poor mortals at their mercy. But then I see these 'black people' are made of stern stuff, they don't flinch, they return the stare. Not provocatively, they couldn't risk that, but they stand their ground. They stand up to the confrontation with a measured righteousness, just enough to maintain dignity without risking violence or being hauled away from their baggage and family. The inquisitors will confer, reluctantly return the papers and look at each other as if to relieve their eyes from the sight of scum.

Police operate only on the platform so passengers find peaceful refuge in high halls of waiting: cavernous, echoing exhibition theatres of cultural diversity. There are old Uzbek men, with square black hats and knotted walking sticks cut from trees far from Moscow; blind, old, bandaged *babushkas* led by puny, reluctant girls with scarves; excited, shaved-headed boys running in circles, engines at full thrust; dark-bearded Muslims sheltering their female charges; and blond, muscular, young Russian men with Adidas bags slung over one shoulder. They chew gum and see nothing.

There are announcements of departure to fairyland: Tbilisi, Yerevan, Baku and Rostov on Don, Samarkhand and Bokhara. And finally: 'Trans-Siberian train number 3 leaves from platform 13 in twenty minutes.'

The ticket said: *vagon* 14, *miesta* 36, *poezd* 3. Wagon 14, place 36, train 3. Wagons are clearly numbered; 14 was about centre.

The *dejurnaya* is a peculiarly Russian occupation. It is an office that carries much power, weight and responsibility. The Russian word is feminine; it's a woman's job. In hotels she controls floors, or sections of floors. She sits at a strategic desk and watches. She knows who is in and out, who is asleep or awake, who is drunk and who is sober. The person at the front desk inside the door assigns you to a floor, but it is the *dejurnaya* who says exactly where you sleep and how you behave yourself. She determines the degree of comfort and peace you enjoy. If you require an extra blanket, a cup of tea, or a headache remedy it is she who says whether you will have it or not. It is a monarchical office and the *dejurnaya* reigns, unchallenged, over long sovereign landings.

Dejurnaya power is such that an entire hotel does not have a reputation as a whole; it varies from floor to floor depending on the individual. She runs a staff of minions and, depending on her disposition, a corridor can be full of chirping, gossiping, happy women, or a galley of slaves, going grumpily about the chores of housekeeping.

Trains have *dejurnaya* too. (Officially they are *provodnitsa* but everyone calls them *dejurnaya*.) They stand on the platform outside their respective wagons to greet, threaten and warn. Each one has three assistants lined up behind her. They wear the same uniform as the *dejurnaya* but while she is the matron they are the ward maids. The *dejurnaya* of *vagon* 14 was two women. The one who met her passengers fifteen minutes before departure was confident, easy, even cheerful. The tag on her mountainous breast proclaimed her to be: Svetlana. She inspected the tickets, slowly. Assessed her clients and then thoughtfully indicated assent for them to find their *miestas* in her *vagon*. Svetlana asked for my passport, pretended that it was in no way unusual to have an Irish passenger and, after thinking for a long time, flicked it back with, 'Correct all! Please engage *miesta*.' One of her assistants followed at a distance to see I didn't sabotage anything.

Each compartment has four *miestas*: two up, two down. During the day there is no change in the arrangement. What are beds by night are still beds by day. Those occupying the upper ones are dependent on the magnanimity of those down for daytime viewing of the passing panorama. To look out of the window from the upper ones involves a manoeuvre that could easily involve landing on one's head on the floor below.

The compartments are well-planned, with space for luggage in bins under the lower *miestas*. Bedrolls are stored in a little loft over the entrance door and when these are rolled out on the *miestas* the space becomes available for more luggage. A *vagon* has nine compartments, two of which are occupied by the *dejurnaya*, her assistants and their trappings. These two compartments are their homes for a seventeen-day round trip to Vladivostok. In fact *dejurnayas* on this longest-of-all-haul trips live two-thirds of their working lives on the train. You can glimpse the domesticity when their doors are left open a crack. Off-duty ones wear rollers and dressing gowns. They have makeshift cookers and photos on the walls. Their uniforms are on hangers swaying to the motion of a 7,000-mile trip at a leisurely, reliable, average speed of forty miles per hour.

The Moscow–Irkutsk train moved exactly as the second-hand of the clock indicated it should. Embraces and kisses ended; some tearful ones, left behind, walked, trotted and then ran to keep up with their departing cousins. Their hot pursuit personified the almost universal desire to be somewhere else, somewhere other than 'here'. And those going were an ironic reflection of those who pursued them: 'Wish I could stay.'

My destination was Irkutsk, the halfway mark, the heart of Siberia. It was the place that the man with the one arm had said I was destined to go to. The trip would be four days and the initial punctuality was maintained throughout. The first shudder of movement that begins this eight-day odyssey is the birth cry of an entity: the *poezdka*, the trip. Every trip has an identity, an individuality. Once it has commenced there is little you can do to change it. Like a surfer riding a wave you go with it.

To this traveller, trips are offspring. You conceive them and then let them take their course. They mature in their own fashion, full of the lovely, unexpected quirks and turns that make life. On its way out of the station the train is forced to snake around revealing its complete length and form. A tame, itinerant, long, low, snaking beast destined to live its life in motion, hauling people over great distances: a slave to the whim of human instability. Its lonesome call as it curled around re-echoed what I had heard in the house of five children in the Pushkin Hill where I took refuge from the 'killer bee' two years ago. And then it modestly straightened itself out, demurely concealing its curvaceous length. 'Enough of that,' it said. 'Stop looking at my body.' So, guiltily, I was confined to viewing close up the section over which Svetlana reigned.

She took her assistants in tow as she set out to inspect her complement of passengers. She sat in each compartment for a few minutes and laid down the law. What the train had in length, Svet had in breadth. She was large standing; when she sat she spread. Her bulk occupied a large portion of the compartment. She had the standard blonde hair, newly peroxided and curled for the event. The nifty soldier hat of her navy uniform was held down with a formation of clips. As she sat, the skirt of her uniform stretched . . . and stretched and finally held her enormous thighs from flowing over the length of the *miesta*. She collected the tickets and filed them away in her important leather portfolio. She tucked each one into a numbered slot. This was her register, and her assurance that her rules were kept. Submission of the ticket was a kind of undertaking to live train life as she dictated. Tickets are returned on arriving at the destination. They act as a kind of documentation. Getting the ticket back means you have served your time, that you have paid the price and now are deemed suitable to spend a spell on terra firma.

She offered laundered bed linen in sealed plastic bags for about six dollars. Her assistants scurried back and forth, fetching. Her nails were long and red and she used them to effect. She pointed like Igor: 'No drunkenness; no swearing; no dumping material out of the windows; no opening the windows. Understood?' Any transgression could incur serious penalty, which would be imposed by the train police. She was firm, but she inspired confidence and there was a touch of solicitude. She told me in an aside, in deference to my being a foreigner, how to use the samovar at the end of the corridor. She said if I couldn't manage it not to hesitate to call for help. All Russians knew how to use such things, she said. It was a minor gurgling monster of flame and pipes and taps and bore little resemblance other than rotundity to the brass tea-makers I had seen on land. 'Don't be afraid of it, just ask me and I will do it for you, no problem!' she assured.

This was the mellow, evening Svetlana. The mornings saw another woman.

My compartment companions were father and daughter. Three people, four *miestas*, the computer had benevolently decided that spare spaces should be equitably distributed. My compartment companions didn't see me for nearly two hours. They spoke to each other in business tones. They stowed and arranged and shuffled and re-did. Zips were done and undone; bags were consigned to bins with a finality that said they would stay there for the rest of the trip and then, five minutes later, they were resurrected in search of toothbrush or salt. She called him Papa; he called her *Devushka* (little daughter). When she was tired or impatient it became Pap–ah—ha!

Their line of vision never crossed mine. I tried to catch their eye but missed every time. They found a hundred imaginative, safe places to look in this confined space. They took off outer garments and hung them carefully on hangers. Street shoes were tucked away, carefully, under seats before they ate. Potatoes, greasy chicken legs and crude, torn-off bits of dark, hard bread (called black bread in Russia). The fare was released from a swaddling of newspaper and I wondered who packed it. She wouldn't and he wouldn't or would he? Most Russian men wouldn't, but he was a little different – deferential to the daughter. Like Russians everywhere the train's off was their signal to start eating. An ancient fear of starvation on a long trek spurs them to get into the food straight away. Trip and food seem to have a one-to-one correspondence:

'I'm going to Kiev.'

'Oh! I'll make potato cakes for you.'

Much of what I remembered about my gulag escapee was about his obsession with starvation. I remembered one vivid section where he was assailed with great hunger and somehow came upon a chunk of black bread. It was frozen solid and he had no teeth. I felt his frustration then and now recycled it as Papa and *Devushka* ate. They ate too busily. They held their chins out over the little shelf table to avoid drips, and chewed excessively. They wiped away dribbles with bits of the bread and then ate them. When there was no business left to occupy them, so they could avoid talking, they made going-to-bed movements.

I couldn't take it any longer. 'Where are you going?' I asked. It was a bold, ill-conceived question for I couldn't face the night without some talk. Russians are given to lengthy silences; Celts are not.

An awful stillness for a minute. I thought he wasn't going to answer, then, with a sigh of relief that I was ordinary and spoke his language, he told me his very ordinary life.

He was a widower from Crimea; this (proud hand sweep) was his daughter. She didn't acknowledge, tucked in a blanket instead. They were on their way to see his other *devushka* who was a teacher in Zema, three and a half days away.

He came to the point quickly. 'How much do you earn?' He mirrored my abruptness but a different set of rules apply. It is a question one Russian would never ask another Russian. But foreigners are different. They are outside reality and they don't need the same delicacy in these matters. A truthful answer to this question has nothing to recommend it. It is unlikely they would believe the truth. Why would one earning so much be travelling by train, and second class? So I answered with a premeditated lie:

'One hundred and fifty dollars a week.'

'Whee! So much.'

Teachers in Russia in 1997 got ten dollars a week, pensioners more – sixty dollars a month; Nina, the eye surgeon, got thirty dollars a month for performing up to eight operations a day. Russians dress well and they love gadgetry. Had things been otherwise, Russia would probably be the most advanced consumer society in the world. In Moscow there are shops selling designer clothes: shoes 200 dollars, *dzheens* (jeans) 100 dollars, cute little tank tops for 100 dollars up. People say these are only frequented by the Mafia, but it is hard to tell. It's hard to tell who is in the Mafia, what it is, or what it does. There are those who cruise around St Petersburg and Moscow in four-wheel-drive Japanese jeeps and dress like Italian men. They carry handbags and mobile phones and look very serious. But no one will say exactly what they do. 'Ooohh! Maaffiiaa shhhhhhh!'

In the *starry system* all groceries were sold through state-run outlets called *gastronoms*. They were large barn affairs with endless lines of shelves loaded mostly with bread and vodka – well, before 1992 they were. Then, in 1992, when the Soviet Union broke up and the shortages became public knowledge they got much exposure in Western media. These *gastronoms* were seen nightly on TV news programmes; empty lines of shelves and many square Russian shop assistants saying *nyet, nyet* to despondent shoppers. But now the *gastronoms* are gone or have been converted to supermarkets like those in the West. They have the same range of goods as any store in Ireland or England, and at the same prices. It is a situation that matches the frustration of the gulag escapee and his lump of black bread: it is there but it cannot be eaten. They are busy. No one earns a decent salary, yet everyone is spending. And everyone is very curious about what people in the West earn. They ask early on in the conversation.

'If I had 150 dollars I would be very happy . . . very, very happy.'

'How much do you earn?' I asked.

'Ohhh, in Russia we don't ask such questions.'

When he retired I took to the corridor to find out what I could. Next door there was a very large granny. She fanned her sweating face as she ate. She sat among a cluster of bags, all oozing evidence of food. My first glimpse of her was with a chicken leg across her mouth, the hairs of her chin glistening with grease. Her granddaughter was busy poking deep into the bags and producing tasty morsels and placing them in her granny's inflated hands. Her son, the child's father, was a very handsome blond man of about forty who sat in a tip-up seat in the corridor doing crosswords. He didn't speak for four days. His mother did. She hollered for the child to lead her to the toilet, or to fetch *chi* (tea) from the samovar, or to dive into the food bags for sustenance. She hollered in wheezes; obviously an unhealthy woman. I pretended intense interest in the passing countryside, but was in fact watching the reflected action of their carriage. The train had left Moscow at nine and by ten it was already dark. There was nothing to see, so my pretence of peering out was like Alice in Wonderland viewing reality through a looking-glass. Eventually I was alone in the corridor, so I reluctantly conceded to the night and went to bed, but not to sleep.

I was aware of the train's battling on through the inky darkness. I felt sorry for it. Lying awake an old refrain or half-remembered rhyme comes into my head . . . the train struggles uphill . . . *I think I can; I think I can; I think I can* . . . then as it is almost there: *I know I can; I know I can; I know I can* . . . and racing down the decline: *I knew I would; I knew I would* . . . carried away I enjoined the refrain aloud and guffawed like the schoolboy I was remembering would. My Crimean friend sprung up worried.

'You all right, friend?'

'Yes . . . just helping.'

'You need *chi?*'

'*Nyet. Spockyniy noche.*'

'Sure you are all right, friend? You need sleep.'

Foreigners!

The dawn was wonderful, but Svetlana was wicked. She tumbled out, a tousled mop in a dressing gown, full of protest and invective. She threw down mops, buckets and orders. Her blonde hair, imprisoned in curlers, jerked in furious protest at those who dared to pass her on the corridor. She squeezed the cord of her dressing gown tighter and kicked imaginary obstacles out of her way. Her assistants sprung to attention but her business was too tumultuous to bear assistance. She threw back compartment doors, oblivious to privacy, and glared at imagined dirt and debris. She punished every rail and sill with polish and rub, as she heaved in protest. Only when she had retired to her compartment, with as much slam as one can get out of a sliding door, did people venture out.

'Women!' my companion whispered, making sure *Devushka* didn't hear. Then he quietly eased utensils out of his bag and set the table. He laid out three cups. He had only one spoon and he set it beside my cup. He padded up and down the corridor with steaming water and only when everything was in place did he gently stir his lumpy daughter. She shook off his hand, so he tried again even more gently. She came too, blinking and scowling, grabbed the spoon to pile sugar in her cup, and huffed back to her bed with it. He cast his eyes gently up, I thought he was going to say, 'Women,' but he didn't.

Despite how remote Moscow is for many Russians it is still the marker that determines time and place. Train time is Moscow time and the most important bearing, distance from Moscow, is measured in kilometres. The milestones (kilometrestones sounds strange) mark the distance from there. They are on the south side of the track and take a little getting to know. At first they flash by so fast that it is impossible to read what they have to say but then you develop a knack. Put your face right up against the glass and look as far as you can in the direction you're going and when you see one approaching don't let it escape. Hold it with your eye and the focus of that eye travels with it and then you know how far you have to go to Vladivostok. I was delighted when I learned this trick. I subtracted this from the total distance and knew how far we'd come and then I saw others looking the other way and discovered that the other side of the stone tells the distance we'd come. So, same trick, head right up to the glass, see a stone approaching, reverse head and in its departure away back towards Moscow you can read how far you've come. No need for subtraction. Maxim was right: 'you must be thinking . . .'

In the train corridor there is a timetable and it also tells the distance from Moscow so you know which town is coming up. It tells the time of arrival at each station and how long it will stay there and what time it will depart.

The shortest stops are two minutes, the longest twenty-five. Last night I had been surprised by frequent stops very close to Moscow at suburban stations and wondered if I had taken a really slow train that was going to stop at short intervals all the way. 'Oh the number 3! Wouldn't dream of it, stops at every station.' But it didn't. Once we got up steam, or rather electricity (as in the West, practically all trains are electric now), there were lengthy intervals between stops. Two hours out, after it had become dark, we passed close to Suzdal where Mikhail and Anna had drawn in their children when I told them of my ambition to go to Siberia. I would have waved symbolically but, though no one looked like they were looking at me, I knew I was under scrutiny, so I just smiled in satisfaction instead. They thought I was crazy, that I'd never make it: *knew I would . . . knew I would . . . knew I would*.

We had crossed the Volga at k.289 (289 kilometres from Moscow) before I slept. I had a problem turning down the volume of 'The Volga Boatmen' that played in my head. The river is to Russia what the Nile is to Egypt and though I only barely saw it through the dark, its greatness resonated.

I awakened just before Svecha at k.818 as we passed through serious taiga. Taiga is a vast coniferous forest made up mostly of cedar, and is so extensive and remote that it has escaped human interference and aged to haunting density. And at about k.880 we crossed a river called Vyalka and pulled away to an area of vast fields and scattered wooden villages. The first lengthy stop was at Kirov at k.975. The town got its name from the man who was expected to succeed Stalin, but while Big Joe cultivated him Kirov shone too bright and ended up dead. He probably started a trend, for it was at this location that Stalin's great purge of the thirties took hold. The town now has a population of half a million.

It made me think of ballet and escaping dancers. Was it from the Kirov ballet that Rudolph Nureyev escaped? Better not ask . . . might be a bad mistake, inappropriate, or maybe no one knows. The slow, groaning, screeching approach along bending rails is far from the glitter of the ballet world. A vast expanse of tracks is choked with weeds. One lonesome, abandoned carriage is overcrowded by growing daisies. The platform is lined with *babushkas*. Their anxious faces take in the possibilities. Good. The sun is bright and hot and as soon as the train stops everyone is on the platform.

Svet has emerged, gushing. Her hair is flicked out in curls around her uniform cap, set at a jaunty angle. Her buttons twinkle and shoes glisten. She counsels care with the steps and offers a helping hand. She tells me this is the place to buy *blini*.

'In all of Russia we have good *blini* – but here in Kirov . . . the best!' kissing her pursed fingers.

She is right. *Blini* are pancakes, folded in squares or triangles around blocks of fillings: cheese, *smetana* (a type of sour cream), marmalade or berries. They are juiced and sugared on the outside and there are as many varieties and variations as there are busy *babushkas*. They wrap and parcel, take money and give change. Their cheer grows as the bundled roubles poke out of their apron pockets.

There are some non-*babushkas* too. Whinging, pinched women who try to sell inferior fare. Their failure makes them even more bitter and they blame all around them for their bad luck: *gizn trudney*. They are furtive and shuffling, of the moment, exploiting it, knowing that they will never again see this set of customers.

But most of them are amazing in their dedication to a passing trade, whose satisfaction has no bearing on tomorrow's business. Sold out, they stand shuffling in satisfaction, curious, but unwilling to ask any questions. I also am shy but know I will regret an opportunity not taken, so I direct a question at a clutch of these women.

'Do you do this every day?'

They crowd around, laugh at my Russian and find out all about me: my age, marital status and that I earn 150 dollars a week.

'How much do you earn on a morning like this?' I ask.

'Oh, in Russia we don't ask such questions . . . very bad.' Then, handling the fabric of my Marks & Spencer shirt: 'How much costs such a shirt?'

They tell me that the *gizn* is *trudney*, but I see happiness in their eyes.

The happiness turns to panic and that is how I know the train is moving. I freeze. I'm wearing my money belt, but my remaining few possessions are on board. The folding steps have been taken in. In a flash the city of escaping dancers and assassinated greats, even a city full of *babushkas* like those facing me, suddenly loses all its attraction. Even Svet, standing in the open doorway, looked gorgeous as the train swept her away from me. A flurry of women scoop me up and bundle me into her waiting arms. She has seen what has happened and is folding out the steps when I collide with her. She isn't prepared for the impact and we land on the floor in a greater intimacy than either of us had ever anticipated. We disentangle and wave thanks to a scrum of laughing *babushkas*.

Gizn trudney.

Papa is surprised at my amusement. He tells me people are often left behind at stations. His daughter isn't interested; she's busy with a make-up mirror. Then he sees that I am feigning mirth, so goes with his cup to the samovar. He puts in a spoon of honey and, setting it steaming before me, he says, 'Drink!'

It is seven hours until the next stop. This is at 19:45 Moscow time. The train runs on Moscow time throughout. This leaves it eleven hours out of sync with local clocks by the time it reaches Vladivostok. At first this seems like another senseless rule, hung over from Soviet days. It is something Westerners comment on with a chuckle and shoulder shrug. But in a country that spans eleven time zones it is sensible; it makes for easy calculation of time taken, without adjustment for local differences. All timetables in all of Russia, from the Caspian

Sea to the Arctic Ocean, and from Europe to the Far East, run on Moscow time.

At k.1,000 there's a town with the unfortunate name of Bum. It has a second half to it but who'd remember it! And after Bum there are miles and kilometres of fields of cabbages and glasshouses, obviously a section of some massive agricultural project of former times. It still looks well-kept and there are loads of villages of bright doors that indicate vivacity and hope and the train is fairly skipping along. Then with a blast of a whistle the train changes its tune to an ominous deep-throatedness as solemnly we cross miles and miles of swamp.

A short stop at Mendeleevo, a town called after the Dmitri who developed the periodic table. Then a full orchestra of sound from the train: bass, drums, trombone and even a cannon: we've reached Tchaikovskaya, called after himself, that eponymous Russian composer of ballets and symphonies. Peter Illyich Tchaikovsky is supposed to have died of cholera but there is a someone-told-me-that-someone-told-her story that he was actually blackmailed into taking poison because of a homosexual affair with the nephew of a St Petersburg nobleman.

I had read that you could figure out the speed of the train by counting the time between milestones so I count and watch and figure out that because there are fifty seconds between stones we are going at sixty-five kilometres per hour.

Perm 2 looks marginally better than it sounds. I half-expected two heads of hair teased and curled and burnt to a frizz. It was home to one of the most infamous gulags of the Stalin era, but is now not significantly different from any other station on this epic line. It is grey, gaunt and full of the signs of decaying, rusting industrialisation. At 1,437 kilometres from Moscow, it is the last European stop. Tonight the train will struggle over the Urals to cross the divide between two continents, Europe and Asia, at k.1,777. It's the marker that I've been waiting for: 1,777 kilometres from Moscow: Asia.

Here, at Perm 2, selling women are oblivious to their proximity to this geographical goal post. They have potato cakes, still steaming and coated with crusty breadcrumbs, and doughy dumplings variously filled. These are cosseted in a variety of saucepans, buckets and bags and topped with swaddling clothes of crushed newspaper and steaming, damp cloths. The timetable is so accurate they can supply piping hot food. It is prepared in their homes yet it arrives as if it just came out of an oven on the platform. The vendors ease off the lids and release a homely gush of steam and smell. They invite inspection and display no insult when one passes to a neighbour for comparison.

Clutching a warm bundle wrapped in newspaper, I am the first back on board and view the line-out from a safe distance. Despite the warm sun of late evening every *babushka* wears a scarf, sometimes over another head-covering. Most have traditional, country, cauliflower faces but there are pinched city ones too. A few have makeshift trolleys and two, of about forty, are accompanied by their men. The pairs are more efficient. One deals with goods, the other with cash, but it is clear they are battling the prejudice of custom. It is not a man's job. The single sellers are engaged first and only when they are overcrowded does the overflow resort to the partnerships. Even then it is with a little guilt, and they deal only with the man's hand. No eye contact is made, it saves him embarrassment at what he is reduced to: sobriety and this!

It is going to be dark for the crossing, I know, but I'm going to be prepared anyway. Vindication is on the horizon: I'm going to ride over the hills into Asia on the other side despite all of the *ochen kolodnays* and *ochen delakos* and *nyets*. Out of Perm we're out of forest and into open plains and mild meadows and trees and . . . what's this . . . daisies? Sure we're not gone astray? What next? Roses?

Night falls and still nothing. Are these Urals Mountains or molehills?

At k.1,747, thirty kilometres short of the crossing, through the darkness I see the shell of a vast factory and Lego-block apartment buildings with a light here and there. What's a high-rise doing here? And then for thirty kilometres I press my forehead to the window, this time really trying to see outside.

I awaited the change from Europe to Asia alone, in the corridor. I cupped my hand to the glass in an effort to penetrate the darkness. I only saw ghosts. Ghosts of other disappointments. The crossing is nothing. There is no wall, no tower, not even a river, and if there is a kilometre marker for k.1,777 it is lost to the night. An earlier traveller, P.L. Jefferson, had written about the crossing:

Hills piled upon hills, shaggy mountains and gaunt fir trees and beyond them dwindling away into the mist of the horizon the great steppe land of Siberia.

I saw nothing of it.

A lonesome whistle sounded at what I estimated to be the vital time but there was no one to ask. I played with the idea of wakening Papa but decided I couldn't explain what I considered so significant. After last night's 'I knew I would' and the Kirov incident, I thought he might be offering me more than tea with honey if I woke him again.

Even the blond crossword-solver had gone inside. My urge to mark the moment was stillborn. I contemplated opening the window to test the Asian air for difference but, although Svetlana now slept, I shuddered at the thought of the morning if she discovered. I crept past her compartment, slid open the door where man and daughter purred in their *miesta* and, slipping under my grey blanket, slept in Asia.

I am ashamed to say I slept through Ekateringburg. A city of one and a half million, it was home to pivotal events in Soviet, Russian and Siberian history. It was here that the last Czar Nicholas II, his wife Alexandria, their four daughters and only son Alexei were assassinated by the revolutionaries. What follows is the Romanovs in a nutshell. Alexandria was German which caused some conflict due to the war in progress with that country. Their son Alexei was a haemophiliac. The Siberian monk and seer, Grigori Rasputin, was supposed to have magical powers of healing and Alexandria sent for him in desperation when her son was lying in a coma from internal bleeding and in danger of dying. The Romanovs didn't want the public to know of their son's illness. As well as his curative powers Rasputin was 'weak of the flesh' and had a deserved reputation for frequent drunkenness and crass behaviour in brothels. He loved all women, but apparently was especially fond of gypsies and 'hot-blooded ladies'. He was summoned to the palace and whatever spell he wove was responded to by the boy. Alexei became well and developed a trust amounting almost to dependency upon Rasputin. The monk often dined with the family and shocked everyone by his outspokenness, drunkenness and lewdness. A rumour abounded that he was intimate with the Czarina. It was never proved or disproved but the supposed goings-on were depicted in graffiti in the vicinity of the palace. Effigies of the pair in compromising couplings were burned in public. But the Czar and his wife were very much in love and when apart wrote sometimes more than once a day. The rumour it seems did not drive them apart. The Czar was afraid of the revolutionaries and the threat to his throne. He really believed in the God-given right of the czars to rule. He said of his people: 'Their souls belong to God, their flesh is ours.'

A male cousin of the Czarina took it upon himself to have Rasputin wiped out. As a member of the Russian aristocracy, this cousin was having a rather good Imperialist time and didn't want it all brought to an end by a troublesome Siberian monk so he summoned him to the palace. His efforts to poison Rasputin proved more difficult than he expected. The monk had at least once exposed himself while doing a dance on a table in a brothel and thus gained himself the reputation of having the genitalia of a horse . . . it seems he had the strength of one too. He couldn't resist food, women, or alcoholic drink. Cousin offered him buns laced with cyanide and plenty of wine. He polished off the lot, sang a song and asked for more. He had eaten five buns. The apothecary who had made up the poison had assured Cousin that all Rasputin had to do was take one bite and he was past tense. They brought him more wine with so much poison in it that Rasputin complained it tasted of the barrel and roared for more 'fresh wine'. While waiting for it he danced. Bored with the waiting, Cousin shot him in the heart.

He lay dead.

Just to be sure, Cousin pumped five more bullets into his body and went for a drink himself, tired out with all the assassinating. He came back with some help to move the corpse, which had escaped not only from the palace, but over the gate and had gone for a walk by the river. Some say that he died from swimming in the winter river, or fell in, but there is still no consensus on whether

Rasputin was poisoned, shot, drowned or died from a heart attack after sudden immersion in the freezing waters of the Neva.

It seems that Rasputin suspected the summons to the palace of being something other than cordiality. He left a note for the Czarina saying if he was killed by the revolutionaries, not to worry, she'd be all right, but that if he were killed by a relation of hers none of the royal family would live more than two years.

Right again, Rasputin. They were all shot in the Ekateringburg through which I slept. Their bodies were discovered two days later by supporters of the throne but to this day they have not found a final resting place. Church and state disagree about where they should be interred. The haemophiliac heir Alexei's body was never found. For many years a woman calling herself Anna Anderson claimed to be Anastasia, Alexei's sister, who is supposed to have escaped before the shooting. However, after her death in the 1990s a DNA test was carried out and it did not correspond in the way it should with that of Anastasia's cousin, Prince Philip of England.

Thus the revolutionaries came to power. Communism and the Union of Soviet Socialist Republics was born and led by a gaggle of various Communist leaders. While Rasputin was busy predicting the future and the revolutionaries were assassinating the Romanovs, Vladimir Illyich Lenin was in exile in Switzerland. The Germans were interested in keeping Russia as unsettled as possible for their own ends in the raging First World War and it was they who arranged the smuggling of Lenin back to St Petersburg. The train in which he arrived is still on display at a station called Finlandia in that city. Churchill commented that the Germans smuggled him back in a sealed carriage like a 'plague bacillus'. He got a hero's welcome and led the Soviet Union until his death in 1924. Had he been succeeded by Leon Trotsky rather than Stalin, the history of USSR and of Communism would have been very different. Trotsky was an intellectual with an idealistic view of Communism as a force for an equitable world. Trotsky said Stalin was Genghis Khan with a phone. The one with the phone got the job and Trotsky had to go into exile, first to Alma Ata (later Almaty), the capital of Kazakhstan, later to Norway and finally to Mexico where he had the ice pick planted in his back courtesy of Uncle Joe. After the demise of the Czar, Stalin's evilness was a close second favourite of the authors of *The Last Shortest Remake of Russian History Ever Written*.

Stalin's vital statistics are astounding and as history unfolds the deaths attributed to him increase all the time. The last highest estimate theory quoted 47 million people. That is a quarter of all Russia. One in four people wiped out by a single man. At the same time 10 million more were annihilated in the Second World War which leaves one wondering how the race survived. Between Stalin and the Great Patriotic War (that is what Russians call the Second World War) almost sixty million people died from unnatural causes.

My slumber through Ekateringburg also saw me sleep through one of Khrushchev's finest hours. He was Stalin's successor and though given to a severe intake of vodka, he did have a dream for the Soviet people and he did denounce Stalin. He also didn't trust America. He had reason. Page six of *The Remake* said:

Forty-six kilometres outside Ekateringburg on 1st March, 1960 Gary Power was shot down while piloting a U2 spy plane in Soviet aerospace. Nikita Khrushchev said nothing. The Americans said: 'We're missing a meteorological aircraft over the north of Turkey.' More silence from N.K. Then the Americans said they were quite worried about it and that what probably happened was that the pilot's mask failed and he passed out and the automatic pilot took over and it was even possible that the plane could have strayed into Soviet air space but that there was 'absolutely no deliberate attempt to violate Soviet airspace and never has been.' Nothing from Nikita. All the time they hoped that Gary Power would have used the poisoned needle they had packed for him or that he would have pushed the self-destruct button in the sophisticated U2 spy plane. They couldn't believe that the Russians had the technology to detect, much less shoot down a plane at such a height. Gary landed alive and well complete with the 7,500 Russian roubles he was carrying, gold rings and presents to please the hearts of Russian women.

It took Nikita seven days. His timing was beautiful, then he went on TV and addressed the Americans. What he had to say he called 'my little secret'. He told them they would be glad to know that Gary Power was alive and well and in his company. He even had his photographs developed for him and they were good pictures of Soviet military installations. Then he said, seeing that he was flying so high, perhaps he intended visiting Mars and leading astray its females with the lovely gifts that he carried. He was shot down from 68,000 feet. That is more than ten miles up. He was sentenced to life but released two years later in return for two KGB spies. The plane is still on display in Ekateringburg.

Having slept through so much I decided on a four-hour vigil. A kind of Lenten preparation for Siberia. We still weren't there. Asia yes, Siberia no. The Urals mark the divide between the two continents but not the beginning of Siberia.

Russia is divided into *oblasts* just as Ireland and England are divided into counties or shires. And like Ireland or England, a county or shire often takes its name from a town within it. For example, the city of Cork is in County Cork; Bedford is in Bedfordshire. It is the same in Russia. They tag a 'skaya' on to the end of the town name. Thus Tyumen is in the *oblast* Tyumenskaya. The old name for Ekateringburg is Sverdlovsk, so Ekateringburg is in Sverdlovskaya. Sverdlovskaya is in Asia but it was not until the train reached the boundary of Tyumenskaya that we entered Siberia. Siberia makes up three-quarters of Russia's land mass and half of its people. Still, when Russians who are not Siberians talk about Siberians, it is almost as foreigners or, at least, very backward country cousins. It was never a separate republic like Ukraine or Georgia; Siberia was always a place within Russia. For years I had searched out this simple bit of information. The boundary has no political significance, merely a demarcation between districts. The demarcation is 2,078 kilometres from Moscow.

And then I missed the second crossing. Nothing to say we were going into Siberia. The first I knew of it was the city of Tyumen, which is the first and oldest city in Siberia. It holds half a million souls and was founded in 1586. It grew out of the necessity to have a holding pen for exiles before they were herded farther east to work in salt mines. Banishment to Siberia was no invention of Stalin though he honed it to a fine art. The tendency to send undesirables to far away places, out of the way, to do the work that no one else wanted to do existed for centuries. It is estimated that by 1900 one million forward-prisoners had passed through Tyumen. 'Forward' indicated neither an over-friendly attitude nor intelligent precociousness, no, merely that they were destined for more remote places and were held there until transport was available to drive them farther.

Tyumen is Asian. It was thus deemed out of danger from the Germans during the Second World War, so many factories were relocated to Tyumen during the conflict. Many people had their valuables secreted in anticipation of a retreat if the invaders took over European Russia. Even Lenin's corpse was sent to Tyumen and looked after by a team of specialists. There is no great and obvious difference from European Russian cities. It is like Perm where I ate last night. It seems as if the women have run over the mountains in the night to stand in wait again.

The morning is glistening bright and warm. The railway workers walk the length of the train, testing with metallic tapping the wheel's functions. They hit every wheel, every spring and every drum a light tap, cocking their heads to one side to judge the echo. Like their European counterparts they look interested and engaged with what they are at. There is no difference.

Isn't Asia brown skin, isn't it oriental eyes? There are tigers, aren't there? Siberia is cold, isn't it? It is dangerous, far away and inhabited only by ferociously hungry wild animals and men banished here to fodder them.

While I'm searching for Siberian symptoms, Svetlana's door hisses open and there stands a metaphor of the myth: cold, snarling, big and dangerous. Everyone retreats to the comparative safety of their compartments while she slaps and hammers and bounds the length of the corridor, barking her assistants into a frightened flurry of action.

From our compartment window I still search for difference. I try to engage Papa in any conversation. The daughter is taking a beauty sleep so he sheepishly whispers reluctant answers while preparing her lunch. He whispers that this area has a long tradition in converting industrial alcohol into something to be consumed by those who cannot afford real vodka in bottles with labels. He talks hesitantly. I don't know if it is the secret he is hushing or if he is afraid of Her. He doesn't look out at this Asian Siberia, just sneaks gentle peeps at the top bunk. Peeved, I establish my own space, shuffle into a comfortable squat and meditate. After a short time he coughs gently. When I don't respond he touches my knee and I open my eyes to a steaming cup of *chi* and my smiling host. *Devushka* is sulking again.

My diary says: *Disappointing first day in Siberia. Nothing to indicate it except salt lakes either side of the tracks at Yalutorovsk. Almost ashamed of wheat flax and sunflowers. Shhhh – who'd believe it?*

Later Papa told me this tame arable land was Khrushchev's idea, he had a plan to develop this area called the Virgin Field Campaign. He had offered irresistible incentives and promised a better life to workers who came here to develop what was then (in the fifties) virgin land. Obviously it wasn't an empty promise.

Omsk is halfway to Irkutsk, one-quarter of the way to Vladivostok. It has some forgotten geographical significance, something to do with time ('Linehan, what time is it in Omsk when it is twelve noon in Greenwich?'). Its importance is not obvious here. From the train, the mammoth statue of Lenin in the square outside is clearly visible, ironically pointing the way forward. The break up of the Soviet Union did not impact people of this side of the Urals as it did their European counterparts. They were isolated before, now they are ignored more democratically. In European Russia, they pulled down the statues of Lenin and other emblems of Soviet rule. Here they didn't bother. Too much trouble; too busy with important things like finding a living. Life is real, not symbolic. They shrug their shoulders at statues. 'What are they; landmarks, things to give names to bus stops.' And it was in Omsk for the first time I noticed that people walked differently.

It's big, over one million people and something about it attracts me, 'I'll come back here,' I think. It was the echo of the school days and that ghost of a question bothering me like a tune you can't get out of your head. And there was one other reason.

In 1849 three prisoners serving time for political offences in a Moscow jail were sentenced to meet their death in front of a firing squad. On December 22nd they were led from their cells to Semyonovsky Square where public executions were carried out. They were offered the last rites. The guns were raised. They heard the rifle bolts being cocked. They drew in their final breath. Then a messenger came running. He said the Czar had changed his mind; the convicts were to be saved. At the very last moment the rifles were lowered. It was in fact a hoax, a mock execution, a punishment. One of the prisoners went permanently insane on the spot, another went on to write *Crime and Punishment*.

After this, Fyodor Dostoyevsky was exiled to Omsk and it was here that he met the characters that inspired his later works. He learned anew the extremes of cruelty of which men are capable but also the human kindness that can survive such cruelty. One hardened murderer who seemed to have attained a spiritual equilibrium beyond good and evil particularly impressed him. He tried to adapt that equilibrium to his own existence. Once he was flogged for complaining about a lump of coal in his soup. Later when he saw a fellow prisoner drowning he dived in to save him though he must have known the consequences of his action. For his bravery he was flogged again. This time so severely he spent six weeks in hospital. I thought if I called in on Omsk I might find out more about his place of inspiration, his gulag.

Outside the city, by the banks of a river, I see a foursome of boys smoking. They are wet and wearing mother's knickers. It's a beautiful day again. Since Moscow, fifty hours, there hasn't been a cloud. It looks idyllic.

Things must be different here. It's so far from everywhere. On the map it is the middle of that huge, brown, vast unknown, where names and landmarks run out. These people must be friendly to strangers. They must look in wonder and envy at passing trains and dream of going away too. The boys sullenly spot me. In a burst of bonhomie I wave. Nothing for a second . . . then the biggest one brings up his right arm and halts its motion with the left to its elbow. He holds it, fist aloft, in the universal salute: 'Up Yours.'

I was still feeling amused and a little sad at it when we reached serious steppe. As far as the eye can see a greenish-grey barren plain stretches itself away to all horizons. Eventually to the left I spy far, far away a forest shimmering slightly like a mirage. Papa tells me it is 'more or less'. Yes, there are trees, aspens, but they are many miles apart and only our great distance from them gives them the appearance of being close together. I'm wondering how he'd know when he says, 'Everyone knows this, it is a phenomenon often talked about.'

This whole area of steppe sits on top of hot water, a thermal area of apparent great potential. Then we step into fertile land again and over the horizon appear what seem to be cowboys. In Siberia? Five horsemen rounding up stock. We ride a bridge. Curling into it and straightening out of it I can see it is more heavily buttressed upstream than down to withstand the icebergs that flow down in the spring thaw. The river is the Ob.

Svet gushed in saying we would be in Novosibirisk for twenty minutes, that I mustn't be late (this with a red-nailed, funny finger-wag), and that I must buy *pelmeney* here. 'In all of Russia we make *pelmeney*, great *pelmeney*, but Novosibirisk . . .' and she kissed her pursed fingers as before.

The name Novosibirisk translates as New Siberia. It is the capital of western Siberia and has the largest train station in all of Siberia. A huge glass affair, it looks like some kind of exhibition centre. The glass is green, the food-sellers licensed; you need a permit to sell. No small-talk of shirts and 'how much do you earn?'. Here business is business. I had *pelmeney* . . . had to have *pelmeney* Svet said. It is like an Italian pasta dish. It consists of little handkerchiefs of dough wrapped around tasty morsels of mincemeat and boiled. It appears white, pasty and unappetising, but tastes like heaven. They scoop it in mugfuls from steaming containers. They lift the lids quickly to release a gush of steam and give the customer a quick glimpse of the prize without allowing it to cool. Steam whooshes up in Morse code dollops along their line and the released flavours seduce. They even have polystyrene containers like Chinese take-aways. Many of the *babushkas* have white coats and assistants, who splat a spoonful of *smetana* on to the steaming *pelmeney*. *Smetana* is the stuff of poetry, prose can not describe it. Barbarians say it is sour cream. Hah! Is honey syrup? At first it slithers around the top and then filters down to fill the crevices. The first bite is bliss. The morsels explode between tongue and palate, the *smetana* rushes in to cool and flavour. It stays to soothe.

After Novosibirisk at the end of the second day my diary says: *The large woman in the adjoining carriage is in trouble. During the day she makes a few trips to the toilet at the end of the corridor. She has great difficulty in walking. Her granddaughter takes her hand and leads her, but her mass hinders progress. She is obviously expanding. She has been eating constantly and she is retaining fluid. Her eyes are bulging and her arms and legs frightfully swollen. She could explode.*

And the entry for the next morning: *Seven a.m. Was going to take a look at the woman next door but Svetlana was occupying the corridor. Hard to believe it's less than twenty hours since we were locked in laughing embrace on the floor. Today she is a health hazard . . . some of her hair has escaped from the curlers and is springing wildly. The train police tried to pass her but retreated when she turned on them.*

By Krasnoyarsk, five hours later, Svetlana was fine but the woman was worse. *I can't see her ever leaving the carriage. It is quite frightening to see her arms stand out from her body like a blow-up doll. She is like an enormous puffer-fish. Her son, the crossword man, is pretending not to notice but he must be worried. Svetlana is up and down the corridor a lot. I think she is worried about her train.*

In 1900 the Eiffel Tower won a gold medal at the World Fair in Paris. So did the wide bridge just outside Krasnoyarsk. The name of the town means beautiful steep bank and in earlier days was inhabited exclusively by ex-convicts. If you didn't have a record you weren't trusted. There is a story of a respectable businessman who set up in Krasnoyarsk and no one would do business with him because he had never been a convict. So he went back to St Petersburg, committed some minor crime and was exiled to Irkutsk where he served his sentence, then returned to Krasnoyarsk and thrived. The bridge sits on the Yenisei, which as it is less well-known than the Seine is one of the reasons why its bridge's distinction is more of a secret. The Yenisei's banks are not as romantic as the Seine's. They are heavily industrialised and they have floating log-piles. Great stretches of them strapped together, a chain-gang. Escaped logs on the banks feed my imagination. To me, they seem to be another image of the universal desire to be somewhere other than 'here'.

Away to the right I see the misty outline of what must be the Sayan mountain range. Snow-capped? Or is it the distance? Below that will be Mongolia.

The countryside is unfenced but everywhere there is wood. Houses are made of wood, and the fences surrounding them are wood too. The landscape floats away in billows. Like, I think, Mongolia would. The earth is dark. Sometimes a dirt road approaches the railway and the crossing is blocked by a single striped pole. Waiting at a crossing I see a few horse-drawn carts with big wooden wheels. In some gardens there are hens and in all women working, wearing only knickers and brassières. I feel guilty for going away and leaving them but, still stung from the smoking boy's salute, I resist the urge to wave. But I like it here. There's a tranquillity and a sort of freedom. Like we've gone far enough to be beyond the gravitational force of bigger, better-known names. The garden life in plots beside the railway attract me too. My dream for the future switches to W.B. Yeats' poem 'The Lake Isle of Innisfree': 'nine bean rows and a honey bee', by a railway, where I can watch, forever, strange people going to unknown destinations.

For moments I mentally transfer myself to one of these gardens and, rather than them pass by, I watch train-people pass by . . . searching.

As we approach Zema Papa is restless. This is his destination and he is about to meet his second daughter. He dons an unused shirt and carefully knots a tie around its unyielding collar. *Devushka* has spent the day with lollipop sticks in her hair and now she is unwinding them and squeezing pimples on her chin. He puts away all the crockery. Then hesitates, unpacks a mug and places it in front of me. I can see he's thinking of the spoon but the daughter is watching now. He leaves me a miniature paper cone of salt and sits uncomfortable and straight. For the first time he shows interest in where we are.

At the station I see the second daughter race into his arms, happily blubbering. He holds her tight, lips squeezed, resisting tears, his travelling *devushka* stands apart. The two girls finally shake hands. He is lost in admiration of his offspring as all three exit under an arch bearing a hammer and sickle. I thought he had forgotten but he rushed back in time to wave goodbye and mouth some advice that I wish I could have heard.

And now everyone is getting ready. It seems half the train is emptying at Irkutsk. People change when they are getting near their destinations; they lose that peace, become fidgety and restless again. The trip is nearly over. Fantasy is ground down by reality.

'Don't forget that bag.'

'Look out . . . tut, tut, tut, look at what you have done to that.'

'Here, take your brother's hand.'

'Yes, we are nearly there now.'

'Look sharp.'

Svetlana had her uniform on and her mouth closed. Morning. She was under great pressure to explode at all the stupid people and her assistants – but she couldn't. Irkutsk was an important stop. The most important between Moscow and Vladivostok. So she had to fly the colours. What might people think of *vagon* 14?

The swollen woman had to be unloaded. She had got worse and couldn't risk continuing to Vladivostok. The policemen had to help prise her out of the carriage and push her down the corridor. Her blubber brushed both sides and a dangling piece of her disarrayed clothing caught the steam valve of the samovar. It hissed cruelly at the poor woman. A fork truck lowered her on a pallet to the platform at Irkutsk station at 6:40 Moscow time – twenty minutes before midday local time.

I walked and walked and walked all along the train's length and couldn't believe its unsuitability to where it was. Positively rude, gushing and coughing and releasing wind and steam from various orifices, not at all like the easy beast of steppe and taiga. Not made to be, not used to being, stationary, the worst came out in this halted train. Like a caged animal it looked awkward and uneasy to be off. I had prepared a farewell but this wasn't the train I had prepared it for. That one was easy, reliable and free. Here was a hissing and gushing juggernaut waiting for release, a fire-spitting dragon in a cave, wanting to be somewhere other than here.

Chapter Four

I tried to say its name different ways: Ir . . . kutsk – too much like irritable. Then Ear . . . kutsk and it became a different place. Any place with an anatomical association is homely and also I could laugh at a mental picture I had of Earkutsk. Old Irish women forever tweak the cheeks of babies and little children, with a kissing sound: 'kutsky, kutsky, kutsky'. So I imagined Earkutsk a country baby whose ear I would tweak with a 'kutsky, kutsky, kutsky'. I saw it small, cute, red-cheeked and welcoming.

Expectations of new places are unrealistic. First-time visitors to New York might expect the Statue of Liberty out to greet them; in London Big Ben to offer one of its hands; in Venice a chorus of gondoliers to form a guard of honour. In Irkutsk I quietly dreamed that the locals would, on witnessing my arrival, come to a halt and say, 'Look there's Paddy. Welcome Paddy. Here's my baby waiting for you to tweak its ear and listen to you say "kutsky, kutsky".' I thought they'd all be wrapped up in rags and shawls, observing and thinking.

Two things surprised me about the place. Number one, that it was so ordinary, and number two, that it was so different. It was typically Soviet. The myth of Siberia is so great that one doesn't expect its cities to be similar to other Russian cities. But Irkutsk station has people and bags and slow bustle like all other Russian cities. It has concrete structures and tilting power poles and the usual array of Lada cars. People don't look much different, perhaps a little more loosened out . . . less into themselves, otherwise the same – Russians.

What was different about it was that it did not match my fantasy. I looked around and thought to myself, 'This isn't forbidding Siberia, this doesn't feel like a place of exile. This is a fine place.'

The square outside the station has a mixture of qualities. It is impressive but seems homely. Its air enters the body with ease unlike some strange places where the atmosphere seems incompatible. I felt comfortable. Maybe I slipped in alongside its European aspects; its columns and pillars. Maybe it is simply because the old station buildings are substantial and yet the scale is small enough not to be forbidding. It would be easy to enter this station, it is not so massive that it deters and yet it is sturdy enough to be serious.

The square itself is not a square but a rectangle of about one hundred and fifty by eighty metres. Facing the station across the shorter dimension is a grassy bank worn into brown earth paths by frequent passers.

It was noon and hot and I stood for a long time on the steps of the station witnessing reality. Long lines of people with bags awaited trams. One rattled noisily in on loose iron rails. It was thin with a single lamp at the front, making it look like it had just clattered off the set of a black and white First World War film. Another rattled in from a different direction; it was patched with flattened-out, corrugated metal, daubed over with light blue, streaky paint. Above the station stood scaffolding supporting a sign made from failing, flickering torch bulbs that said the next train departure was to Kh–baro–k at –5:—. Where the trams halted there were toppling hardboard kiosks selling food and drink. A few beggars looked doubtfully at me and passed on. Three dogs sniffed each other indelicately. A certainty that I was going to like this place oozed through my surprise at its ordinariness. I knew I could handle anything this town had to offer. A railway station is a good place to take the pulse of Russian cities. Irkutsk's heart had a regular beat. It had no physical similarity to Galway in the west of Ireland but it had something of its aura – Galway fifty years ago.

A gravelly voice furtively asked me what I wanted and in all honesty I said, '*Ne znaew.*' I don't know. He shrugged his shoulders and drifted away. Among the waiting cars were a few old yellow taxis with chequered tape. The whole scene was fifties; were it not for a few tell-tales, like fake Nike and Levi logos, it could be a set for an old movie. Gravel Voice returned.

'You want to go to hotel?'

'No, I want to stay in a private house or apartment.'

'You know someone in Irkutsk?'

'No.'

'Then you can't stay in private house.'

'Why?'

'You're foreign . . . you need many things.'

'No! I live like Russian. I don't need anything special.'

'I will take you to a place in my car.'

'How much?'

'Sixty thousand roubles.'

'Thirty thousand.'

'Forty.'

'It's good.'

But he didn't take me to a private house. Foreigners who don't know what they want must be led. He took me up a hill, circling around the place the amblers went, past a Sunday market selling rusty car-parts, avoiding potholes and open manhole covers. Then, after more minutes of motion, we left the partially surfaced road for one that was never covered. It was red and rutted from rain rivulets. We sidled down it to another rutted dirt track and stopped in front of a blocky, red-bricked building. It was surrounded by iron railings with a chained gate. He rang the bell on the gate, took the forty thousand and was gone before Lena answered.

She was in her late fifties and comfortable-looking. In Russian she told me I could share an All-American room with a real American gentleman for fifteen dollars a night. This included a breakfast of coffee and pancakes with maple syrup. It was not what I wanted but I decided to take it until I found something more genuinely Siberian.

In the hall there were photographs of Lena with Santa Claus, of Lena with a Lord Mayor, of Lena on the Golden Gate Bridge, of Lena on a toboggan, of Lena with fur hat and a much older man. There were stairs going up and stairs going down, marble stairs, and at every step there were more photos of Lena. In one Lena was holding a cocktail glass by the stem; in another she was stooped down, beside a wheelchair under a banner, 'Welcome Home Konstantin'. The old man in the wheelchair, rug around his knees, looking very frail. Lena was beaming, holding his scrawny hand in hers. There were rings with very large stones on every manicured finger.

She lapsed into Californian as she showed me the shower and balcony. She was equally at home in both languages and said she didn't know which she was speaking unless someone reminded her. She spent the winters in California 'to be close to my husband's tomb', the summers in Irkutsk 'to be close to my roots'. She kept help; three women working in shifts 'so that I am never alone . . . since Konstantin you see'. In the kitchen she sang Russian songs in the trilly voice of a woman who has enjoyed a comfortable life. Later, the midnight-to-morning lady whispered that Konstantin had been the fourth Mr Lena, and very rich . . . 'American.'

My room-mate Doug was, as promised, American. He was from Baikal-Something-or-Other, one of a series of programmes financed by USAID: Lake Baikal Ecotourism Project. This, in turn, is a branch of something else funded by some other American do-good organisation intent on forcing on the rest of the world the benefits of American know-how. 'Baikal holds a fifth of all the fresh water of the world. But these Russians just pollute it. They don't know any better.'

Irkutsk is not on Lake Baikal, it is on the Angara River, which is the only one that flows out of Baikal: 350 rivers flow into it. The prefix, Lake, is not used in Siberia, it is simply Baikal. The name is uttered with reverence. I asked one Buryat girl why it sounded so like a person's name. 'Oh because it is,' she answered, 'it's my grandfather.'

Russian visitors arriving on its shore for the first time squat down and wet their faces with scooped-up water. They mutter something as they do it, as one would mutter encouragement to the very young or the very old. They splash the water reverentially on the heads of children. Siberian Holy Water.

Krasevee Baikal (Beautiful Baikal) is home to a great variety of fish, including the sturgeon, and it has its own breed of seal called the Nerpa: the only freshwater seal in the world. Its waters are crystal clear. I had been told this over and over but was not prepared for what I saw: water so clear that it is possible to see features on stones 150 feet down.

Even though Irkutsk is not on the lake, anyone doing anything about the lake stays in Irkutsk. So that is how Doug happened to be in Lena's comfortable, red-bricked guesthouse. He was safe there. She spoke to him in Californian and gave him pancakes with maple syrup for breakfast.

He had a lot of bags. One black one shaped like a submarine blocked my passageway to the balcony where there was a makeshift clothesline. Failing to circumnavigate, I tried to move it; it wouldn't budge, nailed to the floor. Curious, I peeped inside, it was full of scientific paraphernalia: test tubes and electronic balances and rock samples with incrustations and some frilly coral rock. This was just one of the bags.

Doug had a paisley silk dressing gown displayed on a hanger on the outside of the wardrobe. He wore striped pyjamas. He had shoe trees in all the ones he wasn't wearing and an alienating shine on the ones he was. Here to do something about the lake, he never really saw it; and he never saw any Siberians. He went to Baikal almost every day in a chauffeured four-wheeled drive landcruiser with the insignia of some international body on the door. He travelled in quarantine, smoked glass windows up, air-conditioning on, once there I presumed he donned wellingtons . . . no, waders. He returned in the evening, weighted down with rocky exhibits for the prosecution: proof that 'these people' were irresponsibly killing the lake.

His driver was Russian but acted American with his passenger. He occupied another room down the marble stairs in the basement. Doug shuffled uncomfortably when I told him I had come by train. 'There is an airport here you know,' he said. When I told him I was going into the centre of the city to check it out he enquired if I had asked Lena to call a taxi. 'She can tell them what you want, she speaks their language.'

I got off the bus at the park by a very Soviet, official-looking building. In front of it a huge Soviet Square, great for marches.

Its vastness is now traversed by noisy Ladas, scurrying like routed ants. It is impossible to tell which direction the confused ants will take. They burst in from one corner, scuttle across the middle, miraculously avoiding each other by radar it seems, and make a scurrying exit on two squealing wheels into invisible side streets. To get anywhere this square has to be crossed. After coming into frighteningly close eyeball contact with honking drivers I make it.

Stressed, I limp into the park and sit down. It is still Sunday. Russian city parks are great. Very large portions of them are not cultivated at all. It's as if bits of the countryside escaped and settled here. The rest of the world insists on mowing and manicuring and in dressing up their greenery to make it acceptable for urban consumption. Not Russians. A small centre section may have fountains and seats but the greater part will be left to its own devices and country ways. Even the centre section is not as cultivated as in the West. You never see or hear a lawnmower and I don't think this is because of the lack of resources. It is because there is a genuine rustic in even the most citified Russian that craves unruly country growth. The parks often abound in briars, bracken and nettles. I like this freshness but I wasn't among it now, I wanted to see the city people in their city mode so I sat in the centre.

A very pretty twenty-something teacher waited with a squad of children. She had a yellow dress with dots and platform-soled shoes of the same colour. She carried a huge bouquet of yellow flowers. The dress, the shoes or the flowers would, individually, cost more than a month's salary. An equally pretty girl entered from another corner and they ran at each other. They locked in embrace and then stood apart admiring each other's apparel. They talked, simultaneously, in wonder. They clapped hands over mouths and opened eyes wide; they laughed and the children watched. This kind of display would not be seen in Moscow. It was June 1997 but looked 1957. Or maybe felt it. A two-way communication, a sharpness of exchange. The same encountered in the West would, I feel, have a fog of interference about it. A fog, or fall-out from excess that has taken the magic glow out of new clothes.

A drunk in a recycled suit approached me and told me about the *gizn trudney*. He wore a dirty white shirt with sick stains. The tie hung unevenly: narrow leg very long. His shoes were down-at-heel but formal, tied with broken laces. Remnants of sock displayed navy/white ankle. His greasy hair fell down over his eyes as his unsteady head lolled from side to side. His manner was obsequious until I refused his request for roubles. Then he became arrogant and, despite his difficulty in co-ordinating movement, he looked me up and down with the disdain of a camel. He snorted and a disgusting mixture came down his nostril: '*Vui govno*,' he managed . . . you're shit.

The gossiping girls, the waiting children, the vendors selling ice-cream pretended to see nothing, as I walked uncomfortably away, carefully gauging a speed that wouldn't look like a rout.

The real town was a few blocks away. The main street is called Karl Marx and it is like a narrow French boulevard, but slightly narrower. It is lined with trees. Banners slung between them sing the praise of Kodak Gold.

Though Sunday, some shops were open and the street was full of strollers – mostly beautiful young women. Many cities claim to have the most beautiful women in the world but there are only two serious contenders: Buenos Aires, Argentina and Irkutsk, central Siberia. It was hard to believe that it was not a parade organised by Pretty Polly or some other manufacturer of hosiery. Females here haven't got the same affection for peroxide as their Trans-Ural sisters. They are amazingly stylish. Natural models. Very many Russians have an innate sense of style and quality. They may possess but one coat, one pair of boots or one summer dress but they can wear it as if it were especially selected from an extensive wardrobe to suit that particular day. And they touch their apparel with great effect – not for effect. It may be a hand to a collar or a flick to a shoulder; it could be a button adjustment but it comes out a poetic motion. Just as working men's conversation in the public *banya* is as likely to extend to ballet and opera as it is to the difficulty of earning a rouble, so all Russians have a range that touches on the artistic. The finer things in life are not the preserve of the privileged. This phenomenon, strangely, is more striking in Irkutsk than in Moscow or St

Petersburg. Perhaps one is over-prepared for roughness. Or perhaps it is its breeding. Like Larissa in Moscow it aspires, with perhaps more reason, to grand lineage. The Paris of Siberia it's called and I hate such comparisons, but Irkutsk had a stylish, smaller similarity to Paris. It administers over an area twenty times the size of France which would leave Paris shrugging her shoulders 'so what' (in French of course). And I remembered how *The Remake* had pointed out it was the Decembrists that gave Irkutsk its intellectual qualities.

They were exiles of a better class, banished not because they didn't matter but because they mattered so much that they were feared. They were of noble birth and from western Russia. They arrived in 1825 and gold had been discovered a quarter of a century before. The adventurers who had become rich in the gold-rush were introduced by these new arrivals to outlets other than gambling houses and brothels for their new wealth. Some copied the habits of the new exiles and hired French tutors and imported French clothes and jewellery for their families. Evidence of gaud and grandeur persist both in population and building. In 1891 Nicholas II, the czar later assassinated in Ekateringburg, dropped in to open a bridge and attend a ball, though he wasn't a czar then. Despite the combined influence of noblemen from the West and a visit by the heir to the throne, the Decembrists' refinement was not wholly embraced and the ruffian element of the frontier territory persisted. In 1903 there were 50,000 inhabitants and that same year there were some 400 reported murders. Allowing for a few unreported ones, one's chance of being bumped off amounted to about one per cent. Gold-diggers, fur-trappers, traders and tea-merchants from the Orient made for a tempestuous lifestyle. Irkutsk is still today the largest supplier of fur to the whole world market.

Tolya wasn't selling fur but blue plastic coats squeezed into pouches the size of a packet of cigarettes. It hadn't rained since I arrived in Russia. But it must, he said. I had never seen such a compact answer to bad weather. The material was not much sturdier than bin-liner but, complete with hood, it was exactly what I wanted; a garment I had mentally manufactured many times but never before seen. Now, at a street corner in the centre of Siberia, Tolya was selling them for about one dollar.

'Where do these come from?' I asked him.

'China of course,' he answered. 'Everything from China.'

With that he showed me his under-the-counter stock of tapes, CDs and electrical small goods. 'Every week my friend goes to China; anything you want I will get.'

Another geographical surprise, I hadn't realised how close The Land of the Dragon was. Irkutsk is only two days by train from Peking. Tokyo is only half as far as Moscow and it would be easier to reach California by continuing east rather than back via Europe. Mongolia is just down the road, a day on the train to Ulan Bator.

Despite this there is a disappointing lack of oriental features in the main streets of Irkutsk. Some selling-stalls are manned by 'black people' from Azerbaijan and Armenia and there are a small number of Buryats but not as many as one would expect, judging from its geographical location. Irkutsk is on the north side of Lake Baikal about seventy miles from its western tip. The Republic of Buryatia is below the lake but still close enough to expect some overflow of its people here. Not so. Russians still insist that Buryatia is a republic but they don't explain what that now means in the new chaotic Russia. It is a region with some autonomy from Moscow – but then everywhere by necessity now has. The mighty Soviet Union suffers from Humpty-Dumpty Syndrome. Russians and Buryats alike expect and get little from four-day-away Moscow. Buryats were Mongolians. They wandered into the area above Mongolia and below Baikal some time in the fourteenth century. They settled in and intermarried with natives. The variety of people who inhabited this region is mind-boggling. There were Chinese and Turkic people as well as white western Russians. The Buryats now predominate. They still look a bit Mongolian and their features are refined to perfection. Sculpted marble. There are 350,000 of them in the zone below a lake called, unsurprisingly, Buryatia. The total population of the autonomous region is 1,000,000. Female Buryats are so good-looking that white Russian men marry them. Actually, Buryats are the only non-snow-white people Russians accept with some degree of equality. Their culture is irresistible. Outdoors in the summertime they join in groups and sing and dance in costumes of colour and fur. Their music so haunting, their movement so fluid, their features so beautiful it looks like the landscape possesses them or they it. It's hard to believe they migrated here, they look more like exotic birds in their own habitat. Even Russians concede it. Russian women rarely marry Buryat men but they understand how their menfolk cannot resist Buryat beauty.

Tolya was standard Russian, except that he smiled first off. There is a hint of vulnerability in these people of Siberia. Extreme weather conditions often do that: make folk dependent on each other, more communicative. Not that the weather in Irkutsk put any strain on people in June 1997: it was a sunny 25°C. Its average June temperature is approximately a maximum of 20°C, a minimum of 10°C, and in January a maximum of -15°C and a minimum of -25°C.

A pedestrianised alley connected Karl Marx to the other main thoroughfare. It was lined with stalls selling the same things that are sold all over the world. The cheap blouses and skirts, the plastic flowers, screwdriver sets and tacky glass ornaments. Then a stall selling musquash fur coats and hats, another selling a mink coat for 3,000 dollars. People come from afar to buy and they are not put off by the fact that the bargain they seek is hanging outside a makeshift blue polythene stall. It seems strange at first. A mistake? Or some great scam? But no, the furs are genuine, so they tell me, *konieshno*: of course, and when I walk away they snootily rub it better where I have fingered it. 'Wouldn't know mink from rabbit.'

At the end of the broad alley there stands a very modern pink and green building that looks like scaffolding. It is the new central market where people rent stainless steel counter space from which to sell their produce. Everything is very clinical, sellers wear white coats and hairnets and the displays are out of a glossy magazine – prices are as in the West. Upstairs there are designer sportswear shops.

At first I couldn't find anywhere to eat. This is a problem all over Russia, a relic of Communist past. There was supposed to be no competition so there was no advertising. They haven't yet fully adapted to a cut-throat free enterprise market where everyone roars what they have to offer. Many stores don't display their merchandise; the windows are curtained in lace like Irish country houses of yesteryear. Eventually I asked. I was taken down a side street, up some stairs, along a squeaky corridor to a fine restaurant. They served delicious vegetables and bacon so good I didn't want to swallow it. I drowned the potatoes in *smetana* and closed my eyes to remember where I had tasted their like before. I thought I must return and asked the waitress about queuing times.

'Yes, we are open from eleven until eleven every day except on Friday when we are opened until two a.m. Of course it is more expensive on Friday because of the strippers.'

'Huh?'

'Strippers, you know, women who take their clothes off.'

'*Konieshno*,' I say, but it comes out like a frog. I look around to see where, surely not on the tables with the red plastic tableclothes . . .

'Tut, tut, tut, *konieshno nyet*. There is a stage on Friday. Very professional, classy.'

'*Konieshno*.'

'*Konieshno*.'

Full, I returned to Lena's where Doug was sitting up in bed wearing his striped pyjamas and reading *Time*. He asked me if I had found the Intourist Hotel. I had, but I hadn't gone in. I told him about the stripping eating-house. Not interested. The Intourist Hotel is the only *safe* place. He wasn't interested in anything else. The next day I had to get interested in it too.

Regulations are constantly changing. Foreigners going to anywhere in Russia cannot get a visa without an invitation. This gives rise to another under-the-counter operation of issuing invitations via fax or e-mail. I had received mine over the Internet from Igor who in turn had organised it through some mini Mafia company in St Petersburg. I was required to register with the police wherever I went; that's what some people said, others didn't agree. Lena said she didn't believe in any regulations and never did anything except bribe them with Konstantin's money if they asked questions. They seldom asked her, she said. I would have guessed.

I went to the police and they told me I wasn't there at all. They told me I was still in Moscow, but that I should be in St Petersburg and that if I wasn't I should be in jail. I had to contact my inviter from St Petersburg who was to say I wasn't there, but here. If she told them that, then they would know that I was in Irkutsk and they could do something about it.

'What?'

'Put you in jail.'

So I had to go to Intourist Hotel to fax St Petersburg this complicated tale.

The Post Office in Irkutsk is an old building selling gum and sticky paper and bottles of ink. It has a back office staffed by a very efficient, pleasant bunch of large ladies who, happily, transmit and receive fax and e-mail. However, my story, in my Russian, was beyond their comprehension, so I had to resort to the very expensive twenty-four-hour bi-lingual service provided by the Intourist Hotel.

I sat in the dark, marble lobby between bundles of purring Japanese tourists for hours. I watched the fax girls talk animatedly about things. They were not watching and I worried that they would miss my message. Eventually it came through saying that if I was in Irkutsk I could stay there. The woman at the police station tut-tutted and said I should have told her before that I was here, and not be putting her to all that trouble. She then gave me an embossed pass to avoid the queue when I came back the following day to adjust my visa stamp. I asked her, why the pass?

'Tomorrow is foreigners' day, there will be a long line.'

'But I'm a foreigner.'

'Not a black foreigner, they will be from the Caucasus, central Asia, dreadful . . . with this pass you can come straight to my office.'

Doug had to spend a night on the lake to do some testing that couldn't be done by day. He packed a few of the bags and lined them on the steps of the stairs for the driver to pick them up. He was going to be away all night. He had taken his dressing gown.

When I came home that night Lena told me I had a new room-mate. She didn't want me to be alone, she said. I climbed the stairs in anticipation of another American.

I couldn't believe my eyes. His face was ruddy-yellow and polished. The eyeslots were forced up by the plump, shiny cheeks and they had collapsed into the nose-place. There really wasn't a nose, just two holes; miniature, inverted replicas of the eyes. He was low and square and wore a silky, blue, crossover tunic, like a benevolent Genghis Khan. The whole face was a smile and he had a pigtail reaching down to his waist. He waddled towards me. Despite the smile as he got close I nearly panicked. I thought he might be a survivor from the Golden Horde and that he might draw a dagger and bury it in my chest. A near death experience transported me to a height from which I saw my twisted Caucasian body on Lena's marble floor; an emerald-encrusted hilt protruding from my bleeding chest.

He threw his arms around me and put his head in turn on both of my shoulders in a very warm Tuvan greeting. I loved him immediately. His name was Kongar-ol-Ondar.

Tuva is a very remote area of the Soviet Union, two hours by air from Irkutsk to the left and below Baikal, close to Mongolia and Kazakhstan. It is still difficult to get permission to visit there.

Unlike Buryatia, Tuva wants to maintain its isolation, or so it seems. I have heard that travellers there are hassled by police and moved on if they haven't got specific permission for visiting. All of Russia has a severe alcohol problem, but I believe Tuva is the worst. Refusal to become unconsciously drunk can give grounds for incarceration. The people of this remote, autonomous area also look Mongolian but, if you can imagine appearance having a spectrum, they would be at the stronger red end of it where the Buryats would occupy the lighter, more delicate-seeming violet.

Tuvans have a unique culture. One of its component parts is throat singing. Kongar was its most renowned exponent. He had just come in from Tokyo, three hours flight away. Before that he had been recording in California. He had worked with Frank Zappa and Johnny 'Guitar' Wilson and the Chieftains, a traditional Irish group with an international reputation. The Chieftains have travelled the world establishing unexpected links to traditional music in the strangest of places. When he mentioned them I realised I had seen a BBC TV program about Tuva and its throat singing tradition and that it had featured Kongar. Then he took out one of his CDs and two tracks were of Kongar accompanied by the Chieftains.

He was born in 1962 near Khernchik River and had, ironically, been drafted into the Soviet Navy. Tuva is one of the most inland regions in the world. While loading a ship in Vladivostok, a bag of something fell on his head and broke his neck. I marvelled at his recovery from such a serious accident and he agreed he was very lucky. 'Imagine never singing again,' he grinned.

He demonstrated his art. It vibrated the room and Lena hollered. He shrugged his shoulders and said that we should drink a bottle of vodka to celebrate Tuvan–Irish unity. I distracted him from the idea. I didn't want to tell him that I hadn't taken a drink for ten years and that, even though I'd love to get drunk with him, I dare not. I wore him out with questions until he yawned and nearly fell asleep sitting up. I didn't want to let the moment go. I don't often share a room with Tuvan throat singers who have broken their necks while working for the Russian Navy. Before he gave into sleep he showed me the doll he had bought for his three-year-old daughter whom he would be seeing the next day after an absence of three months.

He was asleep immediately he lay down and the holes where his nose should be dilated and contracted rhythmically. Every sound he made excites me still.

Next day Doug returned with a new companion, Sergei. He was some kind of park warden. The whole area around Baikal is a type of national park. Its boundaries are not clearly defined but it extends for about five hundred miles on either side of the mighty lake. Sergei was an expert on the area; he clearly loved it. He knew every track and mountain path. Russians are great for the outdoors. They camp a lot or sleep out under the stars. Even in urban areas it is common to see people setting out or returning from treks. It is the trip to the *dacha* on a larger scale. Very often one sees groups of thirty or forty youths with packs walking along the side of the road or through fields or up the sides of hills. They speak in familiar terms of far away places for trekking. They talk about woods where it is easy to take a wrong turn.

Sergei was wonderful – I thought he was wonderful. Later I was to discover his friends were not like him. He knew every inch of the area for hundreds of miles around. Lena's was full so he slept in a sleeping bag on our floor. Doug was overenthusiastic about this, he was anxious to let me see how he fraternised with the natives when they were civilised. Lena said she would give him a special rate, fourteen instead of fifteen dollars, because of the lack of bed.

Sergei had fragile old Soviet maps falling apart at the folds. They were genuine maps he said, true in every detail. I looked quizzical and he told me that in Soviet times most maps were purposefully falsified to conceal strategic information, such was the paranoia of the Soviets. But these were the real thing, genuine old government maps. He treasured them and held a cupped hand under squares that were inclined to fall free. He said that in the time I had I could only expect to see the south side of Baikal. I should first take another day on the Trans-Sib to Ulan Ude and stop there for a few days because it was the best place from which to visit Buryat settlements. Then, he said, from there, if I wished, he could arrange a lift with his friend to a settlement called Ust Barguizin. I don't like doing this. I don't like making arrangements in advance, I want to be free to change my mind if I come across some good 'bad company' and especially I don't like to make arrangements to go by car. I like public transport. But Sergei was so enthusiastic and well-meaning I couldn't turn him down. So it was arranged. I would meet a Stepan at ten o'clock under Lenin's head in the vast square of Ulan Ude. I couldn't miss it: it was the biggest head in the world.

The place he was sending me was not in Buryatia, he said, but a Russian village typical of the area and on the shores of Baikal. Olga would look after me there. I knew from the way he spoke her name she was special to him. 'Olga cooks like an angel.' I was to discover she could also be a demon.

He said I should get in as much practice as possible at speaking Russian because no one in the village would be able to help me out. Olga was a teacher but she wouldn't know any English. The appointment with Stepan was ten days away.

Next day it rained. Plastic coat Tolya was his own advertisement standing on the footpath selling his blue plastics for a dollar. I asked him if he knew any family that I could stay with for a few days to practise the language.

'Stay with me. My wife and I know no English; you will have to speak Russian. We will not charge you much.'

By the time I had picked up my bag and rejoined him, the rain had stopped and he had sold all his merchandise. His eyes twinkled and he led me through Yuri Gagarin Boulevard to the promenade by the river. Girls walked in groups on the shiny, wet pavement and Tolya teased and amused them. He knew most of them and it was clear that his knowledge went fairly deep.

In Soviet times Russians married young to get away from their parents. Many were married at seventeen. The tradition lasts. They are sexually active in their very early teens. It seems that fidelity is not highly prized.

Tolya's apartment was in a rough-looking complex. There was no surfaced pathway leading to it and, after the rain, the overgrown muddy patch looked particularly unpleasant.

Almost everyone in Russia has a dog. They favour very big dogs: Great Danes, Alsatians, St Bernard's. Areas around apartment complexes are overrun in the evening with these dogs and their owners. The dogs are well-fed and groomed in contrast to their owners. Judging by the sleek condition of the animals and the shabbiness of the people who walk them, one would think that they were not the owners of such animals. They look more like servants paid to do the job. Tolya said it was because the czars liked dogs. He said dogs, especially big ones, were status symbols. Their barks were deep and lonesome and carried far after the rain.

The apartment was on the fourth floor and there was no lift. In the downstairs entrance there was a line of vandalised post-boxes and the smell of shit. On the second floor landing snivelling skinheads sat on the stone steps sniffing glue, and on the third a bony human mound blocked the passageway. Without comment, Tolya stepped over it and continued to his own door, which he operated on with a variety of keys. It opened to the second torn, padded one, which was also locked. Inside was not an apartment but a landing with four rooms and a curtained section with an enamelled gas cooker on legs. Four couples had a room each and shared the 'kitchen'.

His wife was a shadowy waif who was frightened by me. She had no place to escape to because the apartment consisted of just a room. The bed was elevated and reached by ladder, like a bunk. The space underneath the bed was the sitting-room. The remaining space was occupied by an expensive-looking machine on which Tolya played his CDs. The frightened Valeria went outside and returned, much later, with two bowls of soup. Her hand shook as she set them down on the table under the bed.

Bedtime was embarrassing for Valeria. Three people: two males, one uncertain female. Tolya did nothing to ease his wife. Eventually she stuttered that I should sleep with Tolya in the bed above, that she would sleep with friends. I insisted on sleeping on the mat underneath, where we were assembled.

In much confusion and embarrassment we all went to bed, too early. I rushed it so they didn't have time to undo my resolve not to put them from their bed. I wondered why he invited me to stay, the money I supposed. Sleeping sounds came from above but I lay awake for a long time, wondering.

In the morning Tolya is already gone when I awaken to a hoarse doorbell. Valeria admits Marina, who stoops down to say '*Dobrey den*,' (good day) and that she will be ready for the lesson in a few minutes. I have never seen her before and nobody had mentioned lessons. These Russians are very quick to see a business opportunity. Her eyes are light blue.

They have both gone out again so I take the opportunity to get dressed. Living in tight places forces a lot of compromise – nowhere to brush my teeth. Why did I let myself in for this . . . Lena's seemed attractive . . .all is forgiven, Doug.

Valeria returns with an enamel basin, a jug of hot and a jug of cold water and places them delicately on the floor like a dog's feed. Just when I wonder what to do with my dripping face she reappears with a towel. It is small and striped with patterned tufts of towelling. It is folded in a narrow strip. It may be new. Then they both appear with tea, bread and cheese.

Marina takes control, her scant frame belies a sharp wit and mind: '*Sechaz me oocheem*.' Now we study.

I am a little annoyed and think of crying halt, but she is far too pretty and bright. Her hair is shiny, her body slim. She hasn't a word of English but is a gifted, jolly, complimenting teacher. Waif Valeria sits apart, interested.

Marina is a street sweeper and will be available every morning at nine for our lesson. Hard to imagine her with a big, coarse brush. She works from four-thirty until eight-thirty on the street with a broom made of twigs. She will come straight from work to teach me. She has a degree in psychology from one of the local Institutes of Higher Education. She lives, alone, down the corridor.

'You must learn where to put the stress in Russian, they will not understand you . . . *Nyet, nyet, nyet* . . . again . . . *staratsa* (try) . . . *da da da* . . . listen to him Valeria . . . now he speaks such Russian!' When she smiles I can see where her strength comes from . . . determination.

My resentment at the manipulation that cornered me into this situation dissolves. She traps me into discussions that she knows will anger me. Then, when I am frustrated and annoyed at her inability to see common sense, I realise she is just leading me into new areas of expression. She's charming. She's sensitive. Eyes blue, eyes bright.

I intend staying just two days, but it runs to four. A pattern develops. In the mornings we have the lesson. Teacher-sweeper sleeps a little; I wander a little, sometimes with Tolya, sometimes with Valeria, often alone. In the evenings we share food and I wander again.

One evening I meet them by the river. They are going to an exhibition of Buryat art. I go with them. They are going to the theatre, it is a modern comedy, I'd enjoy it.

'No,' I insist. 'I wouldn't understand.'

'What nonsense! What does that say about Marina's teaching?'

So I go and don't understand but I laugh a lot and they are happy.

I wonder how much they will charge me; will they laugh at me when I am gone?

'No money! In Siberia, guest is most important person. No! Strictly no money. *Abyazatelno nyet*!' Tolya said.

'Please excuse, that we have no bed,' Valeria said.

'My satisfaction is to hear you speak Russian – and see you laugh,' beautiful Marina says. 'Now you laugh in Russian – hah, hah, ho!'

Embarrassed and emotional I don't know what to do. Unseen, I drop a few large dollar bills on the floor where I slept and I leave . . . far too quickly.

Chapter Five

The Trans-Siberian railroad has to go out of its way to get to Irkutsk. If it headed straight for its goal, Vladivostok on the eastern shore of Russia near Japan, it would miss Irkutsk. But it doesn't. There are two reasons. Irkutsk has been a major hub of exchange for centuries. Precious goods from the East, tea especially, all had to pass through here. A kind of score-card was kept here to record the volume of these goods. The old Silk Route had many arteries; one of them also ran through Irkutsk. The second reason is that until 1902, the branch of the track coming from Moscow terminated here. Engineering in those times was not up to the challenge of the loop around the western end of Lake Baikal. The train stopped in Irkutsk and from there the carriages were taken across the lake by ferryboat to a port called Mysoveye on the south side, whence they continued on the remaining section of track that took it on another three-day trip to Vladivostok. Now the track is complete. It has been since 1904. You now go out of Irkutsk the way you went in and do a 'C' ring around the end of the lake. The ferryboat that used to carry passengers is still on the banks of the Angara in Irkutsk but it now lies on its side. It used to be a museum but it didn't attract enough attention.

I took a chance on getting a train that day. It is not the done thing in Russia. You buy a ticket days in advance and spend a few days cooking food for the trip.

Like most things, distances are relative and I considered the trip to Ulan Ude a mere commuter-hop. I wasn't too picky about what train I took – it was only a ten-hour journey. I'd take the first train I could get.

In Irkutsk station the foreigners' window is in a room on the second floor. A tall, long, elegant, if austere, room. A masculine character imbues even the finest Soviet buildings, like the sculpture of the era. Those statues of groups advancing, fists held out with purpose and ambition, are all essentially masculine in character. Even when they are of women they have a masculinity, cornered and angular, rather than rounded. The Duma in Moscow displays the same characteristic. And the Kremlin, for all its ornamentation, remains definitively male.

The ticket window was centre of the room. It was a large plate-glass affair, like a department store display. Behind it sat a middle-aged lady. She wasn't typical of the women associated with transport throughout Russia. She was refined in appearance and speech. She wore a mohair Lana Turner sweater. It was embroidered with small glass beads in a picture of a bouquet of flowers. The sweater was pastel green, her eyes hazel and her hair blonde; but it wasn't the bus driver blonde, which is yellow – no! It was a fine, ivory blonde. Her hands were bony, veined and delicate. Nails were pink and pointed and she twiddled a sharp pencil between the index fingers and thumbs of both hands.

I told her I wanted a ticket to Ulan Ude as soon as possible. She said there was a train in two hours but she didn't think I'd want to take that one; it was coming from Moscow, she said, and would be already 'very used'. I should wait until tomorrow when there would be one starting from Irkutsk with 'fresh produce'. I understood her very well. Marina had been over exactly this conversation; it was as if it was standard for buying a ticket. 'Always ask if produce is fresh,' she said. 'Yes, even on a train.' I said I thought that question was unlikely to be answered in the negative. She looked offended and said Russians would never deceive you about the quality of produce. If it wasn't fresh they would tell you and sell it to someone who didn't ask.

I thought there was some other reason this lady wanted me to wait until tomorrow but I ignored it and considered myself very lucky to be able to go today, the humour was on me! I bought the ticket and she apologised for the foreigner price. This was extraordinary. She was no railway woman. I dallied and talked about weather and *gizn trudney*. She said life was rather good, that she had never married and that she enjoyed her work, even though I was her only customer that day.

I was very intrigued by this unique specimen until she told me she was a retired ballet dancer. She had danced with the Kirov, taken a fall while on tour in Irkutsk, was in the city hospital for some months, realised she was too old and took a job selling train tickets to foreigners. At the end of the conversation she lapsed effortlessly into

English. We had whiled away the time and the train was due. She advised me to go to the platform: 'It's never late.'

'Which train is it?' I asked.

Her raised eyes searched me as she said: 'It is the 44A, of course.'

Konieshno, of course – even this lovely lady! They use it all the time, get great value out of it. It always insinuates that you have been rather dumb and missed the obvious.

The unlucky 44A had all the signs of a tough trip. It was nothing like the 3 that had brought me from Moscow. There was no carpet. The floor was covered throughout in brown linoleum. There were no plastic flowers and there were no curtains on the corridor windows. There were other signs too: the handrail one grips to climb up had never been shined, and the passengers were different. They were noisy, talkative, a touch raucous. A child ran along the corridor. If Svet had seen that! The 44A attracts a rougher clientele, less discerning. The *dejurnaya* was a man. He smiled. I saw him sharing food with passengers. The people who ride 44A live life on the rim. They are risk-takers.

The male *dejurnaya* put me in a carriage with a lively, twenty-three-year-old, yellow-blonde girl and a stout, sweating *babushka* from Astrakan. She was puffing with the heat and it was hard to understand how she had been on the train for four days. It didn't seem like she'd last that long. She was nothing like the woman who had swollen but still she was under pressure. All her straps and strings dangled in the effort to stay cool. She blew out and fanned the air with her hand. The little blonde kept her going with giggles. This generous girl had pooled all their resources and arranged them around the place; not neatly but with the extravagant touch of one who loves life and food. She giggled like Marilyn Monroe. Her name was new to me so I said I'd call her Marilyn. She said, 'Oy-ya!' and squealed.

She had been on the Black Sea on holiday for a month with her friend. She had a beautiful tan and she wore a tight, lime green, lycra top to show it up. She wet her hand with spittle and polished her forearm with it to show me how it glistened. Her friend had remained on in Moscow because she still had money but M.M. had blown the lot and now couldn't wait to get back to Vladivostok to dish out all the presents. She had things for her parents and brothers, and her boyfriend. She showed me what she had for him; a sweater that looked like a medieval coat of armour. I couldn't resist remarking on how big it was. Marina's Russian was flowing and I wanted to say everything I could even if it wasn't what I wanted to say.

'Oh, but he is huge . . . look!' she gushed, pulling a photograph from a bulging cloth bag. He *was* huge – and much older than her.

We were well-acquainted and cushy when, up above, something stirred. The ghost train! Though the fire I had heard about had been under a seat, the unexpected movement gave me a start. The women saw my frightened reaction and I blurted out what I had heard about the 44A. '*Konieshno*,' they laughed. 'Everyone knows about it. What's life if not a bazaar?'

What stirred above was a man – a boy, rather. The two feet clad in working socks came first, and then the smell. It was heavy: of sweat, tobacco and fart. Before he had made his way down, scratching and straightening, M.M. had some tasty morsels set out for him to nibble. He was seventeen and smiled a sleepy, impish grin. He took a few bites and indicated, with an international gesture that it was a smoke he was really after. She pulled out a half-used bottle of beer and shoved it into his hand as he sidled off to the area between carriages where smoking is allowed. In his absence the women told me he also was going to Vladivostok to join the army there; he had just been drafted. 'To lose his life fighting in Chechnya like my son,' the old woman croaked.

While he was having his smoke and drink, M.M. sliced tomatoes, cucumber and salami. On his return he sat down to the table and ate it up, smiling all the while. He never said a word. The two women, young and old, coddled him. He had soft, blond, curly hair and the smile on his face went deep. In embarrassment he rubbed his fingers through his scraggy locks and the older woman's eyes went wet. She followed his every bite. He was a delight to feed; he ate with young animal noises. He smacked his lips, kicked off his shoes and climbed back up to his *miesta*, snorting, belching, smelling but still smiling. In seconds he had settled into a rhythmic quasi-snore. The old lady shook her head in sweet sadness. 'God help his poor mother,' she intoned.

The drafting of young men into the armed forces is much hated by Russians. They see no purpose in the causes served by their fighting soldiers. Thousands have lost their lives in Afghanistan and Chechnya: useless wars, as they see them. These places are far away, unknown, and occupied by black people. There is another problem, too, but Russians don't like to let foreigners know about it. Bullying is endemic within the forces and there is sexual abuse. One seventeen-year-old wept while he tried to tell me the things that had happened to him. He was ashamed, and I couldn't understand all the words. A girlfriend of another said, 'They take his boots and let him go barefoot; they do bad things to him too . . . because he is beautiful, you see.'

Word ran the length of the carriage: 'Soon . . . come on . . . it is coming up, don't miss it.' The whole complement of passengers piled into the corridor, some in night attire, and gaped out of the window. Then someone almost shouted: 'There it is!' Everyone else joined in the refrain:

'Quick, get the camera.'

'Ah! Isn't it wonderful . . .'

'. . . freshly painted too.'

'*Konieshno*.'

'It' was an image of Lenin embedded in a hill. Enormous, like those desert drawings in Peru, it could only be seen as a picture from a distance. It was probably made from metal and, as someone said, it looked freshly painted. From a distance it is hard to judge scale but I reckoned it to be more than two hundred yards in each dimension. No one remarked on whom it was honouring; it was just an anticipated landmark, a milestone on a long journey, a marker from which to judge how far one had come or how far to go. Like the statue at Omsk, its significance is that it marks a spot, not that it depicts a fallen hero.

Even after it had vanished into the distance people stayed at the window, old-fashioned cameras and cheap modern ones at the ready.

Soon Baikal!

We had done the 'C' ring around the lake but had been a fair way away and so out of its view, but soon it would reappear. These people were hard to silence. The 44A had built up a head of camaraderie that effervesced. Different to the solemn 3 – it had been the grand circle, this was the gods. The clientele of the 44A are easily aroused. They are the Mediterranean people of this great, long track. They touched as they passed. Many seemed to want to be close to me to witness my first impressions. Only the boy soldier slept. I was aware of the burden to react big. Missing my cue could kill my audience.

When Grandfather Baikal loomed, a chorus – 'UUUUUUhhhhhhhh!' – put me and my rehearsed reaction in the shade. It calls for music, Dvořák's New World Symphony perhaps, a clash of cymbals at least. A curtain is drawn back on an infinite panorama of live water.

Now I knew why people make it sound like a person. It is powerful, almost a god, benevolent and beautiful. Its spread is munificent. Though still four days to go to Vladivostok these people sound like they have arrived; the Jews reaching the promised land. People swap greetings and compliments in celebration. M.M. is holding the Astrakhan *babushka* in her embrace. 'LOOK!' Tears stream down the old lady's face.

It takes a half-hour from the first glimpse to wind down to water-level. Mountains are capped in white snow, or lava. There are murmurings about the omul as people prepare newspapers and bags. The ledge-table is cleared and other spaces too. Anticipation. The platform is closely lined and the sellers are in competition even though every woman has the same fare: omul. It is a long, slim fish. A little over a foot in length and thin. It is brown – looks smoked. Even before the ten minutes allowed, every bucket is empty and everyone is back on board. Comparative silence ensues as each carriage lays out its feast. I don't have to lie; it is delicious. Not a fish-eater, I had anticipated another feigned appreciation but it was unnecessary. I hadn't tasted anything like it. 'Such fish!'

The train skirted the lake for some time. Here it boasts a sandy beach. Children play. Sand buckets and spades are incongruous – this is Siberia. A browned Adonis does slow, contemplated exercises on parallel bars; his girlfriend eyeballs the sun through mirrored glasses. She slides the string straps of a skimpy bikini higher up to her waist to prevent a strappy tan. Water-skiers rise up on great arches of spray and more incongruities thwart assumptions. This could be a Caribbean resort complete with sand, sea and rich, indulgent people. But this is not a sea, it is a lake and these people are very poor. In places the lake looks so 'laky' you nearly think of it as a river where dwell brown trout. But here it's Barbados. Are these the same people whose average wage is said to be thirty dollars a week? Yes indeed! One must be thinking all the time. Finally, the long train curls away to a more sombre south, whistling a sad farewell as evening approaches.

There is no platform at Ulan Ude. Well, there is, but the 44A doesn't go anywhere near it. It comes to a halt right in the middle of about nine parallel sets of tracks. I don't know if this has anything to do with the perceived risk status of this particular train, perhaps a place could become tainted by it. It takes an adventurous jump to reach the weed-choked patch between the tracks, and it takes a long detour to get around the beast before crossing the remaining tracks to get to the platform. Russians don't use overhead passes to cross the track. It's part of their pragmatism and disposition to dangerous living. Often no such crossings exist. One girl I spoke with told me she had ground much of Switzerland's railway to a halt. In her early days of a posting to Geneva, she stepped delicately across three sets of rails to climb the platform on the far side. Old habits . . .

It was getting dark so I kept my eye on a man who had just met a student type off the train. He approached him, hand held far out. They shook, maintaining the distance. The bonhomie of 44A didn't extend to the land-bound. But he looked like a father meeting a son. I thought I'd ask advice and maybe cadge a lift. I caught up with them halfway across the track.

He put my bag and his son's in the boot. He never asked me where I was going but took me on a tour of the town.

It's impressive. Many years ago I had got a postcard from Ulan Ude from Klaus, an adventurous German whom I had met somewhere, hitchhiking. He was going to see every country in the world. Consumed with envy I prised a promise out of him for postcards from strange places, 'Any place you think I won't even have heard of.' They came from: Tikal, Guatemala; Cochabamba, Bolivia; Ban Hou Sai, Laos; and one from Ulan Ude (near Mongolia). It had no picture, just heavy black lines for the address. The message: *Twenty below 0°C. Drinking tea with butter to keep warm . . . you can imagine. Klaus.* I did imagine. I saw a small, all-wooden station serving an all-wooden village so remote there were only soldiers living there; some kind of leftovers from gulag days. I saw fur hats and uniforms with red stars and jack boots and snow. I saw and heard these soldiers coming and stamping their feet on wooden floors to knock off the snow before kicking off their boots and shaking the snow out of their *sharpkas*: their fur hats. And they were all Mongolian-looking.

The picture I dreamed was not what this father showed me. The huge square was Soviet style, but it was not decayed, not cracked, not choked with weeds. Though there was still a little light in the summer sky, the square was floodlit and symmetrical. Buildings were attractive in that military, orderly way and the rotating electric sign said it was 18°C and 10:45 p.m. Either side of the huge statue, there were healthy, well-kept, silver Christmas trees, like the ones backing Lenin's tomb in Red Square. It could hardly be missed. 'The biggest head in the world,' Sergei had told me. 'You can't miss it,' he said. Another Lenin monument. I've forgotten its statistics but people standing at its base would be no more than the size of his finger if he had fingers. He doesn't because it is only a bust. Just the head, tapered away to a pedestal below the collar and tie. It was here, in five days' time, that I would meet Sergei's friend, Stepan, who would take me to Ust Barguizin. Even the few kiosks selling ice-cream were shiny chrome. There were magnificent sculptures in front of (what father told me was) the Ballet Theatre. It was built, he said, by Japanese POWs during the Second World War. I was completely lost. What were Japanese soldiers doing here; where were they captured; and how were they brought here? There was another theatre for drama. He dropped me at a hotel that took Visa and didn't serve tea with butter, just cappuccino.

So I had cappuccino for breakfast and afterwards went to stand under Lenin's head both to feel the scale and practice for my appointment five days hence. I then went to the museum. I wanted to know many things but especially I wanted to know how influential Buddhism was in this area.

Though Irkutsk was a smart, modern city I found it permeated by a certain tranquillity that I did not think was attributable solely to the intellectualism of the Decembrist exiles. Not only about Irkutsk, in fact way before Irkutsk after I had got over my initial disappointment with Asia and Siberia, I had felt, or perhaps seen, a certain tranquillity, a mindfulness in people. It was a Caucasian version of a similar mindfulness I'd seen and felt in South-East Asia. The country people I had seen in the last ten days and the people in Irkutsk too, walked with the same deliberation as they do in South-East Asia. And now here in Ulan Ude I was aware of something similar. The only common denominator was Buddhism. A minority religion but yet the earliest here.

Even when religion is no longer practised its basic tenets become part of the genetic code. In the Western world practice and belief has declined, yet the basic fundamentals of theistic doctrine permeate our thinking and action. Crime and punishment in secular society parallel sin and its consequences under the vengeful God of Church teaching. The prison system reflects the Heaven/hell concept. Short sentences are similar to periods in purgatory; serious criminals go to maximum security or maybe death row out of which, like hell, there is no redemption.

Our fundamentals about what constitutes right and wrong, good and bad is commandment-based. Even constitutions and their offspring laws are distant relatives of Moses' stone tablets. The basic fundamentals of theistic societies, Christian, Muslim and Jew, presuppose an omniscient judgmental eye-in-the-sky watching their every move for transgression. Our motivation comes from outside ourselves, '*don't* do that you'll be caught', whereas in Buddhism it comes from within: '*won't* do that, it'll screw up my karma'.

In Buddhism, there isn't a spying god who will take revenge. You are what you have done; you will be what you do now. *Konieshno*, all this is not a conscious process but so long formed through our indoctrination that it has probably become part of genetic coding. It seems to me that an area, over generations, takes on the aura of its people's thinking. Like a house with a good feeling to it. Even empty houses have the aura of past occupants, it can be changed but it takes periods of other occupation. So I surmised that maybe it was the Buddhist past of this area . . . away back to the place where I first saw the Sayan Mountains a day before Irkutsk . . . that gave it that different feeling and gave them that different walk I'd first seen in Omsk.

I had this in mind when I was going to the museum. And there was a large section dealing with Buddhism, or rather Lamaism. Another surprise: the Buddhism in this area came from Tibet, not India or the East. Lamaism is Tibetan Buddhism. In the museum were all kinds of things for making sounds – bells and horns and conches – and there were robes and information about the repression of monastic life during the Soviet era. There was other information too. Some was interesting, some less. Where I was standing, all of Ulan Ude and the surrounding area was off-limits to all foreigners until 1990; Princess Anne of England was the first royal visitor since the assassination of the Czar. She came here in 1993, Genghis Khan earlier, in 1239, heading for Moscow way before the train was even thought of.

The area had many other minor ethnic and religious variants: Kazaks, Cossacks, European Russians and Poles. Ulan Ude is the capital of Buryatia Republic, but it is not independent from Russia, and it is hard to figure out what degree of autonomy it has in anything. It has a population of 40,000 and 21 per cent are supposed to be Buryats. This is not reflected in the streets. There were far too many white people and in some distorted, perverse reflection of Russian racism I was tired of 'whitey'.

White people are all right but I prefer real foreigners. I am white, Western and Christian by birth, so when I go travelling I prefer to meet people who aren't. I like them to have black, brown, or yellow skin. I like them to have unusual features and exotic customs. For what are exotic customs but those which I am not used to? A Chinese man coming to Ireland would be fascinated by daily rain and gaggles of priests. They would probably drink pints of Guinness and buy ridiculously expensive Waterford glass whiskey tumblers. These things are ordinary to me and I hardly see them. Black, brown, or yellow skin, scarred cheeks, or saffron monks with begging bowls on misty mornings are my quarry.

Ulan Ude was a bright, airy, attractive city with a wonderful variety of consumer goods. Its theatres and water fountains and banks that change foreign money are a great source of pride to its citizens, but that wasn't what I was looking for. The receptionist at the hotel desk was Buryat and sophisticated and pointed through the window at all the monuments and buildings I should be visiting. She was multilingual and didn't understand why I wanted to speak Russian and roubles when she was fluent in American and Visa.

I had dreamed of a gradual change from occidental to oriental as I moved east but this was not happening. This town was too smart. I expected more from the capital of Buryatia. Or perhaps, more accurately, I wanted less. So I went in search though I was a little worried about my karma: I knew that my thinking was a little plaited. I wanted to see lots of Buryats and I wanted to see them as I fantasised, occupying the land in its raw, un-urbanised state. In brief, I wanted 'primitive'. It is a mental conflict for many travellers; your theoretical aspiration is that all fellow human beings will enjoy (are enjoying) equality. Yet fulfilment of this aspiration would rob travel of its greatest joy: seeing life and people in a 'primitive' state. Disturbingly, there is no better boast within the fraternity than, 'I was the first white man they ever saw.' And it is further complicated by the dilemma of deciding what is better, 'original', 'primitive', or 'developed'.

In the park, men sit at stone tables playing chess. This is common in all Russian towns. They sit with enamelled alarm clocks between them; concentrating hard and then slamming down some kind of stopper on the clock when they have taken their move. Their partners then study the board and do the same. It is mostly men who play chess but, in this park, there were a few women. One was Buryat. She was sophisticated, like the hotel receptionist, and had painted nails too, but I took her presence here in a traditionally male domain as an indication of enlightenment. She wore a pinstriped suit and looked like she should have a briefcase.

She understood.

She recommended two trips out of Ulan Ude. The first she said was easy, just forty minutes by bus and I could do it today. The other was more complicated, down by the Mongolian border but I should be able to fit the two into the five days before I was to meet Stepan.

So, for the one-day trip I took the bus to Ivolginsku Datsan Monastery, now reopened and in full swing. Well, the thing that swung most was a prayer wheel with special powers. Inside it, written in parchment, are the words of some powerful prayers and, the monk told me, for every spin the prayer gets said one thousand times. High tech. So I did a little repair work on the old karma. Then he told me that this monastery and many others in the area were closed by Stalin in the thirties and that all the monks were sent to the gulags.

'Which ones? Where?'

'Who knows, there were so many.'

Then, in the forties, Stalin realised how valuable the support of any religious group could be to temporal power if they were spun the right way, so he allowed many places of worship to be opened again. The Dalai Lama had visited this monastery five times the monk boasted with raised eyebrows and fingers . . . five. He was Mongolian-looking and his fingers were stubby. Another change of Kremlin mind closed it again and it was 'officially' (two raised eyebrows) opened in 1966 but it was a façade (drop the eyebrows). It was 'monked' by the KGB. They learned the necessary rituals in Mongolia and put on a costumed show by day in the monastery but by night retreated in Zil limousines to mountain *dachas* to relax after a hard day spinning and chanting.

I repaired to my Visa hotel to prepare for the more difficult crusade south. The 350,000 Buryat people living in Siberia represent the largest ethnic group in Russia. This area was first investigated by emissaries of the Russian czar in 1620. They had some difficulty with the rapids of the river Angara and many of them never got this far south. Those who did, however, carried back tales of the great agricultural wealth of the local people and that they were anxious to trade their horses and camels.

More Russians were attracted by the prospects and, by the middle of the seventeenth century, it seems the area was settled by a large number of northern Russians. Here I run into difficulty. The Russian paranoia about race makes them unreliable. They shuffle uncomfortably when asked about the degree of intermarriage and integration. Judging by today's small number of mixed-blooded people, I glean that then, as now, there were problems.

The Buryats are Mongolian people. This is evident in their physical appearance. They had drifted north from their homeland to settle. When the Russians came, it seems they couldn't make up their minds between their old Mongol masters and the new ones from the west. At first many fled back into Mongolia, but they didn't stay long. One explanation of their choice reads: 'Mongolian Khans behead culprits, but the Russian Czar just flogs them. Let us become subjects of the Russian Czar.' This popular view of the ferocity of the old Mongol rulers is at odds with some other symptoms of magnanimity displayed by none other than Genghis Khan himself. He seems to have had no religious prejudice but was eclectic in his choice of gods' threats and promises. In his own clan, never mind his army, there were Buddhists, Muslims and Christians. He himself was a worshipper of Tegri, the ruler of Heaven. Maybe he had an eye to the post for later and perhaps some plan to create a vacancy. Before he slaughtered a worshipping congregation in a

Mosque in Bokhara (Uzbekistan) he proclaimed: 'I am God's punishment for your sins. If you had not committed awful deeds He would not have sent such a punishment as me upon you.' This and the multicoloured 'clasp to the bosom' speech I'd read on the back wall of classroom 5 was what little background knowledge I had of Buryatia, this wedge of Siberia between the south of Lake Baikal and Mongolia. The area and its inhabitants share the same name. The Buryatia Republic some call it, but more commonly it is simply Buryatia and the indigenous are Buryats.

The second trip that the Buryat lady suggested would take three days. It was away down by the Mongolian border but when I told her about my appointment she did a little calculation and said I should just make it. She also said I would find not only a Buryat community but also remnants of displaced Polish, Ukrainian and Belorussian Old Believers.

She told me there was some split in old Russian Orthodox religion some time in the eighteenth century, which led to a ghettoisation of those who didn't go along with the liturgical reform. They are called Old Believers. Those who insisted on sticking to the old ways were exiled to Siberia and these were later joined, voluntarily it seems, by others. They now have a settlement in this area. In small villages many of the traditions of Eastern European countries are preserved and, in a way that often occurs, they seem to be purer in their inherited practise than in the place of their origin. Their song and dance, house style, costume and dialect are redolent of old Poland. Their religion has now been officially recognised by the Orthodox Church and they take great pride in its practice. The lady had told me to spend one night in each of two places, one called Kyatka and the other Visinka. She said the town of Kyatka was an important stopping-point on the old Tea Route.

The Silk Route rings exotic intrigue. It conjures up images of haughty camels laden down with carpets and jewels. It evokes dreams of wealth, boundless power, cruelty and excess. Its image is romantic. The Tea Route evokes no such emotions but in its time competed in importance.

The Tea Route originated in China in the city of Kalgan, which is just behind the Great Wall. Here the tea was picked up by couriers who were responsible for its passage west. In the autumn, winter and spring they moved the precious cargo across the Gobi desert to the border with Russia at Kyatka. From there it went on up to Irkutsk where each *tsybic* (tea bale) was stamped. Irkutsk was made an official custom city in 1861. Tax on goods was collected at this point, not only on tea but also on gold, silk and fur bound for Western markets. It was here, at the Mongolian border, I learnt the facts that gave me a greater understanding of why Irkutsk grew to be such an important city in the 1870s.

I had only one night to spend in the strange town of Kyatka. In the evening I walked up a long incline to look across at Mongolia. It rolled away in front of me, an eternal, undulating steppe. In the distance I saw a trail of dust from a galloping horseman. His raiment flapped ferociously in the wind, but I heard no sound. The wind was blowing hard and hot. I hadn't known what to expect from a Siberia–Mongolia border. The concepts that both evoke are too polarised to anticipate that they rub shoulders. Mongolia: hot and dusty; Siberia: petrifyingly cold. The distant, silent horseman was iconoclastic Mongolia, the village from which I viewed him hotchpotch Europe.

In the centre of the town there is a stone market hall that could be in my local village in Ireland and in the Cathedral I saw a painting, it was original but it could have been a replica of many in Florence. In Tea Route times, the town was famous for its millionaires. The tea cargo that came through here went up to Irkutsk, along the route that I had covered. It then continued by camel and horse west to Nizhy Novogorod which is near Kirov, where, were it not for the quick-thinking *babushkas* of that town and for the welcoming embrace of Svetlana, I still might be.

With difficulty I got to Visinka at the end of the second day and decided that I couldn't leave after just one night. Such a trip deserved at least a full day so I would take a chance on making it back on time for the date with Stepan under the Biggest Head. I'd stay another night. That forward arrangement weighed heavily with me all the time and I was plagued by the reiterate thought that I should never make such plans and arrangements.

The place was an attractive little maze of dirt tracks and wooden houses. It had a gushing, mineral-looking river. It was July but every wooden house and shack had logs piled against it. I started early and not far into exploration came across a galvanised hut by the banks of the rushing river. Its gable end supported an almost illegible sign: *Banya*.

Most towns have at least one *banya*. Except, incongruously, poor ones where individual families have their own *banyas* in their gardens. The village of Visinka had as poor a *banya* as I had seen. It had a stoker; he wasn't Buryat but Russian. All *banyas* must have stokers somewhere but usually they are concealed in the crumbling furnace room in the bowels of the place. Technology has not caught up with Visinka so Aloysha (that was his name) stoked from the street, which was a narrow dirt-path at the narrowest, swiftest part of the river. The *banya* was a black wooden shed and small even for such a village. Women and men had to have separate times. Usually *banyas* are wood burning; this one used coal, which was piled high outside on the dirt-path. The room that contained the furnace was so small that the fire door was just inside and accessible from the street. Aloysha shovelled coal into the raging firebox from outside. It was only eight o'clock on a Sunday morning but he was flat-out getting things ready for the 'ten o'clock women'. This surprised me, if there is a first preference advantage anywhere in Russia it is always the men's. Maybe technology had bypassed Visinka or maybe Buryat women don't take the rubbish white Russian women suffer. Aloysha was one of the few non-Buryat residents of this village. His menial position added to my surprise, but not as much as his appearance did. He was a dead ringer for Rudolph Nureyev. Though only four foot tall, from waist up, he was Rudi. I told him so but he was not impressed.

'Don't know him.'

'He's dead.'

'Yes, shovelling coal kills 'em young.'

'No! He was a famous ballet dancer.'

'He's lucky he didn't have to shovel coal for the women of Visinka. Such women!'

He didn't stop while he talked. The fire savaged fuel as quickly as he could shovel it in. He blamed 'the Revolution' (the most recent one) for all his problems: 'Such coal . . . have you ever seen such coal?'

It was nearly all slack. Just a few small lumps here and there, the rest slack. To add to it his shovel was like a sieve. Age had wearied its metal into filigree so, before he got its load to the furnace mouth, much of it had strained away. It was like drinking soup with a fork. And, like many other ailments in this land of problems, there was no solution. By now I had learnt enough not to suggest one. He said it was definitely the revolution. 'Before, coal was coal. Such pieces . . . this size,' and he paused for a precious moment to make a big fist of his two hands. 'But now we have dust.'

I asked him if I could get my camera and take a picture of him because he was so like R.N.

'*Konieshno*, if you bring me cigarettes . . . maybe a drink.' To make up for lost time he shovelled even faster. 'Such women.'

He was still on my mind that night while reading a book given to me by the Buryat *babushka* of the house I was staying in. It was about the local area and one of its boasts was that Rudolph Nureyev was born on a Siberian train as it passed through the village of Visinka.

I climbed the hill and saw down into Mongolia like a frame from the Middle Ages. And another village was so close I knew I'd make it there and back. I'll never know its name but the one I reached had fair-haired girls with garlands and ribbons in their hair as if they were celebrating a Polish holiday. On the way back I came across a hill temple, Buddhist monks tingled gentle bells and then I could see Visinka where, by now, Aloysha rested from his exhausting task of stemming the wrath of his ten o'clock Buryat women.

I was exhausted from worry. Worrying about getting back in time to meet my ten o'clock Stepan.

I made it.

I was transported in a full and ailing bus. It was piloted by a large lady of rustic appearance but with wild hair blonded like Moscow bus women. The seat was patched with glue and plastic and detached from its legs. The floor was holed, the fishnet luggage rack leaked bundles and a malodorous drunk found rest for his bruised head on my shoulder. He slept there until he sobered up and arrived fresh and well in Ulan Ude. I had caught his hangover and collapsed into a bed in the Visa hotel.

Refreshed and ready for the road again I praised myself for punctuality: I arrived at the Head at exactly ten o'clock.

I waited.

Stepan was to meet me here at ten in the morning. I was not to be late. At eleven-plus I saw him approach in an affected hurry. I speculated: he has just indulged the Russian tardiness in the certainty that the foreigner will be relieved to see him and gush politely.

'Are you the foreigner who wants to go to Ust Barguizin?'

'*Konieshno*! Are you the driver who was supposed to take him there at ten?'

Chapter Six

It was a seven-hour ride and Stepan never got over the slight. Nor did I. I had engaged what I thought was the Russian way in reprimanding him for his lateness. It struck a discord.

The road was corrugated and dusty mostly. Occasionally there would be a stretch of tarmac but it never extended fully from side to side. It would only be wide enough for one vehicle and ended in a ragged fringe at either side, before reaching the edges of the patch that was road. There was very little traffic. What there was came at the narrowest strips.

My memory sees them thundering straight towards us at record-breaking speed. Even now I grip my stool and duck. Each time collision was imminent I would be ready to blurt out an apology, a withdrawal: 'You weren't late, it was me, foolish foreigner, that was early . . . a whole hour early.' I never got to it. My dry mouth glued shut as death approached. We only met nine cars in the seven hours but I can remember the eye colour of each driver. After they'd passed I'd open my mouth really wide so that he wouldn't hear the air gushing in to feed the pumping heart. I began to really miss travelling by train, even the 44A seemed great. I would have stuck to rail transport if it were possible but there is no railroad going anywhere near the part of Baikal to which Sergei had directed me. I wasn't at all sure that where I was going was where I wanted to be. It was not in Buryatia, it was just its proximity to the lake that recommended it. I had an awful lot of faith in Sergei and had jumped at what he recommended. Then I stole a glance at Stepan's jail-door face and wondered.

What conversation there was, was stilted. We had a misunderstanding about an old woman. He said she would be sitting by the river at the side of the road and below the hill. She was to be beautiful. She provided rest and sustenance for all the people who walked her hill. She nearly brought us together. I was in anticipation. She sounded like a lovely person and we must be going to pick her up since he talked so nicely about her. I thought she'd repair the atmosphere.

He was talking about the village of Babushkin, which we were to pass through. I was hearing *babushka*. I shouldn't have told him about the mix-up. I could easily have covered it up. I could have been patronising and said, yes, it was beautiful. But I didn't, I said, 'Oh, I understood it was an old woman.' He thought I was criticising his lovely village. In my efforts to clear up that, he got the impression that I was criticising his beautiful language – foreigner of a thousand words! For the rest of the trip I was lavish with hollow praise.

It took the whole uncomfortable day. When we stopped to eat I didn't know what to ask for. Were I alone I would have had no problem and enjoyed the struggle and eaten whatever turned up, but with barking Stepan I was afraid. Afraid that I'd sound foreign and embarrass him so when he had an enamel plate of *shishlik* and *plov*

I just nodded and growled, 'Same.' It came from a wooden corner kiosk and we ate it standing against the car shoeing away mangy dogs. Even though I was doubtful about where we were going I was glad when we got there.

The village of Ust Barguizin was nearly a town, but without a centre. There are three classes of urban settlements in Russia. The smallest is *direvna*, a village. Anything with a population up to 1,500 falls into this category. The next category is *pasooluk* whose closest English equivalent would be a town. It is a slightly more inclusive term and has a somewhat hazy boundary on its upper limit. A city is *gorad* and comes in, again hazily, at about 20,000 people. Ust Barguizin was laid out in rectangular blocks just like a Canadian town. It could almost be somewhere near Winnipeg except for the logs piled against the houses. Everything is of wood, as in all of Siberia. Mostly round logs, windproofed by stuffing the gaps in between them. The filling material is, appropriately, called *packla*. In Ust Barguizin people walked fast and alone and that frightened me. Nothing like anything I'd seen since Omsk. Whatever gave the Siberian people that mindful walk didn't exist here. Here they walked straight and fast. They looked intent on getting where they were going and getting there quickly. From Omsk to here it wasn't like that. The walk was slow . . . as if they were taking pleasure out of just walking. But here in Ust Barguizin there was no pleasure in it. They nearly dashed and dashing doesn't become any location, least of all a Siberian village of wooden houses. I felt disturbed by it. Maybe Stepan felt my unease because he made an effort at reconciliation. He drove me around the *pasooluk* before dropping me at Olga's house. This was the woman that Sergei had recommended to me. She was the one he talked about in mellifluous tones: 'She cooks like an angel.'

I knew I'd like the part of the town where the *parom*, the ferry, was. It was open and looked at the other side of the river from a big, rectangular, solid-wooden pier. There were people and much evidence of coming and going. The ferry boat itself was a low barge-like boat, constantly plying the four-hundred-yard river. It was hard to guess the necessity that kept it going from eight in the morning until eight at night. It was even harder to understand how it made so many crossings without accident. It was a sick barge that had to be hauled out from the wall by another tug before it could start to cross. At the other side it had to be similarly manoeuvred to port. It was crewed by a selection of drunken men. By afternoon they would be incapable of speech, yet they continued to cross until sunset without mishap. They swayed around the open deck. Deck is a fancy word for the rattling platform that cars, trucks, cranes, bicycles and people crowded on to. It was without surround. A step wrong and one was in the drink. Yet these drunks wove around with stout ropes, dumb from illicit alcohol, and they made faultless crossings.

On the Ust Barguizin side, women sold things. Fish mostly. But underpants and brassières also, and nylon stockings sagging on the card they were wrapped around. There was a new portakabin store with a sign, *Krouglosouthnaya*: round-the-clock. I couldn't see the need, but a woman with a white coat and a hygienic white cap on her head came to the door.

There was a straggling bunch of waiters. The ones who always wait where buses, boats or trains come in. Always in useless, listless hope of something turning up. I knew there was enough here to keep me 'finding out' for a long time. It felt like a Scandinavian place or maybe Iceland but run-down, very run-down, though a few good vehicles made the crossing.

Olga's house was far away from this point. The farthest-away point in town. A distance that spoke a desire to be removed from the dregs of society. It was a newish house, surrounded by a fence and double wooden gates. Almost all houses in Siberia stand alone. Even the most modest is detached and will have a large garden for animals and vegetables. Most have a double garage-type door leading to the garden and thence to the back door of the house. Those familiar know the secrets of entry. Stepan knew it and slid his hand through a hole, easing back a long beam that allowed it to yawn open.

Olga's father came rushing from the garden. He was large, with red leather skin and a chin held high. He was barefoot. His feet were of strong leather too. His wife followed. She was also barefooted. She was large, cylindrical and dressed in black, with something coloured around her neck. An enormous Duracell battery, she had bottle-bottom glasses that she kept pushing up with the back of her earthy hand. Like her daughter, she taught at the village school. Olga was with neighbours but her young son Andrei would get her. '*Bistro*, Andrei! *Bistro*!' Duracell battery grandmother shouted. The English word bistro for a particular type of restaurant comes from Russian, not Italian, as one would expect. It means quickly.

The Duracell battery grandmother was old enough to be a *babushka* but she wasn't. She was a wheezing woman of much motion. Shifting her glasses up crossing her arms which didn't meet and when they fell down crossing them again and then looking out to see if Andrei was coming and then opening the window more and mopping her brow and trying to fold her arms again and then rubbing the sweat off her upper lip but the sweat was still there and the glasses had slipped down again so she started a completely new cycle of motion: push up glasses . . .

They put me into the *zemavu* to wait for Olga . . . where is that boy? Andrei . . . The *zemavu* is the summer kitchen, which stands alone from the main dwelling, most houses in small-town Siberia have one. They are like the *dachas* of city dwellers in other parts of Russia. Russians take off their shoes when they go into the proper house. In the *zemavu* they don't. The *zemavu* is like a children's playhouse, free of restraints. There are shelves of bottled berries, some broken implements and strings of hanging onions.

Shuffling, shifting Duracell and her husband walked around my bag that I had placed on the floor. They prepared vodka, cheese and bread. I worked around the vodka, and maybe they didn't notice. Grandpa told me, in gasps, that once there had been French people staying. Some 'ologists' who were finding out about the lake.

At last Olga arrived ('What kept you? We were waiting.') breathing heavily and trying to conceal it. Andrei had dropped his bicycle in the middle of the open gateway and the wheel spun around for a long time. On his way to get Olga he had rustled up anyone under fifteen in the area. They stared around, over and through the wooden fence and after some wide-eyed time went away, careful not to run.

But Luda lingered and *she* hadn't been looking through the fence. She stood, hand on hip, in the middle of the gateway, very aware of her very pretty self. Polka dots and sandals and I think there was a touch of red on the lips: a little less than Lolita but not a lot. When she had seen what she wanted to, and known that she had been seen, she walked away very slowly, fluffing out the polka dots and perking up her chin. Only then did Andrei look to see what this stranger was made of.

The Irish word for strike is *stailc* (pronounced stolk) and one who is inclined towards strike and contrariness is called *stailcish*. Olga was *stailcish*! She walked with quick jerks, always changing direction and mood. The absolute opposite to what I had begun to think of as the Siberian walk. She took me across the yard to the house, showed me a nice room with a thin bed and a shiny spread that slithered around, looked at my little bag and shot out. Minutes later she was back, spun round, indicating not only that I should follow now but that I should have understood that that was what she intended all the time. I followed her around the garden thinking maybe she'll turn around and ask me what the hell I am doing following her. The garden was mostly of potatoes in long rows. She had two pleasantly grunting pigs and a dozen hens. They were in adjoining pens. I lingered. She had made much progress and doubled back, sighing hard, trying to understand why I'd waste time talking to pigs and hens.

At the other side of the garden from the pigs was the *banya*. A private, well-kept *banya* that would accommodate a family. It had a small anteroom for changing. Like a garden shed, it had dusty garments hanging on wooden pegs. The firebox was in this chamber also. Inside there were three wooden stools and a wooden table sturdy enough to lie out on. A few old, dried-out feniks hung around the wall. There were some tin containers on long wooden handles for ladling water over oneself or sloshing it over another.

There was a vicious dog chained at the end of the garden. The chain around his neck had a three-yard lead of more chain and this was threaded on a wire line that ran the length of the back of the garden so that he could run its entirety with his mane always standing in anger.

The noise the chain made on the wire made the place sound like a prison.

Towns, like people, have their own character. Maybe one inspires the other. People and their dogs are often alike too. Ust Barguizin was like Olga, dark and *stailcish*. Trees had been felled to make way for it. At the place where houses stopped and trees started there was a gloomy, spooky reticence. A dark green barrier stood there, pouting in protest at what had been done to its trees. It was a forbidding obstacle. I had to force myself to cross the naked patch that stood between houses and trees. I felt like apologising as I went: 'Nice trees . . . no, I didn't do anything to you . . . don't be so lonesome-looking.' There were paths through the trees. Lumpy, up-and-down paths with rubbish strewn at the sides: plastic containers and faded rags of summer dresses. I went to bed doubtful.

After a breakfast of porridge and jam I went to see the ferry.

I liked it. Even though there was no high ground on either side it had a fjordish feel to it. It is usually easy to tell the latitude of a place by looking at the sky. It becomes a deeper blue as one goes north. At Ust Barguizin it was deep enough to be near Rovaniemi, which is Santa's hometown in Finland. Its latitude is fifteen degrees farther south than Santa's and the sky shouldn't be as dark as it is. All across Siberia the skies are a deeper blue than they should be, but here it is remarkable. On this first evening there was a horse's mane of gasping white daubed across it and behind this spread the blue of a magnesia bottle.

People circled, dragging their feet and arousing small twirls of dust. Sound carried and you could hear the loading noises from the far side. A pile of telegraph poles provided seating. Ust Barguizin was big enough for people not to talk to each other. An unfortunate, pretentious size. Olga's house was a thirty-minute walk away, along right-angled blocks. Never trust a town built in blocks. It is too young. It is too purposeful. Made for efficiency, customised for easy numbering. It unsettled me. I wished the streets would bend and meander and lead you astray. There were maybe ten shops in the whole town, well scattered, and housed in individual log cabins. Little sheds apart from the dwellings that showed little or no sign of their existence on the outside, nowhere for women to gossip.

I liked the Post Office though. It was old and in the shade of friendly trees. Inside there were large wooden tables with yellow telegram forms and dark ink stains. A wooden floor and deep low counter. A *babushka* sold cheese and milk at one corner and on the other wall there was a hatch, sealed closed with old posters that said stamps were ten kopecks. In the *starry system* there were a hundred kopeck to one rouble. When the Soviet Union broke up the official rate of exchange was one dollar to one rouble. It tumbled quickly. Now, five years later, a dollar bought five thousand roubles.

After a few days, walking home in the almost dark, I was surprised to find a tall building of block and plaster. It was out of proportion with its surroundings and stark. Its windows looked like blank eyes. There was no sign so I had to ask what it was. It was a *gastenetsa*, a hotel and a project of Soviet ambition, to open up the area to tourism. Soviet tourism. They probably envisaged healthy citizens fishing and swimming in Baikal. Russians love taking holidays. In Soviet times workers earned the right to two weeks a year in a government-run and owned Rest House. They still abound – now mostly derelict. They dot the countryside in areas of lakes and woods. Concrete blocks of three or four floors fronted by sculptures of happy workers striding out for Mother Russia. A few still function but they're sad. Cavernous halls now echoing to small, scarce voices. The paint peels, water drips and lace curtains hang torn. The Lada-sized parking spots empty except for dandelions.

I found my way across a swamp and through a wood to the lake proper. The *parom* was not actually on the lake but a river flowing into it. And I liked the shore of this lake. One day I found wild horses on it and they frightened and delighted me. Another day I found Jan.

The place was two miles out of the town, through the lonesome woods, which I apologised to, and here the long sandy shore of Baikal stretches for miles like a dark Caribbean island. Other places on the shore are friendly and pebbled, or bouldered and frightening. Here it is a beach. Jan was drawing a bough behind him, making tracks in the sand. He was from Berlin, a student of Russian and studying at Moscow University. He had come to Siberia to see it. His eyes looked weak and he had ten-to-two feet. In his free hand he carried his shoes, and he was kicking at the sand the way one who walks alone does.

We walked together for two days and understood each other. He had the independence acquired by hurt. He was very honest. He didn't take a great deal of care of himself. He had an open sore on his instep and hadn't thought of turning up the cuff of his trousers to avoid the irritation. 'Thank you for that . . . no! I never thought.' He was staying alone in the *gastenetsa* in a narrow, white room with sagging lace curtains. There was no window or light in the bathroom. With a torch we discovered it was like a cave. Like Tom Sawyer and Huck Finn we searched for crawling or dead things. The walls were streaming, rusty stalactites.

Jan was taking Monday's boat across the lake to Olkhon Island, it was a six-hour trip and the boat went only on Mondays. He knew a surprising amount about the whole area. He was the bookish type who takes in everything, one of those who transfer the written word to inner knowledge without question or debate. He said Olkhon was completely different to Ust Barguizin. 'It has a history, a culture and it has ecological interest.' Though I didn't like where I was I knew I wasn't finished with it. There were people around the *parom* I was cultivating. They didn't trust me yet, but they would. I couldn't waste what

I had built. I thought of asking him to stay for another week and we'd go together, but I didn't. In later correspondence he told me his only brother was killed in a car crash shortly after our meeting. I was sorry but not surprised. Jan had taken many hits. I know him still. I see him walking in front of me in paths through woods, barefooted ten-to-two feet marching. Marching in a way he has learnt to keep going against adversity.

'When were you happiest, Jan?'

'When I lived with a friend like a family. But only for a short time.'

Andrei had problems too. He was seriously in love with the older polka-dotted Luda. He was twelve and a half, she fourteen. She tortured him. She sat on the log outside their house, bored, observing the sky. She had acquired ennui. She could yawn on cue. A very genuine, absolutely bored yawn. I had told him I'd like nothing better than a day fishing.

'Oy! Lud! Want to come fishing?'

'Fishing!' she shrieked, like Lady Bracknell. 'With the foreigner!'

Olga didn't exactly agree that we should go but I knew she wanted us to. She prepared cold meat sandwiches and gave us bottles of fresh water. We made our arrangements: we would take the fishing rod and first try the little lake, Malenky Ozera. It was small and warm enough to swim in – maybe Baikal would be warm enough too, it had been hot for a month now. 'But be careful. Remember until three months ago it was covered in a metre of ice. It doesn't forget that easily,' a neighbour said.

'Don't worry,' Andrei said. 'I'll look after our guest.'

I didn't know how Andrei was such a nice boy with a mother like *stailcish* Olga. I thought maybe Sergei, who had sent me, was his father. He had spoken so gently of Olga and Andrei was a bit like him. As in very many Russian families an absent father is not mentioned.

We were going to cross in the *parom*. The other side was far better. Like far-off hills it held unreal promise. 'There the fish give themselves up and wild animals come and eat out of one's hand.'

Olga said to drink plenty of water and stay out of the woods if possible: 'Mosquitoes!' she said.

We tied everything to the carrier of Andrei's bike and he dashed ahead and circled and came back telling me to hurry up, the fish mightn't wait. The far side was strange and swampy. We met distant cousins who said it was better to take the path through the wood. 'Much better, the road goes so far around it could kill a man; through the woods is short.'

It was not yet ten o'clock but already hot. The path through the wood was good. It was powder-dry and the trees were not the lonesome type like those near the village. They poked at the sky and where they met it it glistened, so blue. Andrei would dart ahead and back and circle me and do wheelies. His forays ahead lengthened. I came to an intersection and waited. Paths, equally travelled, gave no hint where he had gone. 'An—dray–ya!' I yodelled a few times.

The mosquitoes struck. This must be the only habitat in the whole world of the ten a.m. mosquitoes. They are armed with spears. First they struck at the tender, already sun-rawed rim around the receding hairline. Finished here, they worked south in formation, covering every square centimetre.

'Andrei!' I roared.

Twenty minutes later he flashed across the silver ranks of birch and came to a skidding halt.

'What you wait for?'

'You! . . . How the hell do I know which way you have gone?'

'This way *konieshno*, hurry, the fish won't wait you know.'

Where we got out of the wood the little lake (small grandson of Baikal) shone. Friends again, we baited and cast. We shared the waiting. Nothing. He said maybe we were in the wrong spot, he'd investigate. He was gone for forty minutes. When he came back he was thirsty and wanted water. It was hot and he spat it out.

'You let the water get hot . . . how am I to drink hot water? Maybe we should go home . . . Mama said I must have water and you have let it get hot.'

I bit my blistered lips, rubbed my bumpy forehead, counted as far as I could go in Russian and said maybe we'd go on to swim in Baikal.

It was ice-cold but wonderful. I swam out, looked down, and nearly fell. I was looking down as if from the top of a twenty-storey building and I could see clear to the stones at the bottom that were beckoning me down. 'Ho, ho, ho! Thousands of miles from gentle Irish brooks, we'll teach you what real lakes are made of.' I did a careful crawl back to shore. He was drawing circles in the pebbles with a stick.

'I want to go home.'

I knew then it was Luda reeling him in. He couldn't bear to be without her and the child had miscalculated. He estimated we had accumulated enough adventure that, with a little garnish, would get her attention. 'Oy, Lud, guess what . . .' I was going to tell him about women, but considered his tender years and refrained.

'Andrei, we'll see who can skim stones the farthest . . . look . . . one, two, three, four, five, six bounces. Can you do better than that?'

'Want to go home.'

I toughed it out until he hollered. I had lain down and pretended to fall asleep. He made louder and louder noises: taking up the bike, wheeling it away, stopping, returning . . . 'Paddy, want to go . . . ferry will be stopped . . . does too . . .stops at three some days.'

I gave in and sulked like his mother: there were three of us now. Surprising how catching this *stailcish*-ness can be. We ploughed the sand along the beach, too angry at each other to say anything. How different sand is to walk on in different moods. Nothing more pleasant than sand between the toes when all is well and you're sauntering but when you've fallen out and you want only to make progress, then it is like ploughing tough earth. Not a word all along the shore over the dunes down into the swamp across the wood and to the ferry which would be in full swing for hours yet (the ferrymen were still able to talk for heaven's sake). Then down all those boring blocks until we were at the top of our road where she was visible. Despite our differences he had stayed with me all the way. Even when he could cycle he circled around never going too far away but when we got to the top of a road that went straight to their house, excitement overcame him and he jumped on his bike to make a dash to her.

My heart bled at the situation – throwing himself at her as she would have arranged it herself. It was fated.

By the time I got there she had chewed him up and spat him out. He was a mess, everything lost. He looked at me pathetically and I wilted. I smiled long and hard, really convincing and, ignoring her, I said: 'Andrei, such a day! I hope Olga has the fire going so I can cook all these fish – we need a feed after such a day.'

He was stunned for a moment. I winked the eye she couldn't see. Lesson one: Us Men Must Stick Together.

I thought perhaps initiation into the man's world might have been too much when I heard him shriek in the night. They were sleeping upstairs in an attic accessed by a ladder. I made it in three steps and was halfway up when all hell broke loose. I was thrown to the ground and the light was so intense for a moment I thought I was in the presence of my Maker. Then he shrieked again and the end of the shriek was swallowed up by the fearful crash of thunder. The place was floodlit for two seconds before another roar that went on and on. Siberia of the Surprises had delivered again. A storm of the tropics on the shores of recently-frozen Baikal.

It was continuous for a few minutes. I picked myself up and climbed the ladder, afraid of what I might find. A large section of the roof was gone and Olga stood in long, ghostly night attire holding Andrei like a baby to her bosom. All his previous ardour had converted to terror and he didn't even know I was there. She shook off my helping hand and descended the ladder before me. It wasn't easy to assist this woman.

'No problem, it has happened before. You go to your bed!'

I did, and they did. They slept in the sitting-room opposite my bedroom. The doors were warped and didn't close. I heard him give a few more yelps and then these faded away to whimpers as the storm rolled away up the lake. An hour later it was a distant, toothless, low growl.

I awakened to the hammering. Olga's parents didn't sleep at her house. They had their own a few blocks away. But her father was here now with three companions and they were already replacing the six sheets of corrugated asbestos that had been ripped away.

Some splintered sheets stuck out of the potato ridges like the debris from an air disaster. Andrei was fetching hammers and nails and holding the ladder. He never saw me; too busy. A few hours later they were tapping final slight strokes . . . job done.

Olga had pots steaming in the *zemavu* and an extra borrowed stool at the table. Her father took a bottle from the top of the cupboard and swiped it dust-free with a spade hand. It was red, like vermouth, and he emptied it into the five glasses. They swallowed it in a single draught. That was aperitif. Now he poked the bottle of vodka at my still-full glass, indicating that I drink up. I shook my head. He threw out the red stuff and filled the empty glass up with vodka. Next time he pointed with the bottle I shook my head again. Now he was beginning to understand.

'I don't drink,' I said.

'All right, just a glass,' he said.

There is no understanding of 'not drinking'. Later I did meet one, the only non-drinker in all my time in Russia. 'Not drinking' is an unknown concept. People who claim not to drink are just saying they don't get blotto regularly. Not to take a few glasses of vodka after fixing a roof is eccentric, uncivilised, downright insulting. A man who would do such a thing has no idea about proper behaviour. The three companions became restless as his frustration mounted. He was a big man; anger inflated him. His cheeks grew redder as he nodded the bottle neck at my full glass again and again. Olga was moving around too, in disapproval of my oddity. He gave up in frustration. Sitting down with a disgusted sweep of the hand he said to his *stailcish* daughter: 'Psash! Give him a beer, he doesn't drink.' She swallowed my vodka and plonked a cup full of frothing beer in front of me. It sat there untouched and I think he interpreted this as stubbornness. He would never know that there was a man who had learnt he couldn't drink even a beer.

In an hour they drank four bottles of vodka, one of vermouth, and ate plates of bacon, spuds and cabbage. It was like an old Irish wake.

The helpers were 'outside men' and uneasy even in the *zemavu*. Two of them spoke nothing until the third bottle. Then they blamed Yeltsin for everything. One of them changed his mind and said that it was the Americans. Olga's father agreed with that, looking at me. They were in agreement that things were better in the old system but that it would never go back now. One of them eventually said it was the Czar who was responsible. Olga was punishing utensils, banging them down and picking them up to drop them again.

The third man had no teeth and giggled a lot. He disagreed with everything, but without offence. He greeted every statement with a *nyet*. It was a smiling, cute *nyet*, that insinuated he knew something that no one else knew. No one took any notice of him but he kept up his *nyets*. Because I was ostracised and no one was taking any notice of him, we mentally formed a liaison. I was relieved to be accepted, if only by the fringe. He said *nyet* so often and in such a way I began to think maybe he had some fresh angle on the problems.

Stools fell as they rose to leave. The *nyet* man was very bad now. He'd rise and take an unbalanced dive in one direction, before over-correcting and banging into a wall opposite. He took a grip of my arm eventually and, with surprising clarity of speech, said: 'He thinks it is Yeltsin, he thinks it is the Americans, he thinks it's the Czar; who do you think it is?' I said I didn't know. 'I think it is the wind,' he said, and farted.

He had a bike. I couldn't believe no one tried to stop him. I said I would walk him home but he wouldn't have any of it. He'd walk the bike home, that's what needed the care, not him. And it would support him.

As he made his way up the road, man and machine drifted farther and farther apart. It developed into an unbridgeable rift. The front wheel pointed off to starboard and he was too askew to the bike to correct it. They fell in slow motion.

I made an effort to lift him but he was fast asleep, smiling like an angel. He slept it off where he fell as people walked past skirting his human sculpture.

Andrei lent me his bike in gratitude for the alliance against Luda.

'Paddy, you can have my bike today. I help Grandpa in the garden.'

He did help him too. They used a single-furrow plough and ran it between the drills to raise the soil up to the stalks. Andrei pulled, the older man pushed. Andrei told me the raised soil encouraged the growth of the tubers. His grandfather told me nothing. He never spoke to me again. It hurt. I knew a similar situation was bound to arise in other places and I dreaded it.

Olga didn't like me either, she made hard work out of feeding me and lighting the fire for the *banya* in the evening. It was summer holidays and both she and Duracell were on holiday from school. Though her parents were at her house when I first arrived, it turned out that she spent most of her time at their house and resented having to come and look after me. Only for me, she and Andrei could have stayed at her parents' house all day until bedtime but because of me she had to light the fire so I that I could wash and give me something to eat. I would gladly have forgone the ablutions, but I thought this might make an even worse impression. Bad enough being an abstemious foreigner without being a dirty, abstemious foreigner.

I took the bike and started to more or less live life by the ferry. I told her I didn't want to eat until late at night and if she liked I'd prepare it myself. At the ferry there was a group who sat on the telegraph poles there; a woman of fifty, one of twenty and her five-year-old son. There was also a teenage boy and a wiry, seventy-year-old man. They hung out together, an unlikely group with some strange interdependence that bound them together. The fifty-year-old was the cement. She had an old dignity nearly lost behind a face scarred with the ravages of drink.

She was gaunt, but forced refined smiles and words when I was around. She'd tie a twisted red cloth in a band around her hair and tap it, ladylike. Behind the twitching smile and the clouded eyes there was pain.

They drank spirit out of a bottle without a label. She'd conceal it. She pulled her lips demurely over long-stained teeth and made the conversation serious. Wiry-man made jokes about sex and she searched to see how I took them. The young mother said foreigners must have plenty of money if they could travel so far. The older lady laughed off her crude remark, saying it was an experience to meet people from another country and that I should send them photographs when I got home so they could see how we live. She wrote an address in a shaky hand, saying that she had cramps in her fingers.

Sometimes she sold things. Unusual things. Not underpants and brassières, but a barometer, a glass vase, a clock and finally a ring. She carried her goods in a paper carrier bag with a scarf on top. She wouldn't leave her merchandise on display and just drew out one article at a time when a prospective customer came across or waited for the limping boat. She approached the good cars only and with an air of 'we are of a similar class'. She was good at display and tilted the *objets d'art* to catch the best light. The day before I left, a white car with blue light on top pulled up beside us.

Militsia.

Police.

She was mortified by the crude exchange. She drew her breath in and slapped a hand over her shocked mouth as they accused and loaded her into the back. She caught my eye as the door was shutting, smiled weakly and touched the red band to make sure it was not slipping. She was shaking her head: some awful mistake.

Twin sisters of nine years sold fish and tried out words: 'Wot oor nim? Sax o'clack . . . Mawndee, Teesdee.' They offered me a seat among their buckets and worked up to tweaking the hairs on my arm. When a new girl joined them they wanted to show how close we were, and linked me. Each day they waited for the last ferry boat before picking reluctant steps home, turning and waving many times.

A few young boys fished. Line knotted on to light branches they cast into the oily backwater where the boats moored, hoping to catch fish dazed by effluent. Their foreman had a nautical peaked cap and distributed chores: 'Tie it on here. No, stupid! Not there! Here. Hold the bucket, not tilted! Straight! No! Not you, I cast.' Then when hope seemed dim: 'Hold this rod, I have to . . .' He was adventurous in the selection of important tasks that only a man with a peaked nautical cap could handle. At the end of the day they might have two semi-submerged and dying fish at the bottom of a plastic bucket of gravelly water.

Olga got sicker of me. She'd slap the plate on the table and go back to her garden. I felt bad about it and tried patronising. 'Olga, could you help me, please? What is the word for when you are leaving a place and you don't want to go?' I asked. She worked on for a while then *stailcish*-ly stabbed *ad-na-kee*, lonesome, into my child's copybook.

I didn't need to use it. Not yet and not here.

I had decided I would cross on the next ferry to Olkhon Island. It was six hours away and close to the other side of the lake, the northern side. Jan had told me it had a history and a culture. I asked around the ferry people and they all said Olkhon was beautiful and wonderful and mysterious and mystical. They spoke about it the way people had spoken to me about Baikal. I hadn't found its magic here except in that small part where Jan walked and in the part where I swam with Andrei but that was overshadowed by the events of that day.

I'd go to Olkhon.

I knew Jan would already be gone when I got there (it had been two weeks since he left) but I wanted to see it anyway. A woman at the ferry told me I'd have no trouble finding someone to keep me. She said the people there were so kind and generous. She said there was a hut near where the ferry pulled in and I should ask there but she insinuated that really it would hardly be necessary, that they would all be out with banners fighting for the privilege of having me.

I was glad when the Monday came around when the ferry would go. I think Olga was even more so because she revved up the car the night before (I didn't know until then that she had one) in case it wouldn't start in the morning. I told her I could walk but she squeezed her mouth and shook her head (she was afraid I'd miss it and she'd be stuck with me for another week). The morning she took me to the ferry was foggy. No dark blue sky; no sky at all. Just banks of impenetrable fog. The boat is a hydrofoil. It lists, but otherwise looks good. It is incongruous with its surroundings. Probably a product of the same dream that built the *gastenetsa* where Jan stayed. It pulls in about four hundred yards from the ordinary ferry. The port is a bed of stamped-in coal dust. Rusty cranes are like petrified pterodactyls. The few men working are so like the surroundings that they blend in and are almost invisible. The crew, shouting about ropes, are smarter and wear colours. They pull rank on the dullards ashore. Without deigning to look at them they bark instructions about casting off.

The departure was delayed by a couple of hours because of the heavy fog. It hadn't cleared at all when we departed.

The bow rose up with a mighty heave and we splashed over the choppy surface at a frightening speed. It was not possible to see more than ten yards. We were travelling at a great rate of knots.

Chapter Seven

For weeks the weather had been almost perfect. All across Siberia there had been clear, deep blue skies and warm days. But now this was awful. I was terrified. The hydro must have been doing about forty miles an hour but I couldn't see more than twenty yards. What I could see was dark and glistening dangerously and hungrily. This lake was a mile deep. We were just waiting for an accident. The driving man upstairs can't have been able to see any more than me but he kept his foot on the gas and I prayed to God saying I wasn't really serious when I said the things about His religion not being the greatest thing, I had changed my mind dramatically and I would never sin again.

For hours it streaked through dense haze blindly skimming the surface like a ghost, and I thought it soon would be if it didn't slow down. I tried to talk to the vessel and bypass Him and the driver but it just roared back and then slap-slapped as it hit back on the lake's surface after being airborne for a couple of seconds from excessive speed.

After four hours the hydrofoil started to whine lower and settle down and finally stopped and sat among the loitering fog. I thought it would be an awful place to be abandoned and that maybe my request had been granted and I shouldn't have stopped it at all. Then I saw a rowing boat approach in slow motion, say something in a fog horn voice, receive a package like a mail bag and silently slide away again. There is supposed to be no occupied island on Baikal except Olkhon, the one I was going to. I never found out what was delivered, or to whom. When I asked for an opinion on Olkhon they just said, 'Interesting!' and looked at each other: 'Foreigner.' The hydro pulled itself and us out of the water again and slapped off the surface for another two hours before lowering its voice to a mere moan, sliding past a massive cliff and settling down on sand.

I made a vow never to travel by hydrofoil again, even if it meant staying on the island forever.

A kind of chute opened out for me to walk on to the spooky, sandy cove. I was the only one getting off here. The place was deserted except for a bundle, in black, perched, crouching on a little rock.

Then there was The Big Rock.

I wasn't prepared for it even though I had been told about it. But the Shaman Rock nearly demands a prostration. It rises so sharply out of the water you get vertigo looking up at it. It towers powerfully above and breathes heavily down on you. A monster. An eerie grey, a limestoney grey, and even the fog didn't hug it but kept its distance. I don't think the rain fell on it either. Inclination is to walk slowly, it intimidates, dominates. It must be 150 feet high and its base is less than its height, which gives it greater power. It has a dark eye like Cyclops and it follows you. Manmade structures, the Eiffel Tower, the Empire State, the Sydney Opera House inspire wonder but they haven't the power of a natural phenomenon.

There will be no other like the Shaman Rock. It is hard even for the most sceptical not to see it as the work of a Creator. A trademark of an Almighty.

A break in the fog showed the hut I was looking for less awesome, more approachable. I kept it in my sight as I climbed the muddy bank; afraid it would escape again into the fog. Every broken plank and withered board and every flake of dark green paint left on it was so beautiful against its ominous surrounds. I came at it sideways and meekly rounded it to confront, ever so respectfully, whoever manned it.

There was no one, just a yelping, limping dog, tied and circling. I had fallen on the climb and muddied myself. The mud was on my hands and I rubbed my face. No house was visible. Along a deeply-rutted, muddy path brown water flowed in rivulets. A few minutes later I was pleased to see the first potato patch. Then houses: small, wooden, individual log huts with *packla* poking out between them. But there were no people. I walked in the middle of the mud road hoping to be seen, while keeping a distance from the complaining dogs. There were lace curtains in every window and tins of geraniums. But no faces. I went to the very end and panicked. I was abandoned on an island in a sea whose only opening was guarded by a Cyclops rock that watched.

Baikal is a fresh water lake but so big it is hard to think of as such. It holds one fifth of all the fresh water of the world. More than the combined Great Lakes of Superior, Michigan, Huron, Erie and Ontario. The Amazon,

Ganges, Mississippi, Nile and Congo together would take a year to fill it. There is only one river flowing out of it: the Angara. The Angara would take 400 years to empty it. It is one of Russia's greatest natural treasures. Russians speak of it as a person – Baikal to them is almost a god. It is 400 miles long and 50 miles wide and has sturgeon. They always tell you this first: 'Baikal has sturgeon.' If you don't look impressed they will add: 'Caviar . . . *vee znaette*: you know.' Then they will tell you about the salmon and the fifty other species of fish that occupy the lake. They will always rank them. Sturgeon first . . . caviar, *vee znaette*, then salmon, omul . . . oh such omul . . . and down the fishy hierarchy to the common pike and perch.

The dream their boast inspired was quickly quenched by rain, dogs, mud and my seemingly solitary occupation. Alone on an island on the largest lake in the world, only 60 miles from Mongolia, but 3,000 from Moscow. Even remote Irkutsk had a ring of home to it now. That was only six hours away by ferry and from there to Moscow a mere four days on the train. The boat calls once a week. I retreated, picking up speed. I knew it had to be gone, but hoped something might have happened to it. If I caught it I would never again complain about anything. Everywhere would be beautiful; everywhere except this abandoned, dog-infested non-place.

The shore was more eerie. The Shaman Rock loomed out of its mammoth cauldron an animated, up-close, ghostly Gibraltar. People came from as far as Tokyo to worship because of its sacredness and now I had it to myself. Well, myself and the lump on the rock still there and still getting wet. Though less animated than Shaman he was more my scale so I approached him cautiously.

'Excuse me, can you help me? I am a foreigner. I want somewhere to stay.'

He sprang to life, a lanky, athletic, six-foot, ginger-haired Russian man. Stepping out, he took the muddy bank with the expertise of a native.

'Ah . . . where are you taking me?'

'You want somewhere to stay, I've got rooms to let.'

'Why didn't you tell me that when I got off the boat?'

'You never asked.'

On the metro in Moscow Maxim had said, 'You must be thinking all the time.'

Nikita was his name and he had a compound of a typical Siberian house and three other huts. One of them was two-storey – the only two-storey building on the island – and the upper floor was mine. It was accessed by an outside ladder. It had a slanting roof, a built-in bed and a low, shallow window all around. The floor was painted blue. Below it, the village spread out like a film set.

He was a sensitive man, a poet. He had been waiting for inspiration not for the boat. He felt my distress and lingered in the room, settling me in. He slowly got me interested in where I was. He smiled gently as he pointed out the *gastronom*, the school, the defunct TV mast and the industrial-looking bakery. A bare bulb hung low, electrical wire wormed around the doorframe and down the ladder but, he told me, there was no electricity. 'Not for two years now, not since the storm.' The cable hadn't been knocked by falling trees – perhaps that could be fixed – no, it had snapped under the lake. Damage caused by such accidents is permanent in Siberia; it is no one's job to correct it, not since the collapse of the Soviet Union. He told me the end of Communism had affected them more than most because of their isolation. The fog wouldn't last, he said, it was rare and never lasted more than a day, usually not even that. The rain also was unusual at this time of year, in fact it seldom rained at all in Olkhon, its precipitation was in winter snow. And almost magically as he spoke it must have responded because when we came back down the ladder the fog was gone and the rain had stopped.

His mother, totally theatrical, was jigging his infant son on her hip. She sported a wide-brimmed straw hat with a flower, lipstick oozed into cracks in her chin and she displayed an inch of cleavage. Natasha, his wife, looked like she was going to rescue her son from her mother-in-law, but when she heard I was foreign she stopped and smiled. She had very long, silky hair and yellow skin. She was from Moscow, had met Nikita at university there, divorced the drunk husband she then had, married Nikita, who didn't drink, and came to Siberia with him. Nikita was the only Russian I ever met who didn't drink at all. He and Natasha were going to make a business here on the shores of Baikal. It was beautiful and many people came from Irkutsk and even farther. They were setting up a business here to accommodate the increasing number of people who were coming to the island. They had a few huts built. One of the huts was long and had a narrow table running down the middle where they fed guests. It was flanked by crude stools which had Dutch wool blankets nailed to them for comfort. The doors had such blankets nailed to them also. The single home-made table was covered with a light plastic cover, from China. 'Everything from China,' Tolya had said. Because of the rain the stools were now wet, but Nikita said they would soon dry out. Rain was unusual at this time of year. The toilet was a hole in the ground covered with a wooden cage with a strategic circular hole and the lot was covered in blue polythene for privacy. The entrance was a corner flap.

They are building another hut and he shows it to me. The builders, a young man and an older, mannish-looking woman, are finished with the outside and are working on the fire. It is in the centre, made of bricks and covered with clay-like plaster which she is smoothing with unusual hands; lumpy yet fluid. The top of each finger and thumb is bulbous, but as she runs it over, smoothing the wet plaster, the joints unlock and her hand surfs as if she is conducting an orchestra. Nikita asks her to explain to me and she does. I don't understand all her words, she is indistinct and a little drunk, but I do understand her conducting. Skimming over the wavy surface of all the nooks and crannies she has created, I can see where the socks will dry in the winter, where the salt will stay running and where a gaudy ornament will lighten the short winter days. Though the new hut is really intended mostly for summer visitors, Siberians are always subconsciously catering to Father Winter. Its severity haunts and enthrals them. In the summer they are like children on a break: they enjoy themselves, they're full of frolic but you know they are waiting for the bell's toll to call them back to reality. An end to frolic. Now, mid-summer, the temperature is 20°C but this mannish-looking woman's hand is forming the surfaces she has sculpted for a winter where outside temperatures will dip to -30°C. Her front tooth is missing, she smells of spirit. Vyacheslav, her helper, is curious: where do I come from? Where is that? What do they speak? Why do I have to come here?

The village, Kuzhir, is in a dip, like the ring of a saucer in which the cup sits. Or is it? A peculiar thing about this island is that everywhere you are the surrounds seem to rise up around you. I found the same thing down by the Mongolian border, the surrounding countryside seems above you on every side. When you attempt to climb to the height it rises again, extending, unconquerably, forever outwards. The result is that one is always surrounded by a clean-line horizon. The sky meets the grass in a distinct, sharp, very definable line. And this line is constantly traversed by either man or beast in the most interesting way. A very mysterious way. You feel like someone is on the look-out for the return of the Marauding Horde. And people walking the line are always in the wind. Even on the calmest of days they look like they are battling a strong breeze, hair blowing, head back, clothes flapping.

I dipped down to the centre of the saucer, where there were lots of muddy puddles from the rain. The *gastronom* is in the middle, one of two non-wood buildings in the village. The other is the *datesky sad* (kindergarten). *Gastronoms* are the same all over Russia; they differ only in size and number of servers. All serving women wear white coats, most wear ankle socks and many wear headscarves. This one was very big for a small village. Lots of the shelves were empty.

There was a line-out of vodka and raisins and tinned mandarin oranges from Israel. Bread was plentiful and appetising; crusty, big loaves of many shapes. There was chocolate, too, and Nescafé and dried apricots in polythene bags. That was the food section. It was half partitioned-off from the rest of the long counter by a kitchen table and four chairs from Finland, with a price tag of 600 dollars, which is what a teacher earns in a year. In the glass display that doubles as a counter, electrical goods were on show. Demand had obviously not been high since the cable broke. Though there were a few generators in the village – one in the bread 'factory', one in the *datesky sad* and one in the house of an Alexander – their operation was limited by lack of fuel.

Then there was the clothes department: chrome rails on wheels parallel to the counter. There was just one sample of each item, if the size wasn't right you went on to the next item. Some were of reasonable quality, most were not. The better pieces were from Lebanon and Pakistan, the poorer ones, native Russian. Trying on any Russian raiment, pieces just drop off or seams give. Labels are indistinct and badly sewn in. Buttons are missing or not lined up with the buttonholes. For a country with an unequalled tradition in creative art, it is no less than astonishing that they can produce such shoddy material. Wherever one sees Russians working they are diligent and interested in what they are at, even street sweepers – especially street sweepers – put their back into their labour, yet their manufactured produce is very poor. The fault is further down the line, at the level of the raw material, whose poor quality is attributable to . . . the story goes on.

Old traditions take a long time to fade out. The weakness of the Communist system was that no one owned anything so no one cared if something worked or not, or if the end product was good or not. Farmers shipped potatoes heavy with mud because they were paid by weight. There was no regard for, or pride in, the quality of the goods produced.

This persists.

In Communist times no one was fired. There was no emphasis on doing things better or faster or cheaper. During the last twenty years of the Soviet system only oil kept it going. In 1973 as a result of the Middle East crisis oil rose from three to eleven dollars a barrel. This resulted in Russia having enough foreign currency to buy imports to feed its people and that is what she was doing. By 1985 Russia was totally dependent on imported food to feed the comrades. When Gorbachev came to power the resource of foreign currency from oil had run out. Everything was creaking and needed replacing and the money to do it was no longer there. People who lived for seventy years with the state providing everything do not quickly learn that in a free market if your produce is not as good as the competition you do not survive. Russians also find it hard to learn to serve the customer. In the old system your job gave you status: the right to abuse those under you or those you served. This is why Russians have such a bad reputation for service in retail outlets. In the old system they didn't care; it made no difference if you were efficient or not. No one was fired. One of McDonald's' new recruits to serve in their first outlet in Moscow couldn't believe it when he was told he had to smile at his customers. 'Why?' he said. 'They'll think we're idiots.'

Smiling was no problem for the women in my *gastronom*. I didn't know the word for a candle so I drew one. They rolled around laughing; they embraced each other in tears, an unusual display of mirth for *prodavetsi*: shop assistants. They told me that the word was *tsvetchi* and that *nyet*, they had none. It is light until nearly eleven at night. I bedded down in my loft as the stars came out in a sky that, though dark, was still very blue. And I thought of my explanation of night as a child. The angels pulled across the curtains; stars are the holes where the sun still shines through.

Next morning I met fifteen-year-old Arteom and his assistants. They were making a machine. It was mostly from the remains of a kid's scooter. The type with a running board that you stand on with one foot while gaining momentum by pushing on the ground with the other. They had extended the footboard. It was now eighteen inches wide and was to accommodate cargo. They were going into the haulage business. They would start with carriage of small items and build. Arteom told me all this in English. He was a good and magnanimous foreman; he kept his eye on the workers as he conducted the conversation with me. They respected him but were not afraid. Though they couldn't understand a word they kept the volume of working noise down, they wanted to hear their Arteom even if they didn't understand him. His spoken English was very good. He had come to the village only two years ago, his father was a government employee working as a driver, something to do with the harbour. There were two things on the island which I should see: one was a spring well and the other was a gulag.

My heart leapt.

It was reading about an escape from such a place that had set me on the Siberian trail. He quickly spotted my interest in the gulag and concentrated on it, though from his tone of voice I judged the spring well to be closer to his own heart. He would take me to both; but not today, there was work to be done.

I learnt the island's geography. Five hundred citizens in the village of Kuzhir, a total of 1,500 on the whole island. A third of the population of Olkhon is Buryat, but they lived mostly outside the village. The whole island is 280 square miles and is really the top of a mountain poking out of the lake. It doesn't look like this at all; it is rolling and rounded, not at all like a mountaintop, and it is dry. The land is arid and its grass is more like lichen.

I wandered alone a few miles in the three inland directions and returned to the shore in the lovely evening. The rim of horizon had many silhouettes and the beach had barefoot strollers and drinkers. I saw Vyacheslav there, in loose underpants, with bottle and friends. The same Vyacheslav who was building the new hut for Nikita. He was not drunk. I approached him and made his friend Ivan very shy. Ivan was fully clothed and it was easy to see that he had trouble with the sun. He had ginger-blond hair and his lips were cracked and oozing. His skin was peeling and his balding forehead very red. He ran his finger around different parts of his face as he said that he fished. Every morning . . . most mornings, he goes out. Vyacheslav helps him and another couple of friends too, but the fishing is bad now . . . everything bad now . . . But he didn't *gizn trudney* (dwell on the bad times) and nervously returned to stretching his neck, pretending stiffness to cover his unease in talking to a foreigner.

Everyone else on the beach was busy not noticing the stranger. And after much blarney in broken Russian: yes, I could go out with them, in the morning – when?

'Oh! Very early, six o'clock.'

It was cold and the sky that strange deep blue again, the leftovers of the night. They were only a half-hour late and were very silent, Vyacheslav, Ivan and Gregory. Gregory went to university in Irkutsk but didn't like it. He liked the island and the people and, most of all, the lake. A lake that is so large it could easily become one's world. Like flat-earth theorists it is easy to imagine that there is nothing beyond. But there is. The region around Baikal is taiga. It is treated as a great national park. It is inhabited by brown bear, elk, moose, deer and 1.2 million people. Given the dimensions of the lake, this 'beyond' seemed to be a great crescent-shaped halo that fades away into the vastness of Siberia.

While Vyacheslav and Ivan raised the lobster pots Gregory explained why the water is so clear. Baikal epishura are miniature crayfish measuring one and a half centimetres in length. They live on bacteria and waterweed and the other things that make water cloudy. The concentration of these miniature vacuum cleaners is estimated at three million per square metre. I thought that such a concentration would, in itself, obscure the waters but Gregory told me that they move in shoals, cleaning as they go. They have a distant relation, the gammarid shrimp, which is twenty times their size and clears up everything else that pollutes the water: dead fish, insects and animals – but they can't handle industrial pollution.

Gregory was about thirty years old and didn't himself remember when the omul were very big, but he had heard. The dam on the river above Irkutsk upset the ecological balance in the lake. The smaller fish, that were food for the omul, were somehow wiped out. As a result the omul became smaller. The human interference also altered their breeding habits. Fishing was prohibited in the early seventies and things did improve but it's nothing like it used to be.

I told him about the omul that the blonde girl on the train fed to me the first day I saw Baikal. I told him I had never liked fish before but that was special. He was proud and smiled – I thought he blushed in pride but it is hard to tell with Buryats. Gregory was about three-quarters Buryat; Ivan and Vyacheslav were Russian.

We were to meet at the *banya* in Nikita's that evening. He had a big *banya* because of the guests. They would bring some of their cooked catch. With a flick to the throat and a twitching smile they indicated that we would get very drunk together. This flicked finger to the side of the Adam's apple is the symbol for drink, drunkenness and drunkard.

I talked to Natasha and she told me to talk to Nikita . . . he didn't drink . . . no, not at all. Yes, it was one of the reasons that she had left her first husband and married him. She didn't know how but he was able to get around it; ask him. In the event, his solution was so simple it was amusing.

I wanted to write and needed to recharge my laptop. The bakery seemed the best bet. I had heard its generator going rat-a-tat-tat much of the day.

The bread factory was protected by a growling block of a Russian woman with her arms folded, sitting on a kitchen chair in front of the large, iron, sliding gate topped with barbed wire.

'*Nyet!*'

I just want to see if I could plug in my laptop. It wouldn't cost anything but I would reward them.

'*Nyet.*'

Handsomely.

'Roubles no good.'

Dollars.

There was a long pause. If I brought her a can of foreign beer from the *gastronom* she'd think about it; beer not vodka . . . it makes people crazy . . . like her husband, he was crazy . . . and idle . . . bastard! Like I said, most people did their job with admirable dedication.

After a trial suck from the long, gold can of Carlsberg she indicated, with a backward jerk of the head, that I should go in. The gesture was difficult because she had no neck. After getting past the further obstacle of a mangy, howling mongrel I met two more *nyet* women. They were kneading dough in great quantities. Not by hand but in enormous, metallic, rotating mixing bowls. They poked their hands over the side as they refused, drawing out great dollops for quality trials. Then a surly man came in and, hearing their refusals, said that *da*, I could plug in the laptop for no charge. '*Da*,' every day, no problem. He was just saying it to go against them and to show who was in charge.

They drew out even greater dollops in protest as he showed me where I could plug in. There was just the one socket. It was in the hallway where he lay down on a couch that sprouted springs through its old grey blanket. On the wall above hung a picture of an ornate Orthodox saint hanging sideways with a plastic flower stuck through its hanging ring.

I thought Nikita's *banya* was wonderful, but it disappointed the three men. It was a disgrace to let a guest into such a *banya*, they said. Gregory scooped out a tin of water and threw it on the rusty cast iron fire casing. I was very impressed with the hiss and bubble of steam but they shook their heads in unison, tut-tutted more and agreed that Nikita must be told. The reputation of the whole island was at stake. Gregory modestly wrapped a towel around himself and went in search. We sat on the high wooden bench waiting. They had brought three feniks and they dipped them into the steaming water, then, ceremoniously, laid them out. I heard the exchange outside. Nikita was contrite, but his mother was saying that if a cold *banya* gave the guest a bad impression it was no help to let him hear people arguing about it. Logs were shot into the firebox from the outside and something opened that made the flame roar and glow red in the cracks of the cylindrical chimney. Gregory came back, accomplished.

We sat in silence until the four of us were greasy-wet and glowing. I wanted to go out . . . thought I was in danger of bursting something with the heat. Nobody gave in. I stood up for a half-minute but daren't exit . . . could be very bad manners. Fearing I might faint, I went to regain my seat but yelped in pain as the roaring-hot wooden seat burnt my backside. It had reached flash point while I stood. Ivan asked if I wanted to go out and I said yes. The others, pretending mannerly reluctance, stepped down and we went out together.

It was the moment I had been dreading.

After getting as hot as one can possibly bear you go outside to the ante-room which, though still very hot, is cooler. Here we sat around a table made from a tree trunk. Gregory got the first bottle from his plastic bag of clothes. He had four shot glasses and he spread them around like a cowboy. They were filled to the brim and quickly polished off. My heart thumped. Second round. I shook my head. My full glass stood there facing me accusingly. I shook my head.

'*Shto*? What?' Gregory asked.

I shook my head again with pain and resignation: '*Izhoga*!' I whispered loudly.

'Agghhh *izhoga*!' Gregory said.

'*Izhoga* . . . you have *izhoga*?' Ivan wept.

'Pity the man with *izhoga*, no doubt life is hard!' Vyacheslav wailed.

They agreed I should be very careful, a man with *izhoga* can't drink and a life without drinking is hardly a life at all. *Izhoga*, heartburn, is the curse of the drinking class.

I said a silent prayer to St Nikita of The Simple Solution.

After the first bottle we returned to the furnace and they asked a lot of questions. How much . . .? Phwee . . . that was a lot of money to earn. Enough money to buy all the small omul that they would catch in a month in Baikal. Life was a disgrace now in Siberia. Time was when a guest would be fed well and kept in a good warm bed without any charge. The host wouldn't have to be told to stoke his *banya*. No, no, they agreed, sweat pumping, it was a disgrace that a host had to be told his *banya* was cold. A foreign visitor would bestow great privilege on a village by visiting it. A foreign visitor who spoke Russian deserved the best they could provide.

Then I got my first beating. All three worked on me together, with a gentle touch. They stood me in the middle of the floor and spun the feniks around in their hands, only barely touching my skin with the leaves. They themselves took turns laying out on the wooden bench while a friend beat them hard. I only got the wimp's version. I felt a little discriminated against, but these men did not discriminate. One of the fruits of alcoholic life is that it reduces all to a common denominator.

Another bottle of vodka. We ate the fish, wrapped our loins in towels and sat on logs outside in the yard, glowing.

The Russian language is even more complex than the people but, like them, it also has beautiful soft touches of an understanding that transcends the tangible. Feminine words end in 'a' or 'ya'. Affectionate forms of objects and people take on this ending also. The affectionate form of names, even men's, likewise. So Vladimir becomes Voloda, Gregory becomes Grisha, Nikolay becomes Kolya, Vyacheslav becomes Slav, Ivan, Vanya and the cold Dimitri thaws to a rakish Dima. It is difficult to say them without smiling.

The third trip to the furnace was awry. Ivan fell and Gregory helped him up, calling him 'poor Vanya'. Then Gregory got a fenik leaf in his eye and Slav tried to help him out calling him 'Grisha'. He couldn't manage the delicate operation and asked me, 'Padsha', to come to his assistance. We then slobbered buckets of water over each other, spluttering and rubbing.

Towelled off, we dressed. Grisha had difficulty with his shoes. They were on the wrong feet: Vanya pointed it out, reeling around laughing; his cracked lip reopened and bled anew.

Outside, in the moonlight, they told me what a privilege it was to have a good drink with a foreigner. Then they stumbled down to the village, a tangle of arms and legs, stopping many times to unwind their grip on each other as they waved and wished *leokem parom*: light steam. It is the greeting Russians exchange on leaving a *banya*. Sometimes they say the steam can sit heavy on one and make you feel poorly, maybe it was the bountiful good wishes of my friends, but the steam sat very light on me.

It was eleven o'clock and still not fully dark, though the moon was already bright. I was making my way to the shore and the Shaman Rock when Theatrical Mother saw me. She trilled and warbled and tapped her head. She called Nikita and Natasha, to witness my foolishness. Nikita provided the beanie, assuming that it was because I didn't have one that I was going bareheaded. Even a foreigner would know the dangers of the night air on a wet head after the *banya*.

I took the long way round and approached the rock from the crest of the hill. Here there was an edge where one knew for sure that you were on the highest point. I was the silhouette walking the crest, the way Genghis Khan and his followers did. Only time was different . . . and what is time but an arbitrary starting point from which to count? Some claim that Genghis Khan was born on this island, but it is unlikely.

The rock loomed out of the water and it was easy to see why it was the focus of worship for the followers of the Shaman faith. Nikita had told me that a shaman was visiting within the next week. Word had been passed on from village to village, just as it must have thousands of years ago.

I was alone on the shore. The rock, lapping water, the moon and me. And I thought, where does the world end? Since a teenager in a wet tent in the west of Ireland I had wanted to go to Siberia . . . I had imagined cold, snow and tigers . . . I was alone on a balmy, moonlight night in a T-shirt but with my head covered. Then a dog galloped along the crest of the hill. Sorry, no tigers.

Arteom said they had waited for me. They couldn't understand why I hadn't come fishing that morning. They had speculated that it might have been the *izhoga*. Since I hadn't made the fishing, he said, maybe we could go to the spring well. I said that I would prefer the gulag. He breathed deep, trying to tolerate the strange taste of foreigners, and deferred. Theatrical Mother gave me a potato cake, smoked omul and advice: keep your head covered from the sun and drink plenty of water. No need to carry it, the stream is good.

Arteom was going to be president. Russia lacked real leadership. Yeltsin drank too much and Nemtsov was only interested in power.

Arteom was only fifteen so he'd have to wait some time.

I thought what a good president he would make. He ran a tight ship. Before we left he had assigned chores for the day to his subjects. He didn't order them, just suggested and advised. He ran an ecology watch. The beach had to be cleaned, old women had to be looked after, wood had to be cut and piled, because, though mid-summer, the fires for the *banyas* had to be lit. He insisted on English all the way.

'You have much opportune for the Rooskey language, for me not so many English, it is more good that we speak it. No problem?'

None at all, Arteom!

We walked a dirt road and up a hill and sat looking down on the village. He took up a fist of clay and threw bits of it at things. He said he wanted to leave Kuzhir and see the world. What was it like? That look was in his eye; that look I had seen a hundred times before: longing. Not a longing to be in any other specific place just a longing not to be where they are now. Whenever it's asked, this question, wherever I am is always the place that the questioner doesn't want to be. I am often tempted to answer, 'It is like being here,' but that would be too cruel. They like to think, these questioners, that a change of location will transform their lives, that it will change a monochrome monotonous 'here' to a magical kaleidoscopic 'there', that when you step off a boat, plane or train it is straight into Fantasia.

Not so. New location – same person.

To Arteom I said: 'It's good if you have an open mind and don't expect too much.' And quick on its heels I added: 'Home is a great place to be.'

'Why don't you stay at home?'

'I do, I stay at home a lot . . . but then like you I want to go. OK, *we* better go or we won't be back in time.'

'In time for what?'

'Look! Down there – is that where we are going?'

My stomach was uneasy and I felt some guilt. Once again I had failed to strike a balance; had failed to show that if you don't like where you are, chances are you won't like where you are going.

Chastising myself I came on the gulag unprepared.

I tripped on a black plank and only barely missed treading on a rusty nail. Recently, people had built a fire and burned some of the wood and left picnic debris but there was some galvanised iron that must have been there since its labour days. Then a section of ground where nothing grew. At the other end two rusty hinges, some mortar and strands of rusty wire. Not barbed wire, just rusty wire, and evidence of a passageway. And at the very bottom, at the lowest point of the sloping site, stood just one small low section of wooden partition. This is the only monument that stands to whatever thousands perished here.

Lenin's claimed dream was an empire of equality. The greatest empire ever known where all men are rewarded equally. I'd seen the biggest head in the world – the newly painted wrought iron effigy, which delighted the passengers of train 44A – and the gigantic statues all over Russia. Now six inches of charred wood to these, his equal comrades.

I walked what would have been the perimeter and came back to where I'd started. The black wooden plank, other bits of wood with nails and holes where knots had been, some old wire, two rusty hinges, earth and mortar mixed, a few bricks and the rusty door of an old range. That's all. And the earth where nothing grew.

Arteom made a seat of a log and pulled up another for me. A log that had been chopped with an axe.

'OK let's eat!'

'Not yet, Arteom.'

I looked and searched for shoe or cap or any evidence and gently stirred the earth beneath my feet. It must have been a hundred metres square. That would have been the practice yard and there the watchtower and this hole? What might that have been?

I imagined my escapee, running down that hill with an axe-head and a stolen lump of black bread in pursuit of freedom. Then I wondered why I had come here. Why I had spent years trying to get to a place that he had risked everything to get away from. Snobby Larissa in Moscow thought me crazy for wanting to go to a place that 'every civilised person was trying to get out of'. She hadn't taken into account that for me this was freedom.

Like 'fighting for peace', putting men where they don't want to be in the name of freedom is a strange contradiction. Communism's claimed goal was freedom. Freedom from the tyranny of the czars, from discrimination and class distinction, from inequality. In its supposed pursuit they imprisoned those who did not agree with what they were doing. But they couldn't capture their minds; they couldn't rob them of their desire to be somewhere else, somewhere of their own choosing. And, inevitably, some of them chose to risk all to exercise their free will. Their motivation to get out of here was the same as mine to get here: freedom.

'Paddy, if you don't eat I'll have it all gone.'

'Not hungry, Arteom.'

He wondered why I was wondering and asked me if Ireland had a national song and I said it had. He demanded that I sing it and I did so with gusto. I can't sing. I asked him if he would sing the Russian anthem and he said he didn't know if it had one but that the favourite song of all Siberia was about a convict escaping from Olkhon who climbed into a salty fish barrel, made a sail of his tattered shirt and tried to cross Baikal. He sang:

The sacred Baikal, the glorious sea
The glorious craft a fish barrel with sails
The Barguizin winds be gentle on me
Deliver me safely from anguish of jail.

He said that his father told him that in the old days people were always trying to escape but seldom succeeded, and that in spring with the thaw the corpses showed through and they were called the snowdrops after the first spring flowers. His father had told him that his grandfather had been in a gulag and had stayed on in Siberia. Arteom was quarter Buryat; the other three-quarters would have come in boxcars. He had plans to leave in greater style. To get away from here, to be like a foreigner, free to see the world.

What a paradox. I had spent years trying to get here because of a man who had escaped, to talk to a boy with a yen for leaving.

In Ust Barguizin I had been told there was no water in Olkhon – none. Very dry. Arteom and I came to a gushing stream and drank from it. We talked about the beauty and importance of clear water. Babbling, rushing, gushing water always rushing to be elsewhere. On our last lap down into the village Kuzhir looked very inviting to me. I saw my elevated loft and longed for what it had to offer me. Arteom sighed, here again, and said it had been a wonderful day, that he enjoyed it because it was great to talk to people from far away, free places.

I went to the *gastronom* each day asking for *tsvechi* and every day their mirth grew. Eventually Nikita told me they hadn't had candles for a year now and that that was the source of their amusement. Nobody expected candles. Things that were really needed seldom turned up. If I wanted ball-bearings or puncture repair kits there wouldn't be a problem, but candles? *Nyet*.

Nikita had a candle, half a candle, and I could have it, 'But be careful!' He tucked it into my shirt pocket and tapped it, indicating I should keep it there and not leave it lying around. Laptop, camera and anything else no problem, nobody will take them, but the candle: well, you have to be careful! I used it for just a few minutes each night while I set things up for writing. I could have managed without but I wanted him to see I appreciated his generosity. It was the only remaining candle on the island.

Grisha visited me some evenings. He climbed the ladder and sat on my blue floor and told me he liked to hear about other countries but he could never live anywhere other than in Kuzhir. He would die for his friends and they for him, foreigners didn't understand this. No! They didn't really understand because on the surface Russians were rough. It is a façade, the roughness; it is also part of their sense of humour. There are as many rough Russians as there are rough Irish, English or Americans. There are people who are real bears, but there are even more who like to act as bears to conceal a very soft interior. It is a peculiarly Russian facet of a universal machismo. When he was about to leave I took the candle and put it in my shirt pocket tapping it just like Nikita did. I winked. I wanted him to know how well I understood Russians and the precariousness of existence, especially here on Olkhon. He shook his head in disbelief at my naivety: 'Who'd steal the last candle on the island? Light it and everyone knows who took it.'

You must be thinking all the time.

They were suffering badly the next day we went out. They talked at each other in staccato barks. Slav stumbled a lot and Vanya fumbled and dropped things. Grisha was the best. He placed me out of the way, grabbing me with both his hands and setting me to one side. He was glancing and guessing I may have taken it as a slight, so he asked me what things I wanted to know. I was a little shaken and didn't ask anything for a while so he filled the blank by telling me how the locals feed the elk, moose and deer in special troughs during the winter. He knew he had offended so this was a display of 'soft interior'. Then I asked what I really wanted to know. All around the village there were rusty metal frames, a bit bigger than the body of a car. They sat on runners, like sleighs. He had told me they were for winter fishing, now he explained how they worked.

In winter the lake freezes to a depth of a metre. These metal frames are cleaned up and pushed out on to the lake. They are covered in canvas, or whatever can be found, and a fire is lit inside in a suspended metal box; here the fisherman waits. Because the water is crystal clear, so is the ice. A hole is cut in it and the line dropped in. Because of the clear ice it is possible to see the fish approach the bait: 'In life, you will agree, things are not as they seem. Anticipation is rosier than reality. Well, so it is on Baikal in winter – a man sees a whale approach, take the bait and get hooked. But when you reel it in what have you got? A sprat.' The clear ice is like a magnifying glass.

And the lake tells other lies too. He pointed out the horizon far away and it floated in the air above the lake. He told me that at night he often saw a train, he saw its lights and its windows clearly yet the nearest track was thirty miles away. And the fish were ghostly too. The omul cried when it was hauled aboard, 'like a baby'. The sands whispered. Doug the American had told me this. He had said, 'They are so stupid and superstitious they think it is ghosts but of course it is the expansion of grains of sand forcing air out of pockets in the sandy deposits.' I don't think Doug even believed in Santa. Grisha said the sand whispering was a signal that the lake was safe, when it stopped it was time to be careful; soon the lake would be iced over. The loudest whisper was in late autumn; it was like the omul's cry; the sand's last gasp before it was frozen into hibernation. Then it was time to look out; the dangers of winter had to be faced together. That was what ruled in Siberia: not Moscow, not any law but a common danger in the face of ferocious elements. There were huts all along the shore of Baikal belonging to no one and everyone where one could take refuge. They were always stacked with logs and the necessities of survival and always replaced when used. There was no rule about it but people would not leave them empty. If one is lost in winter and gives in to exhaustion he is, in moments, a statue of ice deep-frozen until the spring when he will reappear with the snowdrops. The lake talks too. When temperatures drop so low that the deep ice doesn't know what else to do with itself, it cracks in its depth and resounds like submarine thunder.

Grisha didn't like the scientists who tried to explain away all the phenomena of the lake. 'They have a cause for everything but understand little,' he said. All the marine life that lived below 150 metres in Baikal was unique to that lake and existed nowhere else in the world. One fish called the golomianka lives at a depth of 1,000 feet because it cannot survive at temperatures of over 45°F.

When winter approaches it comes closer to the surface, always staying just under the level where the water was 45°F. It produces 2,000 prodigy at a time.

Then he said it was the sponges at the bottom of the lake that caused it to be so clear. They soaked up all impurities. 'You see, the lake even knows how to wash itself. Sponges a mile down there clean and wash and bathe its waters and clean it like a mother cleans her baby.'

'Oh! But I thought is was those little tiny things, what do you call them? The ones that go around in shoals sucking up all the impurities, I thought it was those that kept the water so clear. Which is it Grisha? Is it the little things like miniature vacuum cleaners or is it the sponges at the bottom of the lake?'

'I don't know. Ask the scientists, the lake is crawling with them, we're only fishermen.'

We had more *banyas* and more vodka and many suggestions about what a man who is afflicted with *izhoga* should do about it.

Then the shaman came. A fairly tubby man with little to distinguish him at the beginning. He was the first occupant of the hut that was being built when I arrived and there was minor buzz about his arrival, not too much. At about seven in the evening people started to gather in Nikita's compound all around the huts and blue loo, and some sat on the log-pile. They were dressed in Sunday clothes, small girls with frilly dresses, ribbons in their hair and ankle socks; women with chiffon scarves, stretching jersey tops and necklaces; men with shirts tied uncomfortably to the neck. 'We're only fishermen' were completely sober and shaved. The whole village was there and some from outside who stayed near the gate. His table was set up by a pair of youths. Like altar boys they to-ed and fro-ed between his hut and the nailed-together table set up at the top of the yard. Books and bells and ribbons, miniature tambourines, one small drum, no candles.

He came out half Genghis Khan, half St Patrick. His robe was green, shiny, cheap material and tied like an old-fashioned cross-over apron. His hat was like a deacon's with fins, black with white embroidered motif and he had shoes to match with some silver thread too. He spoke for a long time in a far away voice. And he spoke and spoke and I understood nothing. They said it was Russian but of a type used in religious things. He picked up books and spoke and spoke and put them down again. Then another book and the same again and I got lost in the sky and how blue it was. I was tilting myself to get him against this blue sky for a mental picture for later development when he raised his hand with another tome and I saw the double thumb. That changed everything.

A shaman is a medium, a healer, a kind of priest who can communicate with the spirit. The spirit is Nature, which is the balancer of everything. Sickness is an imbalance and in a trance the shaman communicates with the spirit, Nature, and finds out the imbalance.

Nature chooses its shamans.

Before birth, Nature picks out the ones who are to be the mediums between itself and humanity and it marks them with a distinguishing feature such as an extra thumb or a cleft palate or an extra row of teeth. Often those picked by Nature are prone to illness in their teens and only when they decide to yield and become a shaman does their health improve. Sometimes shamans are marked by what generally in the West is considered a 'weakness' or disability, such as epilepsy or additional limbs, but in the Shaman faith, it is their proximity to, rather than their rejection by Nature that makes them that way. That is what they believe; it makes a welcome change from shunning the mentally or physically different. Some extremist groups in Burma are often led by either children or someone physically affected by dwarfism and I wondered if there might be some connection. Both are based on Buddhism. But one way or the other I was fascinated by this man's extra thumb. From a boring droner he was suddenly transformed to my shaman with whom I identified. How fickle humans are. If this shaman had not that extra thumb then I might never have been cured.

After much book-raising and bell-ringing we took to the highest point above the Shaman Rock. It was an informal procession. The altar boys took the table and the books and the girls with frilly dresses strung themselves together with the ribbon and we all followed, gossiping about the nice weather and, 'You like Baikal?'; 'Fishing?' Then at the highest point there was a kind of straggling line of holding hands – not everyone joined in but most did – and the healing started. People announced their complaints and came forward and were put at the end of the line of hand-holders and their free hand was pointed out at the rock, at which the ailment left them and they were better. Grisha went to the front and I wondered what ailment he'd admit to. He whispered it and I was bursting with curiosity when the hand of the double thumb beckoned me hither, whispered '*izhoga*' sympathetically, placed the hand of two thumbs on my forehead and with the other, pointed at the rock and intoned a mantra that vibrated my brain.

He left the next day and I was going the day after that. It was probably just as well.

We had a final *banya* that night and I told them I was certain the *izhoga* had gone but that I wouldn't want to tempt fate by drinking so soon after the miracle. Grisha said he understood and I think he really did, because he said to me later, 'If you can stop drinking for *izhoga*, maybe I could too.'

Maybe you could Grisha, maybe you could.

The hydrofoil was due at four in the afternoon and it would take six hours to get to Irkutsk, across the lake and up the river. By five, Theatrical Mother and Natasha had kissed me and gone, taking the child from each other as they climbed the bank. Ten minutes later Nikita said he'd have to go, not to forget to call on his brother in Irkutsk, that he had sent word that I would be coming.

Vanya took out the second bottle of vodka. I knew he had been keeping it for the last moment but the waiting had got to him. Grisha looked a slight reprimand at him but took a good swig out of the bottle. Slav next. The hydro I'd promised never to set foot upon again was approaching sideways laughing at me, and when I knew it was only minutes until it took me off, I put the bottle to my head and made a great display of moving my Adam's apple up and down.

Izhoga definitely gone. Grisha took the bottle held it to the light to see no drop in level. He took a long suck out of it, shook his head and clapped me on the back.

It was empty when the vessel dropped down on the shore and, with the three of them helping me, I nearly tumbled into the drink.

Chapter Eight

Siberia is very big. Before my investigation I had thought of it as a blotch. Some kind of a cancer. I'd visualised flying over Russia and seeing a surreal grey spot; not snow that sparkles but hoar-frost and fallen trees, a desolate spot, a comparatively small, deformed part of a vast Russia. I didn't believe that a place so demonic as I dreamed of could spread in such honest vastness.

The Ural Mountains sound awesome. I thought they'd be huge. I thought I'd have no trouble finding them. In reality I expected them to loom out of the earth like the Himalayas. I thought that even a prejudiced atlas would have to recognise them with a purple scar capped in snow. Wrong. In the atlas they are hard to detect. In reality had I not been watching out for them and the train's struggle I would have missed them. Yet they mark the European–Asian divide. Almost everything from there east is Siberia. If one placed a cupped hand on the Urals – it would have to be a left hand for the cup to fit their curve – and swept it right taking all in its path into the Sea of Japan, then what you'd have would be a sea full of Siberia. There'd be a few other small ingredients in there, too, like the Russian Far East, but mostly you have a sea full of Siberian soup. If you hadn't taken out the 35 million inhabitants before you did it you'd have a truly ethnic broth of people. There'd be Russians of course, many of them forced over the Urals for non-conformity, others adventurers hoping to reap the vast resources. And there would be the beautiful Buryats and a scattering of their Mongol cousins. You'd also have Chinese Tatars and numerous other unspellables down to the indigenous Evenks. You'd even have Huns.

Some soup.

I had taken years to find it and most Russians don't know where it is. They pretend they do. They raise up their shoulders and draw in their breath as they hiss: 'Ffffwwweee . . . Siberia, *ochen kolodna . . . ochen opasnaya*!' (Siberia, very cold . . . very dangerous.) It is cold in winter and, I suppose, it can be dangerous, but in the summer it is beautiful and welcoming. At least the Baikal area of Siberia is. But Siberia is so big that no one can talk truthfully in general terms about it. Thirty-five million people live in Siberia but even these people can't have an overall view of it because it is enormous and varied. I had only scratched a line along its surface and done a little poking around in the region of Baikal. I had done just enough to appreciate what a Pandora's box of possibilities this shadowy, vast region of Earth encompassed.

Natasha and Nikita were both well-educated and had a deep, genuine interest in Lake Baikal and its surrounds. They weighed me down with facts and figures in the hope that a little knowledge would seep out to the world, outside of Russia, and help make people aware of what a wonderful part of our planet remains unknown. I'm not smart with facts and figures. I remember in sentimental spurts rather than along the continuous time line of the historian.

Grisha was smart and sentimental. He was educated too, but he was ambivalent about propagating knowledge of the area. He told me of fish and spirits and the power of the Shaman Rock. He told me of the importance of Buryat tradition and of having friends. His voice and their stories are compounded with my own reminiscences.

Siberia is so big that a person in Manhattan is closer to Moscow than someone in Vladivostok in eastern Siberia. It is inhabited by thirty different nationalities and three-quarters of all people live in urban areas. The remainder farm, some in the nomadic herding tradition of the ancient people. There are areas of great, colourful traditions such as I had seen close to the border of Mongolia. Most people here have no more knowledge of how people in the far north of Siberia live than I have. Their view of the remote corners is as sinister as Moscow peoples' views of the Baikal area. Remote is a subjective word, for what is it except far from where you are? Two months ago, this area to me was remote and a little frightening. Larissa in Moscow shuddered, clasped her poodle and shook her head in despair of ever seeing me again. Yet here now, skimming over the surface of Baikal, I knew with certainty that the greatest danger in the region to the refined life of her beloved, scratching poodle would be me.

Grisha had told me that all forms of life were sacred to his people, the followers of the Shaman faith. Though

Grisha was a fisherman he told me his profession was against the teaching of the Shamans. Originally they disturbed nothing of nature – its animals or plants. Modern demand forces compromise. Though Grisha was an alcoholic and the physical and mental damage showed, his outlook was intact. He carried himself around in a gentle cloud. I felt good when it enshrouded me. I noticed others too were calmed in his presence, though he himself often shook.

Grisha was just one extreme exponent of the calmness of Siberia. As large as Siberia is this is its single common feature. Its people have a freedom from attachment, they are free from grasping. Not in total of course, but there is an atmosphere of freedom from affectation. They are close to the earth and I think the tradition of Shamanism accounts for this. Western cultures use earth as a springboard from which to gain their goals. It is a structure on which to build and the objective is to use it as a platform to separate themselves from it; to elevate themselves above it. Ground contact is made only to gain momentum to get away from it so it seems that even in walking each step is separate and furtive . . . it is analogical. Siberians step and stay with the earth . . . they make continuous contact with earth, they are part of it, their motion is digital. I believe this comes from a long tradition of Shamanism. All nature is one.

This is easier to see when one is dependent on the raw fruits of the earth. It is hard to see a Cadillac car or a glass tower building as a fruit of the earth. It is easier to see horse and wooden cart or yurt as earth's fruits. Ironically, the Cadillac and glass tower take far more of Earth's resources but the process intervening between raw material and finished product rob them of their roots. And I'd know a Siberian by their look. They are spontaneous in their glance. Everyone is customised for that particular experience. In the West we have a database of looks and grimaces and they are shuffled but are basically the same, like a pack of cards.

The Buryats deified the lake, Grisha said, and he showed me a sentence somewhere, which lingers in my mind: 'God forbid that anyone should utter a coarse word on its shores, let alone quarrel or fight.'

From inside the hydrofoil it is not possible to test the clarity of the water. Through the windows one could only see foam rising from our progress, which was rapid. This hydrofoil was wide and comfortable, a bit like an older Jumbo jet, but, like the first one, its lopsidedness was disturbing. Though a wonderful, sunny, calm day I couldn't help tilting my weight to help it stay upright. Any lack of concentration on my part could lead to its capsize. I was very much part of the crew. I was ably assisted. We had a *dejurnaya*. She was exactly the same as Svet, mellow Svet that is. She sat in an office at the back and beamed a toothy smile from under a halo of yellow hair. She was wearing a whole tube of scarlet lipstick.

She told me Irkutsk was dangerous and that it would be dark when we arrived. She supposed I would be going to Intourist. To Russians of a certain class it inspires visions of luxury refinement and all that a Western person would want in life. The glow left her lipstick when I told her I was going to stay in an apartment in Lermontova. How could I? How would I get there? Bus! She didn't think that foreigners knew how to use Russian buses and at night . . . Oh! I told her I had been in Irkutsk already and knew my way around. She was disappointed; she had swollen in anticipation of frightening me about the dangers of a wild city. When we docked she pointed at the steps that led to street level. It was a Lady Macbeth shaky pointing that, as well as indicating the way, warned of all the dangers that lurked in life.

Russians love to indicate danger; they especially love to warn foreigners of the dangers of tough Russia. It is a form of national pride. This is the real world of struggle for survival where man eats man. Not the molly-coddled, silver-spoon-fed nursery existence of the West.

Nikita's brother was appalled that I was late. The fact that the boat was late had nothing to do with it. He had been waiting for five hours. A lot of business to be done and he had waited for five hours. His cousin came in and said he had been coming and going to the apartment all day looking for him and that this was the first time he had succeeded in getting him. Nikita's brother asked what did he think, did he think that he, Nikita's brother, who was having a foreign guest, could waste his time sitting in the apartment waiting for his cousin? Then they united to tell me that they had very important business to do and that they would have to go out. They came and went all night. I slept on the couch in the living-room. There was a bedroom beyond.

One of them would come back, take the phone, dial a number and walk around talking in whispered riddles and dash out again. The other would come in, shake me, ask where the other one was, make a phone call, whisper: 'Arrived? When? No. No. No. Not today. Omsk. Later.' Then slam down the phone and dash out. So it went on until dawn. I awakened mid-morning and went into the blue cubicle kitchen to find them both, heads down on the table, asleep among dried-out tea bags. The kitchen was so full of them I couldn't make it to the gas cooker so I went back to bed. Nikita's brother awakened me in panic saying it was late and that we must hurry, hurry. We were going to his aunt's *dacha* where I was to spend a further week. I hurried and then sat with my little bag at the ready. I wasn't going to give him one more reason to indicate that I was taking up so much of his precious time. Then I heard gentle snoring from the bedroom. Peeping in, I saw the two of them, head to tail, crowding the tiny room on a narrow bed.

Hours later they awakened and walked in scratching and yawning. Nikita's brother said we would have dinner at the apartment . . . he had some fresh fish and would cook it because he had time. It was mouth-wateringly good and he told me I should learn to relax.

On the way to the *dacha* he told me a little bit about his business. He was importing cars through Vladivostok. It was a tough business, full of danger because of the Mafia. Only he and his cousin were honest and even his cousin had to be watched. I asked him exactly what the Mafia did and he said, 'SHHHHhhhh . . . Mafia dangerous.' It was hard to see what danger we were in, inside his Toyota Crown. It had red leather upholstery and almost white carpet. The windows were tinted and the sunroof automatic. So was the transmission. The steering wheel was on the right hand side and he drove on the right hand side of the road. They don't in Japan, they share the English and Irish peculiarity of driving on the wrong side. It was a Japanese car. I had noticed before that most of the good cars in Irkutsk had the steering wheel on the wrong side but until now it hadn't dawned on me why. Nikita and his cousin imported used cars from Japan via Vladivostok. The cars are driven from there to the points where they are ordered all over Russia. It is a big operation.

I was sitting where the driver should be so I was in a position to come into uncomfortably close contact with oncoming traffic. It wasn't like the road to Ust Barguizin where we had met only seven cars – on this road out of Irkutsk it was more like seven a minute. They were travelling at a great speed and the road was not good. It wasn't too bad either, surfaced throughout, but it was narrow, though it did have white lines, which helped. We stayed very close to this line.

We were going to his aunt's *dacha*. I was to spend the rest of the week with her. He explained that the apartment wasn't his home nor was it the home of his cousin. They used it only for business. It was safer to do business from an apartment because of the Mafia, 'Shh . . . hh.'

His aunt lived at the *dacha* for the whole summer growing vegetables for herself and her family, the cousin I had met and another five boys. They called her the Caterpillar and I would know why soon enough. He himself had another *dacha* nearby where he would take me at the weekend. It wasn't for growing vegetables, it was for relaxing, I would see, I should learn to relax.

The Caterpillar was seventy years old and smart. She didn't look her age and she didn't look like a caterpillar. Nor did she look like she worked hard. Her hands had some indications of it but not a lot. No more than one would get from a weekend in the garden. Yet she had been working three months here already. It was a dream place and pretty. Though it provided vegetables that would last her and her six sons the winter through, it was also overcrowded with flowers. Delicate, strange blooms as well as the traditional dahlias. That delicate flimsy stuff that florists use to highlight blooms in a bouquet covered the place like a bride's veil. The colours can't have been planned but their balance suggested that they had. It was just part of her natural expertise. Yet she didn't look like a natural garden person. She was rather pernickety about her appearance. She wore a pleated, tweed skirt and a twin set, like a schoolmarm. She had the remnants of an excellent figure. I hadn't seen another Russian woman like her, except Ida in Pskov two years ago. The girls in Irkutsk were beautiful and the old ladies were tubby and I had seen nothing in between. But here was a lady who held her figure and her interest in her appearance, yet worked like a Caterpillar. It was the machine she was called after, not the burrower.

Nikita's brother had told me to bring provisions. He had stopped by the market while I went in and shopped. This was an enclosed market as most Russian ones are. Vast roofed areas of individual stalls run by different businesses: butcher, baker and yes, even candle makers, though I didn't see candlesticks. I purchased vegetables. Everything I brought she already had. She held them up silently. Her dark brown eyes reflected the extravagance she felt in her heart. Her income was sixty dollars a month and she didn't spend a single penny of it during the summer. She'd need it for the winter when she'd return to her single-roomed flat in Irkutsk, on the fifth floor. This was more than a gardening *dacha*. This was a residence. She spent the whole summer here.

The wooden hut-house was very comfortable. The kitchen was separate, with electricity and gas. The main room was small but with a phone on the table and a cabinet with a centre door that dropped down and made a table on which to cut bread. It had two upper doors with panels of amber-patterned glass. The floor was covered with lino, which had a mock wood parquet design.

My room was full of books and ornaments and photos and it had a single bed that dipped down in the middle and was loaded with blankets, crocheted spread and a folded eiderdown. The big bare bulb in the centre was dragged to one side by a flex attached to a radio that gave news and served old classical music. As well as looking a little like Pskov Ida, she had similar taste. There was even a blue vase exactly like the one I had broken.

Her own room was a section curtained-off from the room with the cabinet. The curtain was of old gold brocade material, hanging by means of light brass rings on a taut string. It was only just wide enough to cover the opening and she kept tugging at it in modest concealment of her boudoir. She said she slept there all the time and that it was no inconvenience, but I didn't believe her. The hollow in my bed looked like it was made by, and for, her body.

She had a cat. He was beautiful as cats go. White mink fur with touches of blond ginger around the neck and ears and a smudge around the nose. She held him in her arms all the time the door was open, stroking him. When she closed the door she placed him gently on the floor, looked to see if I appreciated his beauty, and smiled. He walked like a eunuch, though indeed not it transpired, stretching out one paw ponderously before delicately putting it down and doing the same with the other. When he had progressed a foot he stretched out luxuriously, front paws forward, back legs back; most uncat-like. She smiled.

The garden was compartmentalised and studded with barrels of water. Russians live in preparation for things running out. Between sections she had laid planks. She had arranged them so that the divisions were staggered and the entire effect was of a well-planned wooden corridor. Even the weathering on the wood was perfect. It looked like it had been designed for exhibition in a glossy magazine. But this was no play garden; it was for survival rations.

The house was good, better than most of the seasonal dwellings I had seen in Siberia, but she wasn't pleased with it. She was building. The framework was complete and standing. She climbed its skeletal ribs and hammered, holding preciously scarce nails in her mouth. Occasionally she'd hold the hammer in her hanging-on hand and check with the other that her skirt was modest. She worked in her tweed skirt and twin set. She was doing all the work herself, alone. The timber had come in bits and pieces from her sons. They were more welcome, she told me, if they arrived with a few planks. She didn't ask where they got them, she merely examined the dimensions and coded each plank in numbers that assigned it a future role in the two-storey house. Its only occupant at the moment was a terrier bitch and her three pups that slept in a box there. The cat slept inside.

The area around was nothing like Nina's *dacha* in Moscow. Here, many of the houses had boats and barking dogs on chains. It was on the river, the only river that flows out of Baikal, the Angara. I had passed here on the hydrofoil on its route to Irkutsk. There was an abandoned look-out post. It was very high with zig-zagging steps up. It looked like a POW camp look-out. She said that in Soviet times they had things worth protecting. Now nothing, so it was abandoned; another monument to other times like the statue in Omsk or the picture of Lenin on the side of the hill.

In the corner of the room where I slept there was a pole, half its length wrapped in yellow newspaper. While I lay awake in bed in the morning I speculated that maybe she was a revolutionary who paraded with flags and beat the air with a clenched fist. One day I asked her what it was. She stalked to it and ripped off its newspaper covering with abandon untypical of this lady who hoarded rusty nails. The torn papers strew the floor. She shook it loose of its furling and waved it vigorously.

'Paddy, it is the Red Flag and it will fly again.'

Nikita's brother came at the weekend to take me to the *dacha* he and his cousin used. It was on another river, one of the many that flow into Baikal. Here they had a garden also, but it was for storing boats and skidoos and sailboards. Another of the many surprises of Russian life. The seventy-year-old Caterpillar toiled in her *dacha* growing vegetables for her sons while one of them retreated from his car importing business to this paradise of millionaire sports. His friends came to visit him in powerboats with sleeping accommodation for six. They stayed in the *dacha*, which had four bedrooms all worthy of the title 'master bedroom' and two more with built-in bunks to accommodate anyone who turned up. It had its own sauna with a diving-board that extended out over the river.

Late in the evening, while a bevy of ivory blondes in skin-tight suits designed for watersport cooked dinner, us men sweated in the sauna prior to diving naked into the river to cool off. Later we had dinner and then drinks. I complained of *izhoga*. They exchanged glances and said, 'Oh yeah?' I was cornered in an inside seat and sat through quite a few bottles before making the toilet an excuse to get out of there.

They bedded down in various interesting combinations and I took to one of the bunks. Next day, Sunday, was hot and spent in and on the river. The Caterpillar's son lived a Martha's Vineyard life no more than twenty miles from where she saved up her sixty dollars and grew vegetables.

They took me by Rasputin's house and I made a bad mistake. I said I thought he was buried very far from here – I was thinking of the monk who 'looked after' the Czarina and her son. I thought there was only one Rasputin and that he was well dead – poisoned, shot, drowned, or all of the above. He was talking about another Rasputin: the contemporary writer who claims to be unable to produce anything of merit unless he has a bottle of vodka and a young girl every day. He is the strongest voice in an effort to preserve Baikal. He speaks loudly and publicly about its importance to Russia and the world. He is widely respected for this.

On Sunday night, after dinner and a few bottles, they returned me to the Caterpillar. Four of them came in the Toyota Crown and competed with each other for conversation. A couple of friends who had remained mute for the last two days now babbled a combination of Russian and English. They competed for the finest compliments about Ireland but I heard few of them. The driver was as drunk as them and driving on the wrong side of the road because, he said, the other side was full of potholes. It couldn't have been worse than the side we were on but I was not in a position to argue. I was to return to the city by car with him later in the week but, frightened, I said I would go by bus. I said it would give me more latitude.

I walked a lot by day and tried to help the Caterpillar, but she was too competent and organised. I was only getting in her way. Now mid-August, the evenings were shortening. After dark we sat inside with little to say to each other. The cat played on the floor and she wagged her finger at him and collected him in her arms. Each time he scratched her arm viciously and each time she released him to play again. She talked to it, wagging her finger in prohibition: '*Nilza . . . nilza . . . nilza.*' Not allowed, not allowed, not allowed! Over and over again. The cat was allowed to do nothing except look cute. She didn't let him outside the door because, she said, he got into fights and came back DIRTY. '*Nilza . . . nilza . . . nilza* . . . look he knows . . . don't you know . . . show Paddy that you know . . . can't go out . . . *nilza . . . nilza . . . nilza*.'

I really didn't intend to do it. I went to the toilet in the middle of the night. The toilet was at the end of the garden. When I returned, I thought the room stuffy and it was a beautiful, bright night outside. I threw the window open and cuddled into the hollow and into a deep and contented slumber.

I wakened to her yodelling the cat's name over and over again. Sleeping on my floor, he had seen his opportunity and escaped through the open window. At first I felt relieved that he was getting an opportunity to sample some of the nightlife on the banks of the Angara River. Personally, I diagnosed his scratching of her arm as sexual frustration. But as her yodelling started to slobber a bit with sentiment I began to feel guilty. Day long she crawled around on all fours under plants and planks and up and down the bank of the river. I apologised over and over. She insisted it was not my fault but was not at all convincing. When we paused in the search, to eat, I didn't know what to say. To change the topic would have been insensitive, to repeat apologies boring. I was planning an excuse to leave a day earlier to avoid the embarrassment, when she came down the path with the vagrant feline in her arms. He had drawn fresh blood but she was too happy to say *nilza*. He looked the same to me but she claimed he was filthy. She tortured him with damp rags and, satisfied that he was refurbished, she put him down on the floor for another night of *nilza*. He looked sated.

I planned on leaving on an early bus on Thursday morning. Old Soldier turned up on Wednesday. When I returned from the river he was sitting in the garden on a kitchen chair facing the entrance gate, waiting. He had a hat, a row of medals, braces and a walking stick with a knob. He sat feet apart, with the stick between them. The knob of the stick was home to his gnarled, varicose-veined hands. He had sap in his sad eyes. He had already drunk quite a lot. The vodka bottle was sitting in thick grass and tilted to rest against the leg of his chair. He had heard that I spoke Russian and he thought I would know some allied troops he had met in Berlin.

He had built himself up for it and I didn't like to disappoint him but I told him that I wouldn't know any of them. He didn't believe it. I told him I didn't know anyone who fought in the war. 'Just pretending,' he said. I said I wasn't fluent in Russian and didn't understand all he said, he'd have to speak more slowly. He was very amused. He poked the Caterpillar with the stick saying, 'Look at him, ha, ha! Look at him pretending not to know, he knows all right . . . he knows all right.' As the day grew increasingly boring he got more indistinct and I more insistent on my innocence of the war. 'He knows all right . . . look at him pretending not to know . . . he knows all right.'

Evening approached and we went inside. He was very unsteady now; he was on the second bottle of vodka.

When the first one was finished he had asked for the second and she had brought it. She was angry but tried to hide it. He played with me, she with cat. He'd describe some victory or defeat of the war, point the stick at me saying with conviction: 'You remember that.' I'd tell him not only did I not remember it but that I knew very little about the war – nothing in fact. I began to add frequently that I found it hard to understand Russian unless it was very slow. He'd turn his head sideways and poke her with the stick saying, 'He knows all right . . . look at him pretending not to know . . . he knows all right.' But now that we were inside and she had the cat she ceased to make any effort at answering and just wagged her finger at the cat saying:

'*Nilza . . . nilza* . . . look at him he knows, *nilza*.'

And so it went until he was unable to speak. Then he nodded and she hauled him behind the curtain where she slept. Space was now very tight. I wanted to offer her my bed but didn't know how to put it. She might get the wrong impression, true she was seventy, but she was every inch a woman. Though I had not seen what was behind the curtain I knew from the layout that it had to be very tight. If there was a bed it could only be a single. There was nowhere else for him to go, the new house was a mere skeleton. I went to bed embarrassed at how things had worked out. She told me he would be travelling with me in the morning on the bus. He lived in Irkutsk.

I heard low mumbling. It sounded like she was organising space. He was being difficult; he was very drunk now. When he wasn't responding to her space-conserving instruction it seemed like she tried physically to collect him into a space. He then snorted and there was a minute's silence before I heard the clatter. Definitely open hand to cheek. I think the old soldier had mistaken her physicality for acquiescence to what he interpreted as an opportunity. Then he cried a child's cry and I could barely make out: 'Why doesn't anyone understand me?' A few times during the night I heard a shuffling struggle for space and twice I heard, '*Nilza*!' The pretty cat was in my room.

Old soldiers never die!

By morning, ardour was well in control. Caterpillar was industrious with porridge and *chi*. Old Soldier was very shaky and quiet. He dipped bread into tea and lost bits of it on the way to his mouth. The eye sap was red and wobbly, the hand shook. He didn't speak at all. We were absolute strangers. She gave us both sandwiches of her home-made bread and tomatoes. She put a red and a green pepper into each lunch and added a courgette and an apple. She wrapped them in newspaper and pushed them into our hands. He had trouble carrying his because of the walking stick, so I took them from him. He still didn't speak. She was trying hard to be sentimental about the goodbye but it was obvious she couldn't wait to see the end of us and return to her cat, potatoes, building and bed with the hollow in the middle.

There were only two seats on the bus and they were well separated. It was an old German coach that had been luxurious about twenty years ago. The headrests were high and one was not much aware of neighbour or surroundings. The bus stopped twice during the trip and women who looked like *dejurnayas* came on board to check that everyone had tickets. A few hadn't. One man argued and begged, just passing time so that he would have progressed farther on the trip that he couldn't afford to pay for. All over Russia this system operates. Even in cities. 'Bus police' board in search of freeloaders. Their success rate is high. The offenders are usually very offended at the suggestion they are not paying their way. On city buses the police, male especially, can be very rough. I have seen them physically push people around, even women.

When we got to Irkutsk the bus stopped at a busy intersection. There were loose tram tracks and overhead wires, there was our coach disgorging and many old Ladas struggling. The trip hadn't been long enough to eat what Caterpillar had given us so Old Soldier took his from me without speaking. He then made his way across the busy intersection, shaking his stick in the air at vehicles that threatened him. Without turning to me he gave one shake of the stick that might have been goodbye or could have been a threat. I didn't understand but he'd never believe that . . . 'He knows,' he'd say. 'He knows.'

Chapter Nine

The streets of Irkutsk were so familiar I felt I had come home. An accomplished and enriched emigrant returned. I began to pull rank on the natives. I watched the trolley buses and the trams and watched people waiting and mentally offered solutions that would expedite their passage. I, who knew every nook and cranny of this town. A native son returned from a pioneering trip into the wilderness. I had a chat with my inner self about how things used to be.

Inside: There's the OVIR office, remember how scared you were of that when you discovered your visa was not in order?

Outside: Yeah, remember I thought they might put me in jail? God! It looked so strange and foreign then.

Inside: And now?

Outside: Ha, ha, now it is nothing . . . look there's a guy waiting in line, see how scared he looks, should I talk to him and tell him what to do?

Inside: Easy now, you're still foreign.

Outside: Hmmph! You never learn, do you? I may be foreign to you, you never understand me, but I know more about this place than any other foreigner. Bet I know more about it than most natives. Look!

Inside: Where?

Outside: Over there across the river.

Inside: What?

Outside: That's Lena's; remember? The place we stayed with Doug and then Kongar . . . the throat singer, remember? What amateurs we were then, waaaay back then. That place is miles out, all the way round to cross the bridge and then through the park. I wouldn't dream of staying way out there in the sticks now.

Inside: No? So what do you have in mind?

Outside: We'll find a new place . . . I don't want to impose on Tolya and the girls again.

I go to the Post Office, to the Large Lady who couldn't understand the intricacies of the visa problem. For a minute she doesn't recognise me. I look so different now you see. I don't stand out any more. I've taken on the aura of the place and I blend in. Then she recognises me and clasps her hand over her mouth and points. 'Look at yer man,' is what I hear, as if she were a Dublin lady. I think she squeals, or maybe that's the Dublin lady, too, but anyway, a few of her colleagues gather and piece together the story.

'Yeah! Remember? He came in here a couple of months ago nearly crying, saying he was going to be put in jail if we couldn't help him.'

'*Konieshno*! I remember, and you couldn't understand what he wanted and you sent him to the Intourist. The Intourist where they rob people.'

'Of course I understood! Didn't want him to get in trouble that's all.'

'Where were you?'

'Baikal.'

'Oh! Baikal . . . he was on Baikal. Beautiful Baikal . . .'

'I want somewhere to stay here in Irkutsk. Somewhere near the centre.'

'Listen how he speaks . . . like a Russian.'

'Oh, like a Siberian.'

'Like a native son.'

'I have a friend, lives just round the corner with her mother and father. They live on the fourth floor in a beautiful apartment. An apartment from before Khrushchev, when apartments were apartments. Yes, Khrushchev built boxes. People-boxes. But my friend she has such an apartment . . . with a balcony over Karl Marx Street where people stroll in the evenings. She has parents. Yes, she has parents! But she wants to make a little money so she can move out eventually. Now it is so expensive. She teaches English. She has good English.'

'I don't need English . . . I speak Russian.'

'I know, I know, you speak beautiful Russian . . . such Russian. Doesn't he speak such Russian?'

'Indeed.'

'Such Russian.'

'Like I have never heard.'

'And he a foreigner . . . from . . . a . . . a small place.'

Oxcana arrives in a flurry. You can tell she has stopped outside the door to straighten herself out and make it seem that she is calm and hasn't rushed at all. Her blouse is pulled straight down into her skirt in a way that cannot survive more than five paces of careful walking.

'In what way can I be of assistance?' she asks in impeccable phrase book English.

The building is elegant with columns supporting ornate balconies. It is painted the same green as the Hermitage in St Petersburg. My eye has changed and I now see this as an architectural gem. Last time these buildings looked out of period – any period. I had been categorising them into Georgian and Victorian and they didn't fit. Now I saw a pre-Khrushchev, elegant apartment building of four floors and ornate balconies. The entrance was at the back. Like halls and stairs in all Russian apartment buildings it was dark and dingy-looking. The stairs were of concrete with cold railings. But there was no smell of urine, which set it way above the ordinary. Trees in the patch of ground behind grew to the height of the building making it very dark on the stairs. When we got inside Oxcana's apartment, it was surprisingly bright. The windows were just above the level of the tree tops and got light from the clear blue sky above. The sky was peppered with circling starlings.

Her mother started straight away: 'Oxcana! Where is . . . oh there it is!' Daughter tried to introduce me but it didn't work out. Her mother circled . . . hovered, bent to waist level, looking, searching. 'Oxcana . . . where is . . . oh there it is.' Then she'd scoop something imaginary from the floor and sprint into another room, bent in two.

Well, there weren't that many rooms to sprint into, though it was by far the nicest Russian apartment I had seen. The hall was high, very high considering it was the top floor. I could only imagine how elegant the halls of the apartments below were. The doors leading off it to the sitting-room and two bedrooms reached right up to the roof. They were double doors with nice arms. Russians use the same word for door handles and for arms: *rookey*.

The sitting-room was big. This was no surprise, even in humble apartments the sitting-room is big. The book collection, common to all Russian apartments, was tasteful and varied. It was displayed in glass cabinets with ornate wood webbing. This collection was even better than Larissa's in Moscow. We were looking at the books through the glass when the bent mother separated us at knee level and surged up between us. 'Oxcana! Into the kitchen, quick, into the kitchen, I can't find it.'

The daughter was patient. She answered her each time she made a call. 'Mama–ha, I'll get it for you in just a moment.'

She wasn't a completely mad mother, just an obsessive one who feared losing her daughter. The father was severe but he was there. It seems to me that it is unusual in Russia for a marriage to last. I have stayed in more than a dozen homes and in at least half there is no man. He is not even mentioned.

Russian women are strong. Stronger than the men. More able for the struggle. When the going gets tougher they take their bags and baskets and go foraging farther afield. The men give up more easily. They buy a bottle of vodka and when that becomes more than they can afford they tighten their belt and drink some raw spirit at a lower price. Not all men of course, but it seems to me that more men than women give up and give in. Families are not big, often just the one child. So it is very common to find a household of woman and child. Oxcana's father was present but silent.

I am put into the smaller of the two bedrooms, a very comfortable room with electricity, a desk and carpet on the floor. I am confused. I like it, I keep touching things, soft and warm things, and I wonder what do I really want. I cross the world to live in hardship but now I love the soft comfort of this room. Is the wild calling me or am I faking it?

Last time in Irkutsk I had read about the city but I hadn't taken it in. That's because I hadn't understood the Tea Route or its importance. Irkutsk exists because of it. It was here that the formal bureaucratic things were done, like paying tax and stamping the bales of tea. Tea was the main commodity, but the existence of the infrastructure to facilitate its passage increased other trade. Gold passed through here too, and fur and silk. A fire destroyed the city on June 22nd, 1879. Fifteen thousand families lost their homes. Archives, libraries, churches and schools also went up in smoke as did the treasures accumulated by the Decembrists, their descendants and the *nouveau riche* emulators of their lifestyle. But, undaunted by such a set-back, Irkutsk rebuilt itself and gained prominence anew as a pivotal point on the Trans-Siberian Railway.

The city has a reputation for high educational standards and traditions. As I'd seen from the classroom map, this goes back to the Decembrists' uprising, their protest at the treatment of ordinary people. For their trouble they were exiled to Siberia. Many made Irkutsk their home and they were the founders of the educational institutions here. It still has the leafy feel of a university city, a Russian university city. Russians have a great love of education. They have a feeling for it and an appreciation too. Students talk in groups about Pushkin and Dostoyevsky, they argue science and mathematics and you can see they are enjoying it. It's not pretension; it's pleasure. They like talking about their studies and laugh as easily as if they were gossiping. And they look beautiful talking; strong faces.

When I travelled down to Ulan Ude on the 44A with the Marilyn Monroe blonde, the old lady who had lost her son and the silent, smiling draftee, I had seen uniformed men guarding the openings to tunnels. I didn't know who or what they were, or what the men were defending. The guards were period pieces; they looked like Beefeaters on the bottle of gin that carries that name. They wore ornate uniforms and big, tall, furry hats. I didn't ask who or what they were. Limitation in language enforces certain economies of communication. At the back of my mind I wondered if there was some kind of a revolution afoot here that I hadn't heard about. Now I discovered that they were Cossacks. So the bottle image was correct, except it should have been vodka not gin.

The word cossack is Turkish and means 'homeless, bold, free man'. At least that's what my book says . . . I think if one word can say so much about a man, I should be learning Turkish instead of this Russian. They were adventurous peasants who rebelled against the oppression of serfdom. The Russian government saw an opportunity of channelling the Cossack's aggression and fiery spirit to its own purpose. The Cossacks were entrusted with the protection of the Empire. They were stationed all along the borders with Mongolia and China. Old traditions die hard. Though there isn't a lot to protect now, these Cossacks stand alert still, guns held at the ready and heavy fur hats sending beads of perspiration down their foreheads.

In the culturally diverse area close to the Mongolian border I had stopped, briefly, at a village of small people. They had conical heads, smooth, leathery skin and slightly oriental eyes. I has seen a very similar village years previously on the border between Turkey and Armenia. I mentally recorded the similarity. It was one of those coincidences I like to speculate about. Now, here in Irkutsk, I discover that these Cossacks would have come from just such an area. The realisation gave me goose pimples. How small the world. Long before planes, even before trains, these people had drifted two thousand miles across mountain and steppe. Maps with swooping arrows strive to explain the movements of people over aeons. They strive in vain; at least they confuse me. Turkic people are scattered from Istanbul to Vladivostok and

Peking. Languages with Turkish-sounding words penetrate Russian and Chinese. Orientals selling rugs in Saudi Arabia will flash eyes at you revealing genes from somewhere around the Black Sea. And to confound it further you'll find Turkmenistan not to be Turkish at all but Mongolian, its inhabitants are called Turkmen but they are not Turkish. What meaning have boundaries?

In the evening I drifted aimlessly towards the suburbs. The city is mostly of concrete and stone now but there are some beautiful, old, wooden buildings. The wood is very dark, either from weathering or some protective coating. They are very ornate, especially around the windows. These old dwellings are also surprising. You walk along a modern-looking street, all concrete and brick, and suddenly, there in a break sits this almost black, sometimes slightly tilting, wooden house. A fairy tale building. Strange thing is, I never saw anyone come out of any of them. I stood watch at many, wondering if the occupants were as mythical as the buildings looked, but I never saw a soul. I asked: 'Does anyone live in these old houses?'

'*Konieshno*.'

'How come I haven't seen anyone come out?'

'Because no one has come out while you are watching.' Foreigners!

Then I came to a beautiful wooden church surrounded by other small, ornate, wooden dwellings. In the yard, girls played. They seemed big for the child's game of skipping, but they played a game of fast skipping, where it was easy to lose. Two would swing the rope while one skipped. They'd accelerate the swing until it was impossible to keep up and the skipper was OUT. A severe argument followed each out. I couldn't hear or understand all the words but smiled to myself at the universality of the exchange:

'Are so . . .'

'Am not.'

'My turn.'

They wore cotton dresses, with floral print, almost to the ground. Though it was warm, summertime, many wore boots. All wore white headscarves.

Then they saw me watching and scattered. Adults were sitting on chairs and steps and they stopped talking. The girls cuddled into their protection. One man came towards me slowly. He was very dark and wore an even darker moustache. Turkish-looking. (Not Turkman!) He had a craggy, masculine appearance, deeply creased and weathered, his arms swung malevolently out from his body like equivalent bow-legs.

'Can I help you?'

'Just watching.'

'What do you want?'

The girls were, despite the childish costume, physically mature. I knew that I might have looked like a pervert, so I gushed about my curiosity of races and people. He was wary and pierced me with his black eyes.

'You want to see our ambassador?'

Unwilling to pass up an opportunity for diplomatic exchange I replied in the affirmative. He escorted me to a long building at the back where we walked the length of a dimly lit corridor into a hushed room. There, in the centre, sat a pair of men. They were playing chess on a baize-covered table. A single ancient light was just a foot off the table. It was shaded in cardboard, warped and yellowed from the heat of the faint bulb. My guide said something in a strange language and the players stopped. Then they looked up but I could not see their eyes. They were above the light level. One man was round, the other thin. More strange language and the round one gestured the thin one to leave. Then he spoke in the same language to the guide but this time I understood. *Chi* is an international word. He was to bring us tea.

Then I was alone with him. I still thought I stood accused of 'perving' on maidens at play and I sprang to my defence with long gushes about my interest in all things strange – no foreign – well, me foreign too, but unusual foreign . . . interesting.

Nothing.

I wondered if he understood and asked if he spoke Russian. He did. I was Irish and . . .

'Joyce, Yeats, Belfast.'

'Yes!' I could have cheered.

Tea arrived in sticky glasses. It was just the same as I once had with a goatherd at the foot of Mount Arrarat near the Armenian border.

'Yerevan. We are from Yerevan in Armenia.'

My eyes accustomed to the dim light and met his intelligent pair. Wet, intelligent eyes that could be fanatical Muslim eyes. I asked. About being Muslim, not fanatic.

'No! Armenians are all Christian.' It was the first country in the world where Christianity was adopted as the state religion. They spoke Armenian language, which is close to the Aramaic language of the Bible. He didn't know any English but had read Joyce and Yeats in Russian. Joyce was crazy and wanted to confuse people but he was also a genius. But Yeats was love, love of people and of places.

It grew dimmer. His arms rested on the table and they were like legs from the knee down. They were very hairy. He smelt fatherly. The aroma was of tobacco, but there was also a hint of something out of a church . . . incense, and something from my grandmother's house in Ireland. He took a pouch from somewhere under the table and put a little snuff on the back of his hand near the thumb knuckle. He indicated that I should hold out my hand for some too. We sneezed together and it brought us close.

It was dark and I was alone so he insisted on walking me home, only a couple of miles. We cut through side streets and across open spaces in front of apartment buildings. Progress was slow because we met a lot of people, many with features like the Ambassador's. Then I realised I was walking with a black man in a black community; dreaded by Russians. He caught my arm to steer me around open drains and away from obstacles. He had the easy physicality of an Arab male, a natural, warm touch, uninhibited by Western mores. He called into small shops that I would have missed to see 'an old woman who recently lost her husband', to get 'incense to burn against mosquitoes', 'sweeties for my grandson'.

While I still wondered about how old-fashioned his attitudes might be, we met an attractive, thirty-something, ivory blonde. She liked him. He was gentle and masculine with her and she said he should call on her again like he used to. 'Used to make love to her,' he told me. 'But not any more.'

'Why?'

'I thought she was different, but she's not.'

He told me that in Irkutsk people would not be as antagonistic towards black people as those in far-off Moscow, but they were still prejudiced. Not so much against Armenians as against Azerbaijanis, 'Because they know we are intelligent and Christian.' I told him that Christian didn't mean better and that intelligence was not the preserve of any nationality. He saw the flash of anger and said: 'You're right – of course you're right . . . oops! Watch that hole!' We came to a place where he said we should take a bus for just two stops. It was a link area with no street lighting and many water-filled potholes.

All over Russia there are 'punches' on board buses. These are things like paper-punches that make a pattern of holes in the ticket. An inspector can read this pattern and tell something that I never figured out. The pattern doesn't change. It is a mechanical rather than electronic device. In fact, it is a very ancient mechanical device that often requires a great wallop before it performs its punching. If you are not within striking distance of the punch you pass the ticket to one who is and they do it for you. Surprisingly there is never any reluctance in performing this operation. It is one situation where I never heard a single *nyet*. The punches are fixed to the wall of the bus in the ribs between windows.

On the bus for the two stops I took out my ticket (they are bought in bundles in advance and used in ones as required) and handed it to the woman beside me. She was just about to take it when he saw what was happening. Her hand was about to close on the ticket when his hand grabbed too. Our three hands were clasped together in mid-air like some victorious salute. 'What are you doing?' he asked.

'Giving the lady a ticket to punch,' I answered, defensively.

'But we are only going two stops,' he said.

'So?' I said.

He nodded at the woman and wrinkling up his nose he said: 'He's foreign.'

'Ah, ha!' she said, and turning to the woman behind her she repeated: 'He's foreign.'

Then that lady passed it on in a loud whisper: 'He's foreign.'

The Ambassador and the first woman were already laughing aloud while the word spread. The laughing chorus added contraltos, tenors, basses and sopranos while the word was still finding its way to the people on the broken back seat. It had reached a crescendo before we got to our stop. As the driving blonde pulled a lever to release the door and let me out I saw tears coursing down her cheeks. With effort she barely got out: 'Only a foreigner would waste a good ticket for two stops.' A few of the passengers took up the reprise:

'Two stops . . . two stops . . . a ticket for two stops,' as the folding door clattered shut on a very jolly bus.

He squeezed my hand warmly and uttered blessings and good wishes in his own language. Then, in Russian, he said, 'May the road rise up and meet you.' He had read it was an Irish wish for a safe journey. I watched his large mass move down Karl Marx in the ghostly light of the street lamp. Before he took the corner he turned to wave and he looked like a younger, more solid Charles Laughton.

I thought about revisiting the Ambassador's area at the weekend but Mushroom Fever struck. I heard it whispered reverentially, '*Greebney . . . da ochean koosney . . . greebney ochean koosney . . .*' Mushrooms . . . very tasty . . . mushrooms, very tasty.

Mad Mother laughed hysterically and threw her head in the air. 'Oxcana, tell him we go on Saturday.'

'Mama–ha he understands you, he knows we go on Saturday.'

'Tell him, Oxcana, that mushrooms are very important to Russians. Oxcana! Why aren't you telling him?'

'Because Mama–ha he knows what you are saying.'

'Oxcana, he's a foreigner, he understands nothing and you tell him nothing. All right, I won't say another word. Not another word. In Siberia a guest is the most important person – no! In Siberia a guest *was* a most important person until my daughter grew up. My daughter who I spent all my money educating to speak the foreign language but she knows too much to speak to the foreigner. Oh she knows too much! The foreigner will go back to his country and tell people about us in Siberia . . . about us who won't tell him about mushrooms about . . .'

'Mama–ha he knows . . .'

'Oxcana! How could he know? He's a foreigner!'

And then Oxcana, barely suppressing tears of anger and frustration, would start to tell me again with a hand gesture, weakened from repetition: 'On Saturday we will go to the wood. We will take the bus to the station and then we will get the electric train and . . .'

'Oxcana, I can't find it where is it . . . Oxcana, Oxcana, can you hear me where IS IT . . . ?'

Everyone in Irkutsk had the same idea. It was like an Indian train. People bristled buckets, bags and baskets. Many had large rucksack-like contraptions. They were rectangular metal tanks covered in green khaki, with straps for carrying on one's back. Every inch was packed, but there was no rivalry for space. People were accommodating, helping each other.

'Oh, what a fine container, let me help you fit it in here . . . move over there, son, and let the *babushka* sit down.'

'There, there child, don't loose your cap, you'll need it.'

'Oh yes! For the arthritis, nothing like the mushrooms.'

'Catarrh too, I make a milk from them for the catarrh.'

'The soup is the best, mushroom soup is good for the bones.'

'No! No, mushroom soup is good for the eyes . . . for the bones, it's cheese.'

When we got to the spot, about thirty miles from the city, anybody who hadn't been on the train was there before us. They had come by car. Miles of Ladas lined the road by the wood and many had driven down narrow paths designed for pedestrians. In every clearing there were more Ladas. Some had brought tents and had lit fires to cook. It was a full day's work.

Despite the crowd there was no shortage of mushrooms. They poked out of the soft soil and humus in artistic clumps. Their groupings were choreographed. There were red ones with yellow dots and yellow ones with red dots and brown ones and unbelievable blue ones. They were hushed up in the centre; some looked like velvet and others so beautiful that I thought they must be poisonous. But I saw more than mushrooms. Childhood books came to life and I saw elves and goblins. They lured me from clump to clump in a frenzy. My hands turned navy blue and Mad Mother squealed, 'Oxcana you never told him about the blue . . . look at his hands, what will his people think in his country when he comes home from Siberia blue . . . ?' Then, too late, Oxcana pointed out the ones that leave indelible blue marks. She had plucked one carefully by the stem and was holding it close for me to recognise when Mad Mother erupted between us with a hysterical emergency: 'Oxcana! Quick your father is lost . . . gone . . . Oxcana, I can't find your father . . .' He had taken refuge at a distance, out of hearing.

The return journey was heavy. Everything full and people tired. Children fell asleep across laps and people drew strands of hair out of their eyes and tried to poke them into place. I wasn't the only one with blue hands. Children held them out to each other for inspection. It would take at least a month before the stain would wear away but it was no harm. It just put a taste in all the other food you touched. Mad Mother was talking stew to someone until Oxcana started to tell me about berries. Then she jumped up and, squeezing in between us, said we should be talking and enjoying this great mushroom expedition and not be sitting there without saying a word like two dummies. 'What does he want to know Oxcana? Oxcana, ask him what he wants to know and I'll tell you and you can tell him.'

'Mama–ha he . . .'

The stew bubbled and heaved like witches' brew. The surface was foam with little floating coloured bits. Lots of the red skin came to the top and shuddered gently in the foam. Mad Mother ladled it slowly into bowls. She'd hold the full ladle down low, touching the bowl with it and then, tilting it until it started to pour, she'd draw the ladle away creating a column of steaming, viscous mushroom soup.

It tasted strange and strong and I took it in some trepidation, remembering all the warnings from my youth about the 'pookapiles' that were deadly poison. I had seen nothing like these mushrooms, except in children's books about gooks and goblins. They were the stuff of witch's potions, not remotely like what we call mushrooms. They laughed when I drew pictures of our mushrooms. 'Mushrooms! No, they're *champignons*.'

Now that I knew all about the trains I decided I would purchase my ticket well in advance and get exactly what I wanted. I also thought I'd see the ex-ballet dancer and that I could tell her all about where I'd been. I knew she'd be a good listener. She would have been had she been there, but she wasn't. Her place was occupied by a typical train lady, large, blonde and sour.

'*Stho vui khotete*?' What do you want?

I had decided I'd stop at Omsk on the way back. It was still in my mind as a place of some geographical significance. I couldn't get that echo out of my head: 'Linehan, what time is it in Omsk when it is noon in Greenwich?' There was another reason also. I had a friend, Rose, in Kazakhstan who was going to be in Siberia at this time. She had mentioned Omsk or Tomsk, I didn't know which. Tomsk isn't on the Trans-Siberian line, Omsk is. So I thought I'd take a chance on bumping into her there. Long shot.

The blonde told me sharply that she didn't give a kopeck for my reasons for wanting to stop in Omsk, her job was to sell tickets and not ask questions. There was the 4 going in two days' time, it was a good train.

'No!' I said. 'I don't want the 4, it starts in Irkutsk, I want something more interesting.' It was not the right thing to say and I knew it. I wanted to let her know I wasn't the ordinary foreigner who knew nothing and could be pushed around. Conflict occupied the space between us.

'Oh! The number 4 is known to be the best train on the line.'

'No it isn't, the 2 is better but I don't want it either. It is coming from Vladivostock and it will be very used, the produce won't be fresh.' She loomed large with indignation, but I was really enjoying myself. I was regurgitating all the wisdom passed on to me by previous railway women. She huffed and said:

'All right, I'll give you the 44A.'

'The 44A!' I thundered, with magnificent indignation. I said it so loud that a woman with a scarf and a mop who was cleaning the toilet poked her head around the door to see what violence threatened. 'The 44A,' I repeated. 'Everyone knows it is not the 44A but the 45, which had a fire underneath the seat in carriage 16.' She was stunned. 'No!' I said. 'I'll take the 24 coming from Ulan Bator.' She made a slight recovery; I could see a glint return to her eye. I knew she was going to tell me about the Mongolians and the grease, so to really destroy her I added: 'I know everything will be greasy from their butter, but they are a friendly people.' I said 'friendly people' right into her eye. She was furious. She hammered the details into the keyboard. In the '*miesta*' space I saw her fill in 18 and, taking a real risk, for now she was dangerous, I said: 'Ah ha!'

She halted.

'What do you mean: "Ah ha"?'

'Ah ha! 18,' I said. 'I want *neezhe*, down.' Even numbers are up, odds down. And, definitely taking her to the very brink, 'You wouldn't want me to have to put myself in danger leaning out of the top *miesta* to see the countryside roll by?' She counted my roubles slowly and slapped the ticket on the counter, looking out over my head, trying to take some advantage of her elevated desk. Safe now, I added, smiling: '*OO vas boodete harowshee den*!' Have a nice day!

Being Russian is easy.

I had met Ider Batchylynn in Red Square two years ago, on my first visit to Moscow. He was from Ulan Bator and a policeman on the weekly train from there to Moscow. He had no nose or eyes to speak of, a little like Kongar the throat singer, but he had a smile that lit the whole square. I thought I'd take a chance on his being on the train to Omsk. I was betting on a double, maybe meet Rose in Omsk, maybe meet Ider on the train. Coincidences have a better chance of occurring if you set them up.

The mugger struck from behind. I went for a final evening stroll, recording, for later playback, all the streets and alleyways of Irkutsk. I had woven my way around: through the park where I'd seen the girl with the yellow dress, down Karl Marx, then past Yuri Gagarin's bust to the promenade named after him, ending up on the banks of the river. It was dusk. Mad Mother had told Oxcana to tell me not to be out in the dark. She told her to tell me that I was a foreigner. That foreigners, especially, were in danger of being mugged. I smiled in satisfaction of all that I knew. Me mugged! Me who knows this town better than anyone living here, me who looks more native than Mad Mother or Oxcana!

The heavy hand ran around my throat and froze my reflexes. It must have been only an instant but it felt like an anaconda wrapping itself around my neck in slow motion. I tried to scream but before anything came out the snake blocked my mouth. Then it blotted out all vision and my whole life passed in front of me. I saw all the people I know in Ireland waiting, on the airport balcony, for the Aeroflot plane to trundle slowly down the runway. Then I saw my brother helping big, burly Russians to ease the coffin into the waiting hearse. I saw myself lowered into the grave and I could hear them all competing with each other for wise things to say:

'I told him . . . oh, I told him a hundred times of the dangers.'

'Oh! I told him, too, and shure you couldn't tell him. He knew it all.'

'Aw shure! Where's the use in your talking, missus, he's gone now anyway.'

'. . . and may the Lord look after him.'

'. . . shure that itself is doubtful . . . there isn't any God in that place is there?'

'They're Communist aren't they? Not Catholic anyway.'

Then I felt the hair and the heat and I got the whiff of incense and snuff. It was the Ambassador! Recognising me from behind, he had slipped his hands over my eyes to surprise me. He rocked with laughter at my reaction. His generous girth stretched a floral print shirt. He was like Danny Devito on stilts and with grey hair. He thought it was really funny.

We walked until midnight and he told me more about himself and his people. No, he wasn't a real ambassador, just a Consul representing Armenian interests in Siberia. Mostly he dealt with people's problems with work. He helped them get jobs. He had many contacts. His family, all daughters, were grown-up and married and were scattered all over the former Soviet Union. His wife was dead a long time. He had thought about remarrying but no, not now . . . too old, sixty.

I left him again at the street corner.

This was my last night in Irkutsk.

Chapter Ten

Mad Mother was excited about my going. It would be safer without me and still she'd have had the experience of having to put up with me. I overheard her on the phone: 'No! No, no, no, no! He doesn't know anything . . . how could he, he's a foreigner? No, it hasn't been easy . . . Oh he's clean, fairly clean. Doesn't eat in the morning . . . how could he be right? He has nothing.' And later: 'It was an experience, such an experience . . . Oxcana doesn't understand . . . I have to explain things. Never saw mushrooms . . . No! Never! . . . Yes, he looks unhealthy. Well, most of them do . . . eating out of jars. Oh! I must go prepare something for the train. Must take him to the train . . . How would he know where the train is?'

The food for the train was bulkier than my bag. There were two bags of potato omelettes and another of hard-boiled eggs. There was a semicircle of *kolbasa* (meat loaf) and a small cone bag of radishes. She had them in three separate bundles. I was to carry one, Oxcana another and she, Mad Mother, the third. I got weak when I realised what was happening; they were coming with me to the train, denying me the sweetness of silent reminiscing along the dark streets. She'd be jumping in and out of seats on the bus telling Oxcana what to tell me and then she'd be there at the station, fussing me in. I couldn't take it.

I sat down and told her; I said that I was far odder than she had ever imagined. That I liked to be alone a lot.

That I liked arriving and leaving alone. That I hated people meeting me and that being seen off was worse.

I went into too much detail about this, talking about saying goodbye and the train being still there and then saying it again and everyone getting very embarrassed because it was only a false start and the train didn't leave for another ten minutes and that by the time it did everyone was tired of each other and never wanted to see each other again.

'Oxcana! What's he saying about never seeing each other again? Wasn't it good enough for him? Better than what he gets in a country with no mushrooms! No wonder they all have arthritis. Come on! Lets go.' Though it was a balmy night she had a coat and scarf on because it was dark. 'Oxcana, tell him it is dark . . . he'll have to wear something.'

I got very serious. I said, 'I won't go unless I can go alone.'

That did it. As much as she had cherished all the fuss at the railway station she couldn't stand the prospect of having me for longer. She took off the scarf and pulled it tight over the hanging peg on the wall. She stopped, squeezed her lips into a bitter straight line, took off her coat and nearly bored a hole in it hanging it on the same peg; then, turning to her daughter, she said, 'Oxcana! tell him . . . tell him . . . tell him, Oh! Tell him goodbye . . .'

From behind the bedroom door the wailing was heart-rending. Oxcana mouthed that she'd have to go to her mother. She hung her coat and went in.

I was walking out when the father shouted, 'Stop!' I was stunned. It was the first word I'd heard from him. He had just paced around looking serious. He had moved from room to room keeping out of his wife's way but now he was gallantly coming to her defence.

'No, you don't leave like that. Sit down! Now, think for a little time. Think about where you are leaving and where you are going and why you are going there. Think about what you are taking with you and what you are leaving behind. Then the journey will be happy.' That was all. It is a Russian habit to sit down for a minute, no matter what the rush, before you go out of the door. It works. It relieved the tension and I left tranquil.

I had wanted to walk but I couldn't with all the food. The tram was homely and I didn't want to get off when it shuddered to a stop in front of the station. The display still read Kh–bar–k –5:— exactly as it had done on my first arrival six weeks ago.

Inside the station there was no such misinformation. The board of departures and arrivals is electronic and constantly updated. Passengers and people waiting for passengers stand with their bags looking up at it. When a train is about to arrive or depart the display flashes and, simultaneously, an announcement comes over to say which *pootee* (platform) is involved. People move on cue. When it comes to train travel, Russians change. Everything goes *touchney po rosspecaniu*. Exactly by the timetable.

The Ulan Bator train arrived at platform 5. No one got off and only a very few got on. I was the only one getting on a *coupney*, the others were all for the *platscar*. This is a section of the train where there are no divisions between compartments. Everyone has a *miesta*, as in the *coupney*, but they are hard. There can be a very good atmosphere on the *platscar*. Generous Russian women share meagre rations around and cuddle children's heads on their laps. There are *dejurnayas* too but they have to be very severe to keep soldiers and other men in order. I took a few short trips by *platscar* and liked it, but once a soldier in an overhead *miesta* put his head over the side and was sick on me. There was no apology, he was very drunk. The *dejurnaya* was young but she did her best to react sternly. She dragged him from his bunk and pushed a mop into his hand to clean up the floor. He was too drunk to make a job of it so he fell on someone else's *miesta* and slept it off there. He had other, less drunk, friends who muttered under their breath about the *dejurnaya*. It didn't erupt to anything but it had potential. Other passengers pretended not to notice but I could see, in their absorbed distraction, that they had seen many such incidents flare. Women drew in their wandering children and pointed out things of interest outside the window. Danger dangled. Violence is never far from the surface in Russian life.

So now, in Irkutsk, I was the only one getting on the *coupney*. I was the only one in compartment 5 and the *dejurnaya* was a pale, uninterested specimen. She gave me sheets and a wan smile and left me alone. We eased out of Irkutsk just on midnight and the rain fell in slanting streaks on the lonesome window of my comfortable compartment.

I made my bed and stalked the corridor. No one. No Mongolians, no butter, no grease. I went to bed and thought how nice it would be if someone put his head over the side of the upper *miesta* and was sick on me.

The rain was heavy; it wasn't staying on the window but streaking sideways in blobs. I thought even the rain didn't want to stay with me. 'I am sorry, Mad Mother, for what I did to you, I should have let you come to the station. I think you are right, foreigners are a hard lot.'

After a couple of hours the train started to struggle. *I think I can . . . I think I can . . . I think I can* and then, *I know I can . . . I know I can . . . I know I can.* I didn't say a word but I'm sure I heard it urge, 'Come on Paddy, give us a hand.' I couldn't. My heart wasn't in it.

The morning was bad. Sheets of rain lashed by. At a level crossing I saw a gaggle of geese. They seemed to be waiting for the train to pass, their necks stretched and their beaks very yellow. Gardens were abandoned, no fat ladies in knickers. No lardy-bellied men lounging around. The dirt roads that looked quaint on the out journey were now muddy quagmires leading to desolation. Then another level crossing; a lonesome whistle; a wooden cart waiting, its wet, hairy horse balancing his weight on three legs, the driver with a blue plastic bag on his head . . . or was it a remnant of a plastic coat like Tolya used to sell on the street of Irkutsk? Used to sell.

I found the restaurant car. I was the only one. The waitress was stubby with a miniskirt that looked funny. It was made of purple, bulky material and she had a short-sleeved red sweater tucked inside it. She wore gold, flat shoes with little bows on them and she had gold hair. She brought me coffee and said that later she would have stroganoff. I asked her if she knew the police on the train and she got all excited and asked me what was wrong. I told her about Ider and she said that all the police were busy on the *platscar*, that if he was on the train he'd be there, that I shouldn't dream of going to the *platscar*, and that anyway I couldn't because it was locked off from the *coupney* section.

I was joined in my compartment by two women at Nizhneudinsk and they were going to Novosibirisk. I surprised them with my gushing. It took them a while to adjust to Western advances. I was so pleased with the company I fussed about like Mad Mother, making things nice for them. They smiled slightly at me and suppressed laughter at each other. At first they looked blocky women of about thirty years. When they took off their outer rain attire they were more girlish. Both had gold teeth. One had three and the other had two. Here, gold teeth don't carry the associations they do in other places. These were straightforward females making a living for their families. One of them said her husband had been a policeman, while the other hung her head. They told me they needed boots for the winter. That in Nizhneudinsk it was not possible to live without boots for the winter and that it was not possible to buy boots on what they had. A pair of boots would be two months' salary and what would they do for food if they were saving for boots?

They would be in Novosibirsk how long?

'Who knows? Maybe two weeks, maybe a month,' one said as she stood up and busied herself with bags. I didn't ask how they were going to earn the money. They knew that I knew and they were embarrassed.

Covering the moment, I insisted they take some of my food, that I couldn't eat it all. I said I'd be grateful if they would make tea for me because I had none and I had no cup. They were happy then.

I reduced my salary to one hundred dollars a week and told them how expensive it was to live in Ireland. They just stared and wondered what I would know about having to work for two weeks, maybe a month, to buy boots. I said I had very tough times when I was young, no boots, no electricity and they said yes, that it was tough.

Later they made jokes among themselves that I did not understand. When they saw that I felt isolated, maybe laughed at, one of them tried to explain the jokes. Around midnight they wanted to go to bed and couldn't stop giggling between themselves about how much clothing they would take off with the strange man in the carriage. I went into the corridor and when I returned they pretended to be asleep. I sat thinking in the dim light of my *miesta* and when they were really asleep I could see how their rounded and very womanly shapes could provide great comfort for some lonely men in Novosibirsk.

The train got to Novosibirsk early in the morning. I was still in bed, bleary-eyed, when they left, whispering goodbyes at me and fluttering their fingers in a jokey way. Alone again, I went to the restaurant and my miniskirted woman told me she preferred the Vladivostok train. She didn't mind which number it was as long as it was Vladivostock. It was better business. She could get Japanese goods in Vladivostock but only Chinese things in Ulan Bator. As well, Mongolians took butter in their tea and made everything greasy. People from Vladivostok were gentlemen. As she said this I noticed a man sitting alone, listening, smoking. He was about thirty with greasy slicked-back hair, a black shirt with white tie and a leather jacket. He was a caricature of a second-rate mobster, complete with cigarette held between thumb and index finger. He looked sideways at his moll in conversation with the foreigner. She was a kindly soul with interest in things. Business was fairly good but you had to spend a lot of money on bribes to police and to *dejurnaya*. The *dejurnaya* could refuse you permission to take on board the large quantities of produce that one carried from place to place. This trip she had a cargo of children's clothes from Peking that she had picked up in Ulan Bator and which she had dropped off in Novosibirisk. There she had got some Pakistani shirts that she was taking to Moscow.

Novosibirisk was good for all kinds of business. It was a kind of crossroads where businessmen met and exchanged things. Some of these businessmen had a lot of money. Good business. My companions of last night had picked their pitch.

It was still raining. It had been raining for nearly two days and three thousand kilometres. I learnt grammar from my book: there are fifteen verbs that always take the dative and twenty-two that always take the genitive but some of them could take the accusative in certain cases and the only reliable way to find out for sure is to ask 'a good native language speaker'. The book didn't say 'not a foreigner'.

Second time round, Omsk looked different. The rain had stopped and everyone seemed to walk faster. The statue of Lenin had looked strange, old-fashioned, the last time; now it was vibrant and shiny. This square was a terminus for many bus routes. There was a large clock that was stopped at 11:17. 'What time is it in Omsk . . . ?'

People were smart and looked as if they knew where they were going. I judged by the flow of traffic which way the centre might be and set out on foot. It is difficult to ask directions when you don't know where you want to go. I walked all along Leninskee Prospekt, a street of elegant four-storeyed apartment buildings. Two months earlier I would have thought it dusty and old-fashioned, now I saw it as Soviet architecture at its best. The street was lined with trees, whitewashed to waist level. There were trams, buses and trolley buses as in all Soviet, or ex-Soviet, cities. Some of the trolley buses were very modern with concertina bits in the middle. They were long and the doors opened with a hiss. There were no naked hinges either, they were cased in more concertinas, these ones of rubber. These vehicles were, I discovered, rejects from some German city where they failed to meet the emission requirements for healthy living. Vehicle emission is small beer in a land of ailing nuclear power stations.

I saw a girl in yellow just like the one I had seen in the park in Irkutsk. The one with the flowers on that first Sunday morning when the drunk told me I was shit. I asked her if she could recommend somewhere to stay. She was standing at a bus stop in a queue and I could see she wanted to help, but that she was embarrassed. The whole line was looking at her and, like children, they were dragged between curiosity and ridicule. She left the queue saying, 'Come with me.' Then she asked me the things she had wanted to know: Who I was? Where I came from? Where I was going to? And, what I earned? She was beautiful. She was all in yellow and her toenails were painted red. Her sandals were just a few flimsy straps of patented yellow. Her skin was snow-white, eyes blue. Her hair was blonde of course, but not peroxide. She took me down an underpass and across a park and I felt good that a beautiful girl could do this for a fairly weird-looking foreign man without being afraid. I knew it had to be a good city. She wiggled beautifully.

The first hotel was too expensive and the second was at the far side of a high bridge.

Though one of the most inland spots in the world, Omsk is an important port. It is possible to go by boat from here to many of the major cities and towns of the former Soviet Union. Near the bridge where we sat there was a sign advertising sailings to Semipalatinsk, which is in Kazakhstan. I couldn't tell her that I was afraid to walk across bridges. She was in great awe of my adventure so far; I couldn't bear to shatter it with a confession about my fear of bridges. I'd have to wait until she was gone and get a bus to the other side. I watched her walk away and turn around to wave a few times. Only when she was out of view did I retreat and cross by bus.

The hotel was under *remont*: repair. The street leading up from the bridge was really beautiful, lovely low architecture, of what period I didn't know but at least pre-Khrushchev. It was lined with garden seats and many were occupied. I picked on a bony elderly man who rose straight away and moved puppet-like, in many directions, chasing possibilities. He was over-anxious and darted around, stopping people and telling them about me. I felt embarrassed and wanted to call it off. I'd find something on my own; he wouldn't dream of it.

Some hours later we found a place miles away, near the agricultural university. It was in an apartment complex and almost invisible. The door was closed so he rang the bell and he was so relieved to have found somewhere that I knew I'd have to take it no matter what the cost. It wasn't the cost that scared him off, it was the Azerbaijani woman who answered the door. She had dark, wet, gypsy eyes and was dressed in black frilly things. She held a bunch of skirt in one hand. He didn't even pretend to make an excuse, he grabbed me with one bony claw and started to drag me off. The other hand he held aloft as if to shield us both from her eye. I pulled myself free and said it was fine. In defiance, I didn't even ask the cost; any room she had would be fine. And it was. At eighteen dollars it was way outside my budget limit, but it would only be two or three nights. He left, darting back frightened, big-eyed glances.

The room was a voyeur's paradise. It was semi-basement. My window opened to a courtyard within the compound and there was a seat outside it where groups sat and talked. I blush in confession; I listened by day and at night I sat in the dark listening some more.

Old women's tales:

'I'm tired now, always tired. Don't come out because I can't, always tired.'

'In Soviet times roubles were worth something.'

'If I die, who will know?'

'Now I can't buy anything without dollars – where do I get dollars?'

Wives' tales:

'He's no good, only for drinking. And if he could get my money he would drink that too.'

'Of course he has no other woman, he can't do it, I miss that too.'

Boys' tales:

'Natasha is dirty, you'll get thing off her.'

'Listen to him, you can't get thing because you can't do it.'

'Can too, and I'll do your sister too.'

Drunks' tales:

'Tomorrow, I'll give it back tomorrow . . . you don't believe me? I have work tomorrow.'

'Can't work . . . no more than me . . . anyway I'll only have one . . . Cough, cough, cough . . . spit.'

There was an exhibition of Kazakhstan artefacts which surprised me until I saw a map and realised we were less than a hundred miles from the border of Kazakhstan. Then I thought about meeting my friend Rose and I decided I didn't want to, not now. Maybe it was because I had failed to connect with Ider and now I was telling the coincidences that I had set up that they needn't bother occurring. But I think it was because I wanted to stay in character. I didn't want to start talking about Siberia, Russia and Omsk in the third person. I was in it and didn't want to get outside it. Later, I discovered I needn't have considered it at all, because Rose stayed at home in Kazakhstan.

In the evenings, with most of the city, I sat in the square in the centre of town. They sold flowers at three dollars a bloom and Snickers and Mars bars and *got doags*: hot dogs.

Kids roller-bladed on the concrete and did fancy tricks on the steps. Lovers kissed and locked thighs. Girls wore very short miniskirts, had streaked hair and platform shoes. Large, sturdy, middle-aged women walked hand-in-hand and there were a lot of men in uniforms but not on duty. They were healthier and happier than I had seen elsewhere and they filled their uniform. They flirted with and chased the girls who squealed and smiled at the game. Their squealing and giggling didn't take over; it was contained in tight pools. In the West people want to be heard, Russians are more private – especially in public.

I walked the few miles home late at night. I had company all the way. The old tramlines were being replaced. A modern monster drew the old lines out of the ground like a bird pulling a worm, and in its wake came a steamroller spewing out tarmacadam and levelling it out in a steaming carpet. There was a roundabout where trolley bus cables intersected overhead and here there were all-night, plastic-signed take-aways. There was a twenty-four-hour ATM machine with a queue.

When I got home, I heard an argument outside the window. A young couple:

'No, not here, we can't, we'll be seen . . .'

'Pleeeease! I must . . .'

I felt too guilty so I turned on my light and coughed. They spurted out laughter and went somewhere else.

For the journey to Moscow I chose a train coming from Semipalatinsk. It had a good number: 12.

The *dejurnaya* put me in a compartment with a young man of twenty-three. He looked as though he had slept a lot. He was like the soldier on the train to Ulan Ude except that this man spoke. He spoke a lot. He was, though only twenty-three years old, an engineer and was going to Moscow to buy machine parts for the factory where he worked. In my Linguaphone Russian course the main character is a *molodoey enjineer*: young engineer. I hit him with off-by-heart phrases, in exactly the accent used on the tape and he didn't believe I was foreign. I shrugged my shoulders nonchalantly and yawned, pretending that this happened all the time, that people always thought I was Russian. I stayed silent for a while, to maintain the illusion. Then I got down to the inquisition.

'Where are you from?'

'You wouldn't know it, it's a small place.'

'Where?'

'Temirtau.'

'Oh! Is that the Temirtau in the Kraganda *oblast*?'

He couldn't believe it and I had to stop talking again for a while, so full was I with satisfaction. It was one of those times when everything was going my way. It was as if someone above was looking into my small store of knowledge and setting things up for me. I knew about the scheme to move the capital of Kazakhstan from Almaty to Akmola, which is near Temirtau. There must be a god who was setting this up for me. It was a long time before I asked him his name. It was Dimitri.

'And your family name?'

'It is Marchuk.'

'Ah! I know that name . . . I had a friend one time by that name.'

'Not possible.'

'Why?'

'Because it is a Ukrainian name. My father came from the Ukraine to Kazakhstan. Everyone of this name comes from the Ukraine and they are all related to each other.'

Dimitri wasn't a mean character, he was enthusiastic, personable and hearty but he was glad he had caught me out. I didn't blame him. I would have been happy to catch out a know-all like me, too. I didn't argue about it but I knew that I had known a Marchuk. I had a picture in my mind of a girl, a young, shy girl with glasses who had difficulty in talking to me. I knew she was someone I felt good about and I knew that under her shyness she had been enthusiastic, personable and hearty too.

He didn't want to sleep, he had been on his own since Karaganda and he had slept all the time. We talked about the movements of people after the Second World War. How Ukrainians and Hungarians and natives of Eastern European countries were displaced because of the Soviet pressure to spread Communism. He explained many of the things I had difficulty in understanding. The contradictions of a life where people claim to earn ten dollars a week yet have all the trimmings of a comfortable life. I told him about the man I met on Olkhon who had no income but was on holiday. I told him how, on visiting this man later in Irkutsk, he had got so drunk he had to get his son to drive me home. I told him that the son drove me home in a new Land Rover. He said it was easy to explain. He said how he himself earned 200 dollars a month but that now he had 50,000 dollars in cash on him to buy what he needed in Moscow. He said that is the way things are in Russia, an opportunity comes your way and one may seem wealthy for a while. He said Westerners didn't understand because everything happened gradually there. He said it was different in Russia, movement was in great jerks . . . sometimes backwards. It was a collapsed system and sometimes within this collapsed system opportunities arose because the basic infrastructure of transport and communication still existed.

'You must remember,' he said, 'that less than ten years ago, this country had the most advanced scientists in the world. Trade and commerce spanned eleven time zones and was assisted by the largest airline in the world and a good train network. Your friend in Irkutsk lives on the main artery of commerce between Japan, China, Korea and South-East Asia. An opportunity arises to have a part in the big business of transporting vehicles from Japan to the west of Russia, so that is how he happens to have a new Land Rover. He may not own it, he may be passing it on or he may be given the opportunity of selling it and sharing in the profit. That is how things are done in Russia now. Business is conducted through a network of friends and relations. People call it Mafioso business but most of it is legal, working within the constraints of a system that has collapsed.'

Dimitri was very intelligent. I could see why his employers didn't have a problem entrusting him with 50,000 dollars in cash to do their shopping for them in Moscow. He assured me that it wouldn't all be spent sensibly: 'There's also girls you know – in Moscow many girls!' His eyes glazed at the prospects ahead. He eventually yawned and before he went to sleep I asked him to write down his name and address. He put it on a scrap of paper and rolled over, completely clad, into a healthy, young, animal sleep.

Written in the Cyrillic alphabet it didn't look familiar but when I transcribed it into Roman letters I knew I had seen it before. I wasn't going to pursue it further; he'd never believe me anyway.

I have had the same address book since 1967. As well as addresses it has train tickets and receipts and currency notes. I picked through it and under 'M' there was one space for Dimitri. The space was below one filled in with: Marchuk Sophie, Picture Butte, Alberta. She loomed up before me, the lovely, shy, bespectacled, feminine Sophie. In the first year of my teaching career, many years ago, I had taught her in a tiny village on a dirt road in western Canada. I tried to wake him. He gave me a dead look, which held a threat, turned his backside to me and slept like a log.

There was no *chi* for breakfast. Dimitri had a beer and I had a Coke. He did a lot of shaking of the head and scratching before I could get him interested in the genealogy. We argued about what constitutes first and second cousin. He had never met Sophie . . . he wasn't born when her father left to take a quarter section (160 acres) in Alberta. But her father must be a brother to his grandfather. He remembers getting parcels of clothes from Sophie. He remembered his parents told him she had married another immigrant Ukrainian, a farmer, and had many children. She had sent their hand-me-downs to Dimitri and his brothers and sisters in far-off Karaganda.

I felt I had got my own back on coincidences. They had failed to respond to my manipulation to meet Ider and Rose but unbeknownst I had got them to send in the Marchuks. I was gloating.

Chapter Eleven

Another thing I liked about Dimitri was the luggage. He carried but a single bag. When the train pulled into Moscow he was ready in a flash. He hadn't been preparing. He walked down the platform in front of me even though it was I who knew my way around. His youthful vigour made him a natural leader. The bag swung, almost empty.

When I was last in Moscow Maxim had pointed out a place to me in passing one day. He had said it was a very good place for Russians to stay. He said it was not for me, only for Russians. I didn't say that to Dimitri; I just said I knew a good place.

The place was just off Prospekt Mira. There was no indication on the outside that it was a hotel. The lady at the desk didn't know how to handle the situation. My passport was Irish and his Kazakhstan. She deferred to the *dejurnaya* on the third floor, sending us aloft without saying whether we could stay or not. The *dejurnaya* was the standard model of fifteen stone and red nails, but she had dark hair and a streak of decency. She looked us up and down doubtfully. I could see she liked Dimitri. Any mother would. She returned her gaze to me, saying doubtfully, 'We don't usually take foreigners.' I said that the Marchuks were a good family, that I could vouch for them. I said I'd known them for years.

She assigned us room 337, just across from her own desk, where she could keep a close eye on things. There was a light over each bed and other symptoms of luxury. The window looked on to Prospekt Mira obliquely, close enough to get a full view of all that happened there, yet distant enough from the din. There was a phone. One of the lights worked. We transferred a bulb from the three-pronged affair in the centre of the ceiling, leaving one working there. We stood in admiration of the rearrangement. One light over each bed, one in the centre. Neither of us had ever seen such extravagance in Russia.

The shower at the end of the wide corridor was amazing. It had three cubicles and three washbasins. Each cubicle had a hose with a spray attachment, each had two taps. They had blue and red markings and delivered as indicated. I checked the washbasins and they had stoppers. One basin, one stopper. I was wracked with emotion. Such facilities I had not seen for ages. The tiling was like that in a Roman bathhouse, marbled, elegant and complete. The force of the spray hurt.

When I returned, Dimitri was stretched, but not asleep. I gushed my enthusiasm and, opening the window to its limits, said he must try it. I think he hadn't taken off his clothes for five days. He left his gear strewn. Across the bed lay his money belt. I didn't check, but it must have contained the 50,000 dollars. The room was fifteen dollars a night each. It felt like we were cowboys, in town for the shoot-out.

When he returned he looked even younger, even stronger and even brighter. He sniffed indelicately at his trousers and asked me if I had a spare pair for now. Negative. He shook the old pair, like flicking a towel in a locker-room and pulled them back on. We were ready to eat.

Dimitri's animal instincts were a joy to behold. The menu and a shapely waitress halted him mid-sentence. He was torn between them. From the menu he chose *borsch*, to be followed by dumplings. He teased the waitress with flattery and touched as much of her as he decently could in returning the menu. When she was gone he said, 'I like girls.'

After delivering the *borsch* she returned with a bowl of *smetana* and a mini ladle. She asked him if he would like it. He said he would. She poured it on. A drop hung from the ladle. She wiped it with two fingers, slurped it up and wiggled off to get his dumplings.

On our way home he bought trousers and a shirt from a kiosk in the metro.

'What size?'

'Big size.'

He was tired and full and slept as soon as he lay down. He snored a bit.

Next day we arranged to meet at five, he would have most of his purchasing done by then. I would have done my revisiting.

Moscow had changed enormously. I had been away just two months but the city had been transformed. Yuri Luzhkov, the mayor of Moscow, had worked miracles.

No one knows where he got the money from but he has transformed the physical face of the city. In the area around Red Square there is a maze of old streets, more French than English in flavour, but resembling Mayfair in layout. I never before realised the beauty of these streets. In the past this area was so riddled with gaps in the pavement that all one's attention was consumed in finding safe footfalls. But now it was splendid. When it comes to aesthetics, Russians are way ahead of anything in the West. It is hard to reconcile this with a rough exterior. Their art galleries are so surprisingly good they spook you. Their ballet has a quality unknown elsewhere and their sense of colour, despite the blue kitchens, is impeccable. They seem to use a wider palette, their spectrum is broader. They use shades between the main bands of colour. The Mayfair Maze is decked out in shades of green and blue that are hard to describe. They are not pastel and they are not dark, they are from that in-between zone, shades that go very well with the gilding that they use on the ornate friezes and cornices. They seem to be able to pluck true shades from the normally fuzzy border regions of the green-blue-indigo band of the colour spectrum.

Red Square is buzzing with workers busily painting and washing. It is being floodlit. Everywhere there are machines and workmen. And these workmen are busy and contented. Beside Red Square there is another called Manezh. The last time I was there it was so filled with machinery I couldn't see anything. The time before it was filled with Ladas, so rusty and broken I couldn't tell if they were parked or abandoned. Now it is an underground shopping mall, surrounded by walkways rich in sculpture. One piece is particularly imaginative. It is of an old Russian storyteller. He holds a violin in one hand and the other is held out in a semi-embrace. To get to it one has to make a small jump across a gush of water. The successful are rewarded with the privilege of standing within the embrace of his arm for photographs. All this refurbishment was by way of celebration of the city's 850th birthday.

Red Square and Manezh are separated by the Iverskaya Chapel and Gate. The highest point of this building is dominated by a pair of gilt-sculptured, twin-headed eagles. They lay on the ground being re-gilded by men with spray guns.

I met Dimitri in Red Square and took him on a miracle tour. I told him about the Saviour Tower and that it was called Saviour Tower because it was here that dead saints leaving met dead saints coming in and that led to the defeat of the Mongols. Then I told him about the Iverskaya Icon surfing over the waves and waiting 200 years before it sprouted flames and was found. I told it all exactly the way Maxim had told me, but Dimitri said the miracles didn't sound Russian at all but Irish. He said that he always heard that Irish people were full of such stories and that he would prefer to see the hotel I had told him about.

The Metropole Hotel is central, comfortable and posh. The foyer is huge and has excellent, luxurious furniture. The toilets are impeccable and, overall, it's hard to beat for hanging out. You can read all the papers in Russian, English and German. There is a desk where one can write letters using hotel notepaper and envelopes. Even if you are tired of reading and writing it's hard to be bored, the place is full of rich poseurs. Dimitri fitted in a treat. He was no poseur but he had acting ability and common sense. He knew how to behave and get the best out of his performances without being obvious as a crasher. We hit on a good night; there was an International Film Festival on.

We relaxed.

He stretched out his legs in their new trousers and told me he had had a very successful day. He had found nearly all the machine parts he required. In one factory he had met a Ukrainian girl. She was a secretary and helped him to locate everything he wanted. Her name was Katerina. He liked her.

'I like girls.'

In another day he would be finished business and ready to play. On the way out, he approached the desk with calculated boredom to enquire how much the rooms cost. Rooms 200 dollars, suites 300. He waited until we got outside to whistle in shock.

We walked all the way home, turning up our noses at McDonald's and stopping for dinner in a Japanese restaurant. He said there were none in Temirtau but he handled the chopsticks beautifully. He wouldn't let me pay. I had saved him a lot of money, he had expected to pay more for a hotel. He would say it cost him more, a lot more. The parts had cost him less than he expected, but I was the only one who would ever know. Katerina would fix the receipts.

We didn't get home until one a.m. Back in our room of individual lights he asked me if I had a pen. On a small scrap of paper he did calculations in a combination of dollars, roubles and tenge (Kazak currency). He was satisfied. Very satisfied. He would make money. He would fly home. I was surprised he hadn't flown in with his money belt of 50,000 dollars but he said he couldn't get an Aeroflot flight, only Kazak Air. He said Kazak planes were the ones left behind by Aeroflot when the Soviet Union collapsed. They left them behind because they weren't capable of being flown out. He'd get an Aeroflot flight home . . . but no hurry, lots of time yet. We would meet tomorrow back here in our room. He snored a little more.

He was late in arrival and he brought Katerina. She was a plump Audrey Hepburn. Teeth pearls, eyes huge, handshake hot. She said to call her Katya, everyone did. Dimitri said they were going to spend a few days together; he had finished his shopping. She had got time off work, did I mind? He said he'd continue to pay for his bed in the room. I said no need; he insisted. They wanted me to come with them sightseeing, I didn't want to be playing gooseberry. Nonsense! They wanted me to come with them, they had a little surprise. He threw his bag over his shoulder and patted Katya on the bum as she ducked out through the door. The *dejurnaya* saw it and glared, Dimitri winked and she nearly smiled.

We went to Red Square and he told her all my miracles. He put in extra bits that sounded Irish to me but she loved them all. She had been living in Moscow for five years and never knew; how did he know so much? He said he was interested in such things. She asked me if he had told me the stories. I said he had and that I was fascinated. He never flinched.

We went to the new shopping centre in Manzeh, it wasn't yet open for business but everyone was talking about it. Dimitri had a new, small, clever camera that did everything itself. Katya jumped across the water-gush and he took a photo of her in the storyteller's embrace. Then he crossed and pretended to fall in the stream, she shrieked and grabbed me. He loved it and only barely managed to save himself. She was shy of using the camera, would I do it?

'Only if the two of you squeeze into the arms of the storyteller together.'

She jumped. He pushed. She shrieked. He just saved her from falling in. They put their cheeks together and I hit the button. Through the viewfinder I saw more white teeth than I thought possible to fit into a photo.

Dimitri said we'd go to the Metropole. Inside he took Katya by the hand and pushed me in front of him to the desk. Then I heard:

'Key please.'

'Number?'

'207.'

'There you are Mr Marchuk, suite 207.'

The surprise: they had arranged to stay in the hotel. They wanted me to go up with them, just to see. I said tomorrow, I'd see it tomorrow. We sat for a little time in the foyer and then I said I'd have to go. Katya turned to Dimitri to persuade me to stay. He shrugged his shoulders: What can I do? I left them with a wish and a promise: See you tomorrow.

There was a fuss back at Prospekt Mira. Joseph, who was on his way from Lima, Peru to Warsaw, Poland, had been dumped in Moscow. His visa for Poland was not the correct type and the airline would not take him on board. Airlines are now responsible for their passengers until they have passed through immigration. If he didn't get into Poland they would have to bring him back. They weren't taking the chance. He had got a temporary Russian visa and a taxi driver had brought him to this place. He spoke Spanish and English, no Russian. He had three cases and he was overdressed. I should have known. He was nearly in tears, I felt big because I could translate so I took over. Everything would be all right.

I told the *dejurnaya* that Dimitri had moved out and that Joseph could have the bed. She was reluctant, so I asked her what she thought. Then she said that if my companion had moved out that there was no reason why Joseph couldn't sleep in a bed so vacated. I said that was a very good idea and why hadn't I thought about it. She said we were all foreigners anyway and that she had no trouble until the likes of us started to come here. Passports and tickets and rubbish like that, and visas. Who needs a visa if they are sensible and stay at home? But some people just have to be creating problems.

Joseph didn't smell of sweat. He put on a bathrobe and took a large, zipped toilet bag with him to the shower. It was locked. Where was the key? Couldn't open the door. Will my money be safe in the room while I'm showering? This is the wallet with dollars and, in this one, zloty. The pesos are in with the ticket in this bag. Oh! My camera, I'll put it in this drawer here, don't let me forget it.

When I thought he was safely dispatched for the Big Wash he returned to tell me there was a Walkman and that I could listen to it while I was waiting for him. It wasn't a tape Walkman, no, it was a CD: better sound. Some of his CDs were in the other bag, the all-leather one, and there was some Peruvian music. That was for people in Poland. They would be very interested to hear Peruvian music, they wouldn't have heard it but he would explain it all to them.

He was an hour in the shower. He locked the door on to the corridor so that he had all three cubicles to himself. He had forgotten to leave his watch in the room and he couldn't risk someone reading the time from it while he was busy washing his body. He smelt of fancy toiletry. He didn't snore at all.

In the morning we had to go to his embassy to explain to his ambassador how bad things were in this country. His shoes hurt; the embassy was far from the metro station; couldn't we get a taxi? Surely you could not risk just flagging someone down on the street like that? He never took a taxi unless it was stamped with a seal of approval. These people are all robbers you know. Oh yes, hadn't anybody told me that? I said yes, that an Igor told me that once but that I was glad he reminded me. The complaining took the whole day and I never got to see Katya and Dimitri. I wanted to see them. But I had to look after Joseph. He couldn't manage the metro, no he didn't want to learn, who cared where the Kolsivouu Line went, and those silly plastic tokens! He'd only be here long enough to get things in order and tell them at the airport how to treat transit passengers. Exhausted, after a hard day, he had to shower.

The next morning he had to have another shower. He returned after an hour and a half and checked his camera in the bottom of the wardrobe. Then he counted the dollars, the zloty and the pesos. All correct. He asked me if I had remembered to ask 'those women' to wash his clothes and it was then that I exploded.

I told the *dejurnaya* I was leaving and she said she never had people coming and going like this until she started to take in foreigners.

Larissa said I looked good, fairly good. Amazing. She took my arm, with the hand that was not supporting the poodle, and turned me around. Well, she didn't really take my arm, she pinched a tiny bit of my T-shirt between her thumb and index finger and indicated with her eyes out over her glasses that I should spin for inspection. She was fairly satisfied that I was not contaminated but it took her a long time before she released the poodle. When she did, he went straight for my ankle. '*Nilza*!' she shouted, scooping him to safety. She didn't say you could catch anything from that ankle.

Then she dressed. She looked like she was going to the opera. There was glitter in her blouse and a black, slinky skirt sank in below her posterior. She had shiny nylons, black suede, court shoes. Russians never wear shoes in the house. Her hair was swept back and held in a comb, with an ornate bit poking out. She was going to prepare something to welcome me home. She handled saucepans delicately, staying as far back from them as she could. She lit the gas with an old, scratchy, sparking implement, keeping her coiffure well clear, and then she filled two saucepans with water and placed them on the rings. She put them on the rings that she hadn't lit. These descendants of the czars never quite adjusted to the lack of servants. She rearranged the two pieces of chicken on the table, not quite knowing what to do with them. She asked me to light the oven. 'Never could do it . . . Oh! You are so clever.' Then she placed a tin opener and a tin of soup in front of me, saying we could start with that while we were waiting, and it was only then I realised it had all been arranged. She wouldn't have all this food in if she hadn't been expecting me. I had said I would be back about the 20th August, it was now the 21st. If it hadn't been for Joseph I wouldn't have called at all. I told the poodle he was a good doggy. He whimpered and, very carefully, I took him on to my lap. The soup was delicious and the chicken was different and we looked a very odd couple eating lunch at eleven-thirty a.m.

I told her I had to look up some friends staying in the Metropole.

'OOOOOhhhhhh, such a nice place. I'm glad you are enjoying yourself after that awful Siberia. Don't you think you could do with some clothes? We'll have a little party tonight . . . nice people.'

I didn't want to call early in the day. I walked around Red Square watching people taking pictures and workmen washing down Gum Stores with power washers. I looked at the window display and thought how like Milan or Paris, but with that extra little bold flair that made it Russian. I walked under the Iverskaya Gate and the twin-headed eagles were still on the ground, but now newly gilded and ready for replacement. Then I went to the Metropole.

'Mr Marchuk checked out just an hour ago . . . a message? What is your name? Yes, there is a message.'

Hope you are well. Come to Kazakhstan. My phone number . . . Dima.

And in English: *Why not come? We wait we wait. Have very nice time. Katya.*

I went up Treverskaya Street. I wanted to stand in the spot where Sasha, with the one arm, sold maps under the statue of the prince of the long arms, to people like me who wanted to go to Siberia. Only Prince Yuri Dolgoruku stood there still, indicating the way to go. Even the woman who sold prayers was gone.

I went into an expensive shop and bought Italian-tailored trousers and a woven-leather belt. I got a blue, silky shirt, cufflinks and a bow-tie. I put the tie in my pocket and the rest of the gear on me. They gave me back my old cotton trousers and T-shirt in a plastic bag. The assistant held it out to me just the way Larissa had fingered my T-shirt, between her thumb and first finger. I hated parting with them but I poked my nose into the bag and there was quite a pong. I dropped the bag in a bin and picked up my step. Shoes? I supposed I might as well . . . I paid the earth for them. I saw my reflection in a window and I laughed and laughed and laughed. People walked around me. Past the Iverskaya Gate the eagles had been re-erected.

The party was good. Just eight people. Larissa wore a white dress with drop-pearls sewn to the bodice. They swayed as she walked – no! – tripped around. She had clipped earrings to the black suede shoes and transformed them. Early on she wore a stole. There were two couples, one po-faced, the other doddery. And Maxim was there with a girlfriend. She wore something long and maroon and too loose around the neck. Her skin was corpse-white and sometimes you could see her small breasts down the loose neck. When she noticed, she'd press the neckline in with her open palm.

Maxim had a Sanskrit book and another in ancient Irish that he had got in the library of the Celtic Languages department of the university. Oh yes! They had a very important Celtic Languages department. He had started to wear glasses; small and round with wire frames.

I had brought Larissa flowers and a bottle of champagne. I put the champagne on the kitchen table, where already there were three others like it and a bottle of vodka. Champagne is cheap in Russia. The vodka was good; it had a label. She started to pour but she was missing the glasses so I took over. She was proud of me. 'Nice shirt . . . mmmh! Silk . . . love silk.' She tweaked my bow-tie and flicked it in approval. Poodle was confused and coiled around my legs, whining a little. She said he had good taste and approved of the way I was dressed, compared to . . . she trailed away to the po-faced couple where she became very serious and then to the doddery ones where she became doddery. Many times she held out her glass delicately. She didn't start to hic until all the champagne was gone. Then she said she'd have just a small drop of the vodka to get rid of the hic. It worked, so she had some more. She loved the way I poured drinks. 'How clever he is – isn't he clever? All the way to that awful Sebbrrria . . . but he's back so weeerrr cebrillating his return.' The Russian 'r' is rolled like the Spanish. It can carry a lot of saliva.

Maxim and Maroon were the last to leave. Larissa said we'd relax, just her and me, with a small, little, quiet drink. Poodle was traumatised and circled the legs of the kitchen table where we sat. Larissa's pinned-up hair fell, one earring was gone from the shoes, stole missing. Very slowly her head sank on to the table, her legs stretched out and the swaying pearls came to rest. I dragged her to her bed. Poodle tripped around, touching her dangling gown with his nose and sniffing my ankles, judging intent. I put her head on the pillow first and then drew her legs on to the bed. She was a little askew, so I straightened her out. I knew she'd be mortified if she wakened askew. Poodle didn't approve. For a while he traversed between the two rooms and finally decided to sleep in mine. He had a bad night. It took him a while before he got the courage to jump on my bed. I wanted to shush him down to the floor but he was so sad I couldn't. He couldn't settle. He'd stand up and circle around my body. Eventually he settled into the alcove of my bent knees and I nearly said something to console him.

Morning came. On my way out I saw her prone. She hadn't stirred. I went to Intourist. I had lost my *declaratsia* and wanted to replace it.

Nyet! nyet! nyet! Impossible. Don't know what will happen . . . put you in jail I suppose. Oh yes, the jail is full of people like you who forget their *declaratsia*. She was very disappointed when I didn't go foreign and scream. I said that I was very stupid and didn't understand these important things. I was foreign. I lost it in the early days when I was still foreign . . . but now that I understood how important such things were . . . blah, blah, blah. She said she wouldn't worry about it, that things would be all right. She wrote a note, signed it with a flair, stamped, dated and embossed it. I think she winked.

Couldn't hack the shirt . . . checked the bin . . . my beautiful T-shirt and cotton trousers gone. Bought a new second-hand T-shirt from a woman selling things and felt a lot better. I shoved my blue silk in a bag. It had been too expensive to throw away.

Larissa trilled about what a wonderful night we'd had. Did I feel all right because I did drink rather a lot? No she never drinks . . . well, just a little when she has nice friends. But not with nasty people. Never! And never vodka, just a drop of champagne to celebrate. Everything deserves a celebration, even such a ridiculous thing as going to Siberia. She said the po-faced couple nearly wore her out and that she thought she'd never get rid of them and into her bed. She said that Poodle was exhausted with the night and she had found him sound asleep on her bed when she got to it . . . she wondered how I had got to my bed because I had been so inebriated. But she didn't blame me because I was leaving Moscow and that called for a little celebration or mourning. She just admonished me slightly and sent me early to bed to compensate.

Next morning she said I was being absolutely ridiculous on insisting on going to the airport by metro and bus. Why? She'd come out on to the street and wave down some little man in a Lada to take me there. 'These people do it for a few thousand roubles, they need the money – the poor we will always have with us.' Huh! I had such funny little ways she'd never understand me. It was all quite ridiculous leaving Moscow when the ballet and opera season were about to reopen, and going by public transport. She made the poodle give me a kiss and she stayed in the doorway while I made my way out of the building. She waved Poodle's paw: 'Byeeeee.'

Moscow's metro is very good. It is personal. In London, advertisements shout at you, in New York the graffiti screams and in Tokyo they employ pushers to cram people into carriages. In Moscow it tells you in slow, languorous tones where you are coming from and where you are going and, in a chastising voice, it tells you to be careful and not to lean against the doors. I hadn't noticed before, but now that I was leaving it reminded me of Oxcana's father in Irkutsk and how he had sat me down for a few minutes to contemplate where I was going and what I was leaving behind.

Before I got to my station it reminded me not to leave my baggage behind and that if I thought anybody else had left theirs, to take it to . . . The buses are good too, when you get to know them. They rattle and scrape along and ask for encouragement. The blonde drivers know the peculiarities of their individual machines and they coax and cajole, without forgetting to chastise their passengers. And, when the engine falters, these passengers become silently involved; they seem to shrink to lighten the burden and help it along.

The buses nearly always reach their destinations.

The airport is dimly lit. There are lots of uniforms and questions are answered with a silent point. Reminds me of Igor. Everyone is diverting questions to another area. The response to all enquiries is, 'Over there, of course.'

My note from the Intourist is not enough. Without *declaratsia* it is impossible to leave. Without *declaratsia* how can they keep track of people coming and going and what they bring in and what they carry out?

'Did you buy anything while in Russia?'

'Yes, a pair of trousers and a shirt.'

'This is a very expensive shirt.'

'You can have it.'

Stamp, stamp! Next please!

You must be thinking all the time.

Epilogue

I think it was the same plane that had brought me from Dublin but I can't be sure. I know I felt a lot different about it. The hostess was soft. She smiled and ignored my down-at-heel appearance. Maybe it was the trousers I'd bought for Larissa's party. She said, 'Welcome on board,' and showed me to a window seat. She even made an effort to relieve me of my bag and put it in the bin above. I held on to it in an embrace and then I thought of the man whose escape from Siberia had led me here. He had arrived in India after four months of walking. Though physically weak he seemed mentally OK. When they tried to relieve him of the few scraps of clothing that had survived the trip he resisted violently. Having attained what he sought, he fought violently to hold on to what he had escaped from. He made a barricade of his mattress and took refuge behind it with his rags and their fleas. Now I would not part with my bag either. I didn't like this soft living of air travel. It was a sop to Western mores.

My first Aeroflot flight had been taken as a young student flying to the Iran of the Shah. I had gone Aeroflot because it was cheap. Flying with this airline was considered very adventurous and that influenced me too. I remember the seats seemed very big. They enveloped me, not in soft comfort but, like an electric chair, they made me feel I had chosen them and deserved what I was getting. The hostess asked me if I wanted something.

I did. I have forgotten what it was but I'll never forget her response to my timid request. She loomed above and addressed me in a voice that was an example of the volume she required of me. 'SPEAK UP,' she thundered. It wasn't very nice but it was very Russian. Today's hostess whispered wishes for a comfortable trip. She said her name was Svetlana and that we shouldn't hesitate to ask for anything that would make us more comfortable. Unlike the Svet of train number 3 to Irkutsk, she laid down no ground rules. She could have been American or British, definitely not Siberian.

Cruising at 35,000 feet over Europe, she brought plastic trays of wrapped food. Cutlery was swaddled in paper napkins and pepper and salt were in neat little envelopes. The Coke was icy-cold. There was no *pelmeney* or *blini*; there wasn't even *smetana* . . . no, it was sliced prime Irish beef with brown gravy. There was one neat scoop of mashed potato, well placed. And a pat of butter, wrapped in silver foil and rock-hard out of the galley fridge. Dessert was 'fresh' fruit salad. Marina in Irkutsk had warned me always to ask if the produce was fresh. She told me that the *prodavetsi*, the shop assistants, wouldn't volunteer the information but that they wouldn't lie. That if it wasn't fresh they would tell me and hope that the next customer was not as choosy as me. But I looked up at this manicured, slim, elegant Svetlana and I couldn't ask her if her produce was fresh. She was too nice for that kind of haggle. What could she say? She was doing her job in the manner she had been trained. Like the Moscow staff of McDonald's she had been told to smile at the customers and wish them an enjoyable meal. She was a good hostess.

The women at Kirov, where I nearly missed the train, would have oohhed and awed at the wonder of all this convenience. Imagine not having to cart around basins and saucepans to wait for trains loaded with awkward passengers! Imagine just being able to pass out a plastic tray of neatly arranged morsels of thinly-cut beef and dollops of vegetables all equal in size, shape and form! Imagine not having to collect bags and newspapers and anything that could be used to wrap one's produce!

What would the Svet, into whose embrace they launched me, think of the meek performance of this hostess? The Svet who sported a tousled head and temper in the morning and a pressed uniform in the afternoon?

This Svet's uniform was light blue and well-tailored. Maybe some designer label, or some couture house, probably Paris. The women in remote Kuzhir on Olkhon Island had designer labels too. They sat on wood-piles in the evening after their *banyas* as the sun set out over Baikal. They wished each other *leokem parom*, light steam, as they wrapped scarves around their heads and pulled up zips in their designer bomber-jackets. The logos shouted Nike, Levi, Adidas and, on a ski hat worn by the oldest *babushka* I remember a 'Let's Go'. I don't think they were from Paris. No! Probably Peking which was only two days away by train. Or they might be from Ulan

Bator which was only one day away. Those women wouldn't like it if Chinese people or Mongolians, with their greasy ways, came to live on their island home. But proximity to these places had its blessings. It meant they could get cheap clothes like those people in Europe and America wear. They were able to masquerade. They were almost Western. Were it not for the square Russian faces and stout girth, were it not for the wood-pile and the beautiful, the *krasevee* Baikal, were it not for the fact that Genghis Khan had walked their shores, they could nearly be European or American women. Not as rich, not as smooth of skin, not as pampered, but they had the tags – and if you have things tagged correctly they will surely reach the indicated destination.

Svet politely excused herself as she lent across the aisle passenger to take my tray of paper and plastic debris. Her golden cross, on a golden chain, dangled and she reached with her free hand to prevent it from getting in the way.

In Soviet times religious practices were prohibited. Before that, in czarist Russia, the Orthodox Church was revered. Now religious practice is returning and it has its own tag. Maxim was to be baptised. He spoke Sanskrit and knew as much about ancient Irish culture as I did. He had shaken the yoke of Communism and embraced the new freedom with gusto. Being baptised would complete the liberation – he would now have a new and definite set of rules to live by. He had considered

Orthodoxy but decided Western Christianity was more progressive . . . you must be thinking.

He took me down a cobble-stoned street just behind Red Square. It is a beautiful surprise of a place, separated from the Kremlin only by Gum Store and the square itself. It has an old stone wall and behind the wall, a monastery. I had found it myself on my first visit to Moscow. Then the gate was heavily bolted. There was a bell-pull on the wall and I had tugged at it. I heard it clatter, but it was not answered. I pictured a cobble-stoned courtyard with bearded monks in prayer. Though I knew there was no one to answer the summons I felt guilty for having broken the silence and went away.

The next time, with Maxim, the gate stood open. Business boomed. The cobble-stoned courtyard had come to life with selling stalls. Behold! Free enterprise. Wooden home-made stalls dangled scapulars and beads and prayers in plastic coverings. There were ornaments, statues mostly, but vases too. Coloured vases that could hold bunches of flowers to be put in front of the statues. And there were replicas of churches and saints inside transparent, spherical globes.

These snowed when you shook them.

The stalls were worked by pious women in white scarves knotted under their chins. Monks circulate collecting excessive cash because everyone knows that Moscow is dangerous and these women would be in danger from robbers if they weren't relieved of their money. The monks are busy and people pester them.

People touch their long black robes for cures; they beg blessings and the serious monks make the sign of the cross over them and warn them of the danger of eternal damnation.

Maxim thought this wasn't what he wanted, he thought the Western breed of Christianity would be better. Many share his view. I met Mormons in St Petersburg, Seventh Day Adventists in Almaty and Jehovah's Witnesses on the shores of Baikal. They all said Russians were now free and able to make their own choices. They would see the light and make the choices they, the preachers, were free to make in the Western world.

I eventually saw the light too. Svet, the hostess, had to point it out to me. It was concealed above my head. One flick of a switch and my book was illuminated. This convenience is amazing. Enlightenment ensues. In Kuzhir I had only a candle. There was only one candle for the whole village. My quest for light had given the large ladies of the *gastronom* much joy.

There was a light switch in Nikita's loft and, force of habit, I flicked it on after I climbed the ladder each night. It never worked, the cable under the lake had snapped and nothing was coming through. In time it will be fixed. USAID will open the flow. Then Grisha and Vanya and Slav will be able to flick a switch and get instant pictures from Washington and Los Angeles. They will even know what is happening in Moscow. By then there will probably be a barrage of candles in the *gastronom* and the laughing ladies will not be able to sell them.

The touchdown was smooth. The day was bright. I didn't have to wait for the carousel because all I owned was on my back.

Everywhere matching luggage, smooth trolleys and welcome kiss.

My sister met me; she always does. She makes a great sandwich, loaded with care and mayonnaise. She brings these sandwiches and some iced drinks in a cold-box and we sit and eat them at some wayside picnic table. She told me a presidential election was coming up, that an ex-singer was running, that this singer didn't have a chance. She said she thought my answering machine had been cut off and the garden was overgrown but that I'd have things back in shape in no time.

I said my head was full of Russia and she said I should write it down.